WWII

Duty, Honor, Country

The Memories of Those Who Were There

Steve Hardwick
and
Duane E. Hodgin

iUniverse, Inc.
Bloomington

WW II Duty, Honor, Country

The Memories of Those Who Were There

Copyright © 2013 Steve Hardwick and Duane E. Hodgin

All rights reserved. No part of this book may be used or reproduced by any means, graphic, electronic, or mechanical, including photocopying, recording, taping or by any information storage retrieval system without the written permission of the publisher except in the case of brief quotations embodied in critical articles and reviews.

iUniverse books may be ordered through booksellers or by contacting:

iUniverse
1663 Liberty Drive
Bloomington, IN 47403
www.iuniverse.com
1-800-Authors (1-800-288-4677)

Because of the dynamic nature of the Internet, any Web addresses or links contained in this book may have changed since publication and may no longer be valid. The views expressed in this work are solely those of the author and do not necessarily reflect the views of the publisher, and the publisher hereby disclaims any responsibility for them.

Any people depicted in stock imagery provided by Thinkstock are models, and such images are being used for illustrative purposes only.

Certain stock imagery © Thinkstock.

ISBN: 978-1-4759-6659-6 (sc)
ISBN: 978-1-4759-6657-2 (e)

Library of Congress Control Number: 2012923563

Printed in the United States of America

iUniverse rev. date: 12/26/2012

This book was written in honor of the men and women of World War II who responded to serve during America's darkest and finest hours.

To those whose memoirs are contained within this book, we appreciate the many hours you spent sharing your personal, and at times emotional, experiences. We deeply respect you.

All of you have passed the legacy of "hero" to your friends who were lost in battle and never returned home to be honored for their service. You witnessed their heroic deeds, some of which were their final acts on earth. You have told us they are the "real heroes."

For one brief moment, let us and your country call you "heroes," for we were not there to witness the actions of the "heroes" of whom you speak. You, the liberators of World War II, have carried the mantel of hero in their absence for over seventy years.

Through you, we know of heroes;
through you, we see their character;
through you, we learn of their heroics;
through your humility, we see their selflessness;
in you, we see a hero.

"The tree of liberty must be refreshed from time to time with the blood of patriots and tyrants."

—Thomas Jefferson

Contents

Foreword ix
Preface xi
1. The Third Reich 1
2. London Bombed and Battered 11
3. Heading to the Gates of Hell 23
4. The Imperial Empire 37
5. Remember Pearl Harbor! 43
6. The Home Front 51
7. Island-Hopping in the Pacific 67
8. Guadalcanal 95
9. Marines Storm Ashore on Iwo 105
10. Bloodiest Battle in the Pacific 113
11. Victory at Sea! 127
12. China-Burma-India 155
13. Italian Campaign 165
14. Utah, Omaha, Gold, Juno, Sword 181
15. Through the Hedgerows and on to Berlin! . . . 201
16. The Ardennes 239
17. Supremacy in the Sky 261
18. The Bomb 285
19. The Liberators 297
Their Legacy Will Live Forever 303
Acknowledgments 333
Bibliography 335
About the Authors 337

Foreword

This personal effort, WW II: Duty-Honor-Country The Memories of Those Who Served, is perhaps one of the final efforts of WW II.

Steve Hardwick and Duane Hodgin began a personal quest to assure that students and those who will populate the future will recall with detail and accuracy the great challenge of this world at war and the men and women who were engaged in the vanquishing of a great evil.

"We Americans of today, together with our Allies, are passing through a period of supreme test. It is a test of our courage—of our resolve—of our wisdom—of our essential democracy. If we meet that test-successfully and honorably—we shall perform a service of historic importance, which men and women and children will honor throughout all time."
President Franklin Roosevelt
Fourth Inaugural Address
January 20, 1945

In this book, Hardwick and Hodgin are about that task of providing memory so that indeed children, and men and women too, will remember and honor that "service of historic importance."

The authors have produced a volume that gathers succinctly an expansive overview of World War II; key and decisive moments, dominant figures, evaluation and analysis while it explores the war's legacy impact.

Time's swift current takes those who participated. The Greatest Generation continues to diminish. Hardwick and Hodgin have opened their own action against the loss of individual memories of the historic strife. They have gathered personal memories—the rich jewels of those who were part of what Roosevelt called a "supreme test" of courage, resolve, and democracy. Before these participants depart this earthly realm, Hardwick and Hodgin provide them a place in the hall of time. As the last warriors are called home, Hardwick and Hodgin answer the war's call to remember and honor.

As a journalist I was often saddened by what I saw as a lack of understanding of, or a sense of, history. I am the son of a World War II combatant and a mother who played her role on the "home front." They are gone, but the memories they left have certainly shaped their son's life and sense of duty, honor, and courage. Hardwick and Hodgin have done us all a great service by their labor. They help us to remember, recall, and learn.

"We have before us an ordeal of the most grievous kind. We have many, many long months of struggle and suffering. You ask what is our policy? I will say: it is to wage war, by sea, land and air, with all our might and with all the strength that God can give us; to wage war against a monstrous tyranny, never surpassed in the dark, lamentable catalogue of human crime."
Winston Churchill
House of Commons 1940

There is something here for all of us, not only to remember but to honor.

Tom Cochrun
author, journalist, Emmy and Peabody Award Recipient

Preface

Many people consider World War II to be the single most significant and influential event of the twentieth century. During America's nearly four long years of war, Allied Forces of the United States, Britain, France, and the Soviet Union fought against the Axis Powers of Germany, Japan, and Italy. At the beginning of the war, Germany and Japan had the world's two largest and most powerful military arsenals.

This global war was one of the bloodiest and most costly wars in history, involving more than sixty nations in battle. The major battles were fought in Europe, the Pacific, North Africa, and the Far East. America's entry into the war came after the Japanese Imperial Navy and Air Force conducted a surprise attack on the American Naval Fleet at Pearl Harbor, Hawaii, on December 7, 1941.

Victory was finally achieved with the surrender of Germany on May 7, 1945, and the surrender of the Japanese on August 14, 1945, one week after America dropped atomic bombs on Hiroshima and Nagasaki, Japan. Victory and freedom came at a high cost. Over 400,000 American military men and women lost their lives during the war.

This book was written to provide and preserve an oral history of the eighty-four men and women who were interviewed for the purpose of sharing their memories of World War II. The stories include seventy-six veterans and eight women who served as USO volunteers, Red Cross service workers, a Holocaust survivor, and women who worked on the home front.

We are grateful to the individuals who shared their stories by means of personal, telephone, or videotaped interviews. Every effort was made to record the story as told to the interviewer. Each person interviewed made the final edits of his or her story. All of the veterans and the women who served in various support roles have a connection to Indiana. They lived in Indiana when they enlisted or were drafted or returned to Indiana to live after the war.

(Authors' note: The eighty-four men and women interviewed for this book told their stories, based on their personal experiences and memories. Historical facts have been checked; however, some facts and dates may be incorrect, due to their recollection from over seventy-one years ago.)

MASTER OF EVIL

ADOLF HITLER

"DER FÜHRER"

Holocaust

Shoah

Holocaustos

SACRIFICE BY FIRE

The Final Solution.

NAZI PERSECUTION

SIX MILLION JEWS...

ENGLAND

stood alone.

Until...

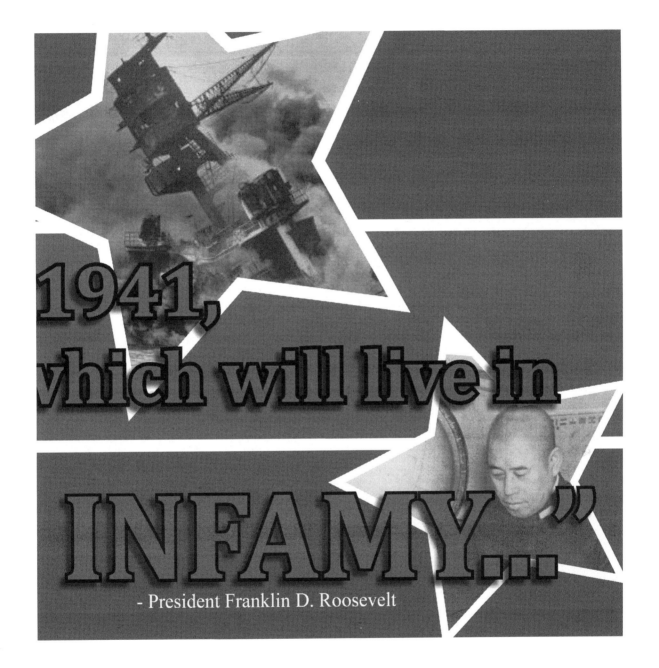

The Homefront Delivers

U.S. builds the world's most powerful war machine ever assembled.

"Soldiers, Sailors, Airmen,

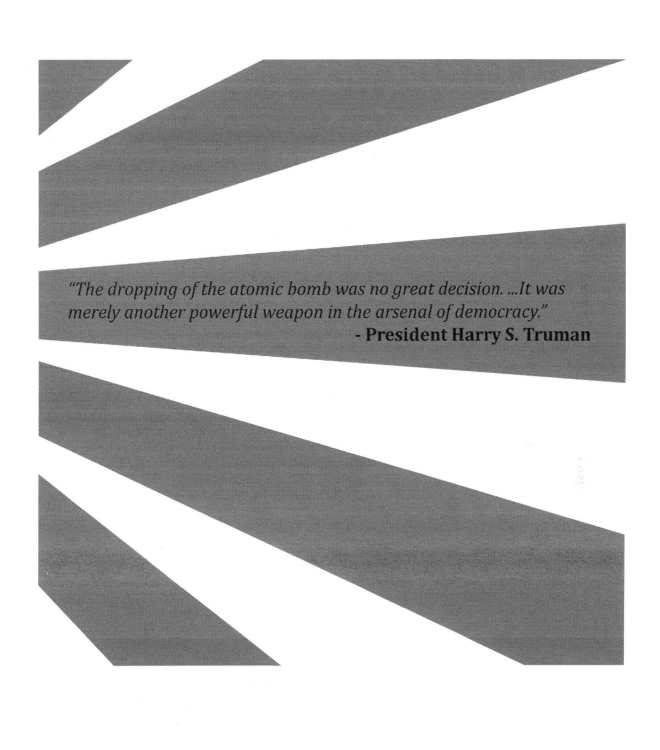

"The dropping of the atomic bomb was no great decision. ...It was merely another powerful weapon in the arsenal of democracy."
- President Harry S. Truman

Freedom...

for us.

In Solemn Salute to Thousands of our Comrades –
Great, BRAVE MEN that They were –
For Whom There will Be NO Homecoming, EVER.

Ernie Pyle, *Brave Men*

1

THE THIRD REICH

(courtesy Yad Vasheem)

"Today we rule Germany, tomorrow the world."

—Adolf Hitler

Germany

"Ein Volk—Ein Reich—Ein Fuhrer"
(One People—One Empire—One Leader)
German propaganda poster

World War II was all but inevitable because of one angry and bitter World War I soldier from Germany. He was infuriated that Germany should shoulder the blame for World War I, and he believed the economic and military sanctions outlined in the Treaty of Versailles were unfair, as it attempted to keep Germany from ever becoming a military power again. This soldier, who received medals for bravery, was Corporal Adolf Hitler.

In September 1919, Hitler joined what was to become the Nazi (National-Sozialistische Deutsche Arbeiterpartei) Party. The Nazi Party, like Hitler, resented the Treaty of Versailles and its harsh restrictions thrust upon Germany. In 1921, Hitler became the party's leader, and with his determination, drive, and charisma, the Nazi Party grew rapidly and began to assert itself in an attempt to gain political power. Hitler and the Nazi leaders attempted to create a national revolution in 1921, by taking over the Bavarian government in Munich, which became known as the Munich (Beer Hall) Putsch. The revolt was successfully defeated by the army and police, and Hitler was put on trial for treason. He was sentenced to prison for five years but served only nine months.

During his time in prison, he formulated his vision for a strong and superior Germany outlined in his autobiography, *Mein Kampf*. Hitler believed that the white Aryan race was superior to all others, and that among the races there were those that are superior or inferior. Since the Aryans are the master race, it was Germany's right to obtain more living space (Lebensraum), and it was justifiable in obtaining it by force.

Hitler stressed that the roadblock to obtaining this world domination was its enemy, the Jews, which he often referred to as parasites, maggots, repulsive, and a menace. Hitler declared the Jews were the ones who sought world control as they conspired to control the world press and financial institutions. In *Mein Kampf* and in future speeches, the German people, including its youth, would be indoctrinated with Hitler's racial hatred of the Jews and his belief that the Aryan race was in a battle with the Jews.

Through the 1920s and into the early '30s, Hitler and the Nazi Party focused on taking over the German government and establishing itself as leader of Germany. With Germany, and the world, being devastated by the Great Depression, Hitler used this as another reason why his party should be in control. With the Nazi Party gaining an unprecedented number of seats in the national election of 1932, it became the largest political party in Germany. Since Hitler's popularity was growing, it was only a matter of time before he would reach his goal. On January 30, 1933, after illegal maneuvering and conspiracies, Adolf Hitler became chancellor of Germany. Hitler's Third Reich, seen as a thousand year reign, was officially beginning.

Hitler's plan for obtaining more living space for Germany began when the German army invaded Austria on March 13, 1938, and annexed Austrian land that he said rightly belonged to Germany. He triumphantly returned to his homeland and was greeted by massive crowds cheering and waving Nazi flags. As Austria was taken over, the world stood by and watched.

In September 1938, in an attempt to appease Hitler and keep him from invading other countries, British Prime Minister Neville Chamberlain and French Premier Edouard Daladier traveled to Germany and worked out an agreement with Hitler to redraw Czechoslovakia's boundaries and give Germany the disputed territory of the Sudetenland. Chamberlain, believing he had halted Hitler's aggression and a war, traveled back to Great Britain proclaiming the Munich Pact ensured "peace for our time." In March 1939, ignoring the Munich Pact, Hitler gave the order for his military to invade and occupy the rest of Czechoslovakia. Again, the world's leaders passively stood by and appeased Hitler.

Seeing he was not being challenged by other European countries, Hitler continued his aggression, and Poland became the next victim of the Nazi war machine. On September 1, 1939, German troops stormed across the Polish border in a lightning fast assault known as Blitzkrieg, which combined land and air forces to overwhelm the Polish military. Within weeks, Poland was defeated and occupied by German forces. Honoring their treaty with Poland, Britain and France declared war on Germany. The world was at war.

Adolf Hitler

"Demoralize the enemy from within by surprise, terror, sabotage, assassination. This is the war of the future."

Hitler was simply known as, the "Fuhrer," which meant leader. Using his charisma and powerful public speaking skills, he convinced the German people he knew what was best for them. To achieve his plans outlined in *Mein Kampf*, his subordinates carried out plans in a brutal and deadly manner. Per his directive, the Jews, and other so-called less desirables living in Germany and occupied territories, were rounded up and deported to labor and concentration camps, where millions died through neglect, shootings, or extermination in gas chambers. On April 30, 1945, with the Soviet army on the outskirts of Berlin, and realizing Germany would not win the war, Hitler committed suicide in his underground bunker.

Hermann Goering

"Education is dangerous. Every educated person is a future enemy."

As a leader in the Reich, Goering was the one who organized the Gestapo, the German secret state police, established the first concentration camps, and commanded the Luftwaffe, the German air force. Throughout the war he remained loyal to Hitler, but as the war drew to a close, Hitler began to distrust Goering because he felt Goering was trying to undermine his authority. At the Nuremberg War Crimes Trials, Goering was convicted of war crimes and was sentenced to death by hanging. Instead of facing execution, he committed suicide by taking cyanide.

Heinrich Himmler

"Ordinary citizens don't need guns, as their having guns does not serve the state."

(courtesy Friedrich Franz Bauer)

Himmler served with Hitler from the time of the Munich (Beer Hall) Putsch, and was considered the most powerful man in the Nazi regime next to Hitler. Himmler was the leader of the Schutzstaffel (SS) and the German police, which used strong-arm tactics of brutal force and repression against those deemed enemies of the Reich. Himmler established the first German concentration camp, Dachau, and eventually supervised all Polish concentration and extermination camps. Himmler was the main Nazi in charge of implementing Hitler's Final Solution—the extermination of all Jews from Europe. When it was obvious Germany would not win the war, he unsuccessfully attempted to negotiate with the Allies. He was captured by British soldiers before he could escape Germany. Before going on trial, he committed suicide.

Joseph Goebbels

"Think of the press as a great keyboard on which the government can play."

(courtesy Sandau)

As Hitler's Minister of Propaganda, Goebbels delivered his pro-Nazi messages to the German people without interference because he controlled the press and radio. He convinced his countrymen to burn books of any writings considered un-German, and helped create an aura of fear by telling lies to the German people about the Jews. As the war progressed, and as German military defeats mounted, it was his task to raise the hopes of those on Germany's home front. In the last days of the war, after Hitler committed suicide, Goebbels and his wife took their own lives along with the lives of their six children.

Soviet Secretary General Joseph Stalin

"Don't let people have ideas."

Stalin was the brutal communist dictator of the Soviet Union who had millions of Soviet citizens and political leaders imprisoned or murdered. In August 1939, the Soviet Union and Germany signed the Nazi-Soviet Nonaggression Pact, which outlined trade agreements and specified that neither Germany nor the Soviet Union would go to war with one another. However, Hitler reneged on the treaty and attacked the Soviet Union on June 22, 1941. As a result, Russia became allied with the United States and Great Britain. Brutal fighting occurred between the two armies, and with a terrible Russian winter, and a determined Russian army to protect its homeland, the German attack was repulsed.

Joseph Stalin, Franklin Roosevelt, and Winston Churchill at the Tehran Conference in 1943

2

LONDON BOMBED AND BATTERED

"We shall fight on the beaches, we shall fight on the landing grounds, we shall fight in the fields and in the streets, we shall fight in the hills; we shall never surrender."

—Winston S. Churchill

Their Finest Hour

*"Hitler knows that he will have to break
us in this island or lose the war."*
—Winston S. Churchill

The German war machine displayed its power in the year 1940. In April, Germany invaded Denmark and Norway. The following month Belgium, France, Luxembourg, and the Netherlands were attacked by Germany. On June 22, France officially surrendered to Germany. To add to France's humiliation, Adolf Hitler participated in the surrender ceremonies.

England stood alone! The British people and their new prime minister, Winston Churchill, knew they were the next target of Hitler's Wehrmacht (army) and Luftwaffe (air force), as they nervously awaited the inevitable, an invasion by Germany.

The initial assault, the Battle of Britain, began in July 1940. German and British fighter planes tangled in "dogfights" high in the skies over southern Britain, while German bombers attacked military targets on this isolated island. Through August and into September, the heroic pilots of the Royal Air Force (RAF) dueled with the Luftwaffe, and both sides endured heavy losses in the process. Realizing they were not defeating Britain's first line of defense, the Luftwaffe's strategy began to transform from daytime raids to nighttime bombings of London and other British cities.

However, this strategy changed as well and turned into an all-out bombing blitz of London. For 57 consecutive nights, from September 7 to November 3, the citizens of London were forced into subways and makeshift bomb shelters to escape the terror from above. Two-hundred German bombers a night unleashed their bombs, turning sections of London into blazing fires. The blitz to destroy British morale and force them to surrender continued until the spring of 1941. Hitler's planned invasion was eventually postponed and never became reality.

With the leadership of Winston Churchill, the valiant efforts of the British military, and the tough-minded and determined citizens of Britain, Hitler and his military never brought down Saint Paul's Cathedral, never scaled the White Cliffs of Dover, never occupied Buckingham Palace, and never goose-stepped through Trafalgar Square.

*"If the British Empire and its Commonwealth
last for a thousand years, men will still
say, 'This was their finest hour.'"*
—Winston S. Churchill

James McDowell

Army: Corporal, 231st Station Hospital
Hometown: Indianapolis, Indiana
Career: Radio and television broadcaster and professional photographer

McDowell with Major Glenn Miller

When the war started, I was seventeen-years-old and was living in Lincoln, Nebraska. One Sunday morning after church, I stopped by my girlfriend's house. She looked out the window and said, "There's a big special on the radio. A place called Pearl Harbor was bombed by planes from Japan." We listened to the radio for about a half hour, and then I told her I better go home because I feel my life has just changed.

I went to Omaha, Nebraska, and was inducted into the army. On a Saturday night, after our physical exams, I went to a local dance hall and saw a band called Claude Thornhill and His Orchestra. I thought, "Wow. His music is great." He played a tune called "Where or When," and I liked it very much.

I went to Little Rock, Arkansas, and did my basic training. When they found out I was a good typist, I was assigned to the clerk typist school and learned to type up medical forms. After we completed our training, we were transferred to the General Hospital at Camp Atterbury, Indiana in September 1942. This was a training hospital, but it was also a working hospital. Our commander was Colonel Lynwood Gable.

We had two jobs to do. One was our medical job, and the other was using our entertainment talents. Colonel Gable organized a dance band, a polka band, a classical quartet, and many more.

This was part of our duties for the rest of the war. Sergeant Harry Miller was a piano player, and he organized the band in which I was the lead singer. Our band was called Gable's Gators, and we played at the Circle Theatre in Indianapolis, Indiana, on WIRE radio, and performed shows at Camp Atterbury and Fort Harrison. We put on a radio show called *Meet the Yanks* that was performed on the radio and broadcast around the Midwest region. We became well known in the Indianapolis area.

On Mondays, at 6:00 p.m., I went to Pearson's Music store, where you could buy sheet music and records. This was located on Pennsylvania Street in Indianapolis, Indiana. One evening, I followed a girl into the store and found out she worked there. I asked her for the latest Bing Crosby record and ordered some sheet music. While I listened to the records in the music booth, I would glance at her and smile, and she would smile back at me. I thought, "What sparkling brown eyes she has; she's a good-looking gal."

Two weeks later, I received a card from Peggy Million telling me my sheet music had come in. On the card she wrote, "Dear Soldier, I have your music. Could you come in as soon as possible?" I found out she lived just outside Broad Ripple right on the White River. She was going to the Arthur Jordan Conservatory of Music in a big house on Pennsylvania. It was part of Butler University.

I would come up from Atterbury to the bus station and take the street car (trolley) to Broad Ripple; right up College Avenue. Peggy would meet me, and we would go to the Broad Ripple Park. We became real close friends, buddies, and sweethearts. She was a singer and dancer, and belonged to an organization that entertained the troops at Fort Harrison and Camp Atterbury. We became engaged, and I took a picture of her that I carried in my wallet for the whole war. I still have it in my wallet.

When our outfit, the 231st Station Hospital, received orders to go overseas, I met Peggy downtown at the bus station to say good-bye. It was the most tearful scene I have ever had in my life. We just bawled, cried, and hugged. It was very traumatic to leave your sweetheart. But the good part is we had "paper love" for the next two and a half years. Every night at eleven, before going to bed, she would write me a letter. I would go to our service club each day and write her. I have all the letters today; we were married for sixty-three years—a great, great love story.

Before our unit left New York City, I got to see Benny Goodman and his big orchestra with Gene Krupa on the drums. It was at an outdoor venue, with thousands of GIs. What a night. They even played "Sing, Sing, Sing." We shipped out in September 1943, and it took us six days to cross the Atlantic. We landed in Ireland and then traveled to Scotland. From there we boarded a train and went to Red Grave Park in England and stayed there for six months.

I visited London on a pass, and the fog was so thick, I could not see the buildings. When the air-raid sirens went off, we knew German planes or buzz bombs were coming over. We went down into the subway, and there were blankets, food, and water for those who stayed all night. When the all-clear would sound, we would go back upstairs. I went to the famous Rainbow Corner in London. That's where all the GIs would go to dance. Glenn Miller, Bing Crosby, and Dinah Shore performed there.

Our band put on a lot of shows at Red Grave Park. We put on dances for the enlisted men and officers stationed in the surrounding area. The big boys (high-ranking officers) loved Colonel Gable and how he took care of the injured and entertained them with the band. Our band initially played dances for our own officers' and enlisted men's clubs. But, when the word got out, a lot of the units asked if we could play for their boys. We also played for English units. Everybody liked the band, and it had a high reputation.

After six months at Red Grave Park, our unit went to Norwich, which is about one hundred miles north of London. We were stationed in the middle of the 8th Air Force and were surrounded by all their units. We were close to the White Cliffs of Dover. The main bomb group stationed near us was the 466th Bomb Group. We could see the planes form up in the sky and wait to take off on their missions. Late in the afternoon, we would hear the planes coming back, and if we could, we would go out and watch them arrive. Some of the planes had holes in the fuselages and parts shot off. We watched and hoped they could make it to their airfield and not crash.

When the pilots and crews came back from bombing Germany, there were a lot of casualties, and the 231st Station Hospital serviced them. We had the best surgeons in the country, and they did miraculous things to mend the air force crews. If they came into the hospital on stretchers, it was my job to take scissors and cut up the pant leg of each airman to see if he had flak wounds. If he did, the guy next to me would sprinkle sulfur on the wound, so it would not get infected. Another guy determined if the airman went straight to the operating room. If he was not hurt too badly, he would go to a bed in the ward.

One day we heard that Glenn Miller's band was going to play in our area. Actually, his band was not stationed too far from the 231st Station Hospital. They were going to put on a broadcast and record it, and all the GIs in the area could attend. We also got word that an officers' dance was going to be held afterward. We were asked if Gable's Gators would play for the dance. "Oh yeah, we could play for that dance. You bet!"

It was held on August 18, 1944, in a large B-17 hangar at Attlebridge. Many of the guys sat on the wings of the B-17 bombers and watched the band. Miller was very popular! After we saw Glenn Miller's program, we went to the officers' club and started playing for the dance. All the big brass was there. Miller was promoted to major the day before, so it was an exciting day for him.

During the intermission, one of the nurses in our unit, came up and grabbed my arm and said, "Jimmy, you're going to meet Major Glenn Miller."

"I can't do that. I'm a corporal, and he's a major. He's surrounded by the brass," I said.

She said, "You're going to meet him." She grabbed my arm and pulled me through the crowd, and went up to him.

She told Glenn Miller who I was, and he said, "I know. I have been listening to him." He said, "Corporal, follow me."

And with that I said, "Yes, sir."

Miller and I went into the men's latrine. We stood there talking with each other, and a photographer came in and took our photo. He chatted with me for fifteen minutes about the vocalists I enjoyed. Miller told me to have my own singing style and not to sound like other singers. He asked me what I was going to do after the war, and I told him I was going to be a singer. Miller told me he was going to live in California and form a new band after the war. He told me look him up if I came to California, and he would help me get started.

After the show was over, six of us went to the bar to order a beer. Major Miller came and put his arms around two of the guys and asked, "What are you guys buying?"

We told him, "Beer."

"It's on me," he said. He liked musicians, and talked with us for twenty minutes. He just wanted to join the guys who were in the band.

One day, we went to London because we were scheduled to broadcast at the BBC (British Broadcasting Corporation) recording studios to play a half-hour show on the air. On the same day, we went to Rainbow Corner to play a dance on the second floor, but we did not know what was going to happen that day. When we were on the second floor, we heard a crowd outside at Piccadilly Circus. We looked out the window and saw thousands of people gathering and shouting. One of the band members said someone was shouting, "V-E, V-E." We did not know what they were talking about. Then we heard people yelling the war with Germany was over. The guys got out their instruments and leaned out the window and started playing, while the people were waving at us. We went downstairs and joined the crowd. Everybody was laughing, hugging, and cheering.

On May 7, 1945, V-E (Victory in Europe) Day, we did a half-hour broadcast on the BBC, and we played our hit songs, including my solo, "Where or When." Gable's Gators disbanded on September 13, 1945, as our hospital was split up and sent elsewhere. The band gave nearly 200 performances during our time in England.

McDowell (standing) with Gable's Gators in England

Roxie Remley

Army: Captain, Women's Army Auxiliary Corps
Hometown: Darlington, Indiana
Career: College art professor

Queen Elizabeth sitting at Roxie Remley's desk signing papers.
Remley is standing next to the photographer. (Courtesy Roxie Remley)

I graduated from high school in Darlington, Indiana, in 1937, and attended business college in Racine, Wisconsin. I was employed there until I joined the Women's Army Auxiliary Corps on August 13, 1942. My three weeks of basic training was followed by training in motor transport school. I was assigned as the driver for the post chaplain. In November, I was accepted for Officer Candidate School and graduated from OCS in January 1943 as a third officer. I was given top-secret orders to report to Bolling Field in Washington, DC, and was assigned to a composite gun battery in the District of Columbia.

Gun batteries covered the East Coast and were part of our Coast Artillery Anti-Aircraft Eastern Defense Command. This composite battery, made up of men and women, was requested by General George C. Marshall to be an experiment. The army wanted to know if women could learn to operate radar equipment controlling the direction of 90mm guns loaded by men. Our battery was known as "Battery X" and was made from borrowed equipment previously used by other batteries in the area. For this special trial experiment, "Battery X" was located in a combat area, and women were not permitted by law to be assigned to combat areas in 1943; thus, the need for our orders to read "TOP SECRET."

Nazi U-boats and planes were creating havoc at this time on the East Coast. Seventy-four enlisted women and four WAAC officers received a few weeks of training on radar equipment and became part of the defense of our sector's military district on the East Coast. We also rotated duties at the motor pool and mess, and held executive positions of the battery along with a male officer of the same position. In early spring 1943, we were transported to a Delaware beach to test this new experiment by tracking and shooting down a sleeve trailing from the back of a plane. Guns and equipment were transported to the beach, and the battery was in full operation. The women lived in beach houses, and the men in tents. We ate K-rations for three days. Our female range crew and director, blind tracking with the 268 radar height finder, brought the 90mm guns on target. The WAAC commanding officer gave the command to fire. The sleeve target fell, not the plane. General Marshall's experiment was a success. It proved women could replace men on radar equipment, if the need should arise. Our "Battery X" was disbanded, and we were sent back to Bolling Field to await orders.

Things on the war front were changing by the summer of 1943, so I decided to volunteer for overseas duty. I left for England in March 1944, and after sailing for thirteen days, we docked at Gourock, Scotland, with 800 women and 10,000 GIs on board. The women were transferred to a staging area at Litchfield, England. I was a second officer at the time and was assigned to the headquarters of Service and Supply, United Kingdom Base WAAC detachment. I served as the unit's executive officer (XO), which was second in command of our unit. During off-duty hours, many of us women would take a bus to visit orphanages in Cheltenham, England. The children had been moved away from London and into countryside homes beginning in 1939. GIs and our women took the children candy, oranges, pencils, paper, and other items we received from home.

Historic D-Day arrived on June 6, 1944. We knew it was happening because on the night of June 5 the sky was completely covered with planes. Our planes were flying in some terrible weather, and it was a sight and noise one never forgets. As our Allied forces began advancing in Europe, our Service of Supply Headquarters began moving to London. I was the last to leave Cheltenham because I had to close out our WAAC company.

The very day I arrived in London, German V-2 rocket bombs were exploding over much of the city. The Nazis had been using buzz bombs, a flying Vengence-1, for many months. You could hear the buzzing sound when they were coming in, and, hopefully, you could take cover before they hit the ground and exploded. This was not true for the new V-2s. Nothing could be heard or seen until they exploded on the ground. Londoners seemed to be used to the bombings, since they had lived and died with bombings since 1940. We endured them almost daily, day and night, until the Germans surrendered in May 1945.

After V-E Day, we began plans to celebrate the third anniversary of the WAAC, no longer an auxiliary to the army, but a part of it. We were now called the Women's Army Corps (WAC). With an invitation to Her Majesty Queen Elizabeth, word spread that she had accepted the invitation to visit us, and a tour was arranged for the queen. When I returned to my office, Her

Majesty was sitting at my desk writing her signature on the Pallas Athene poster. The WAC ensign was a replica of the Greek Goddess of Victory.

In the summer of 1945, I became the commanding officer of the unit. This was a time when we were awaiting orders for all army personnel to either return to the States or be sent to the Pacific Theater. I closed out the London detachment in October 1945, my third unit closing in three and a half years. On November 5, I sailed on the *Queen Mary* ocean liner with thousands of GIs and WACs on board, and five days later we arrived in New York Harbor. I returned to Crawfordsville, Indiana, on November 12, 1945.

During the war, many women did things greater than I. Whatever job we did; I believe we left the service feeling we had made an important contribution to the war effort. I feel proud to have been a part of breaking ground for women in the newly organized Women's Army Auxiliary Corps and the Women's Army Corps.

Prime Minister Winston Churchill

"All great things are simple and they can be expressed in single words: freedom, justice, honor, duty, mercy and hope."

On May 10, 1940, the much-embattled prime minister of Great Britain, Neville Chamberlain, resigned his post, and Winston Churchill took the reins as prime minister. From that moment on, the bulldog style and "never surrender" attitude of Churchill would set the course for British citizens and the military, as they were the last European country left to stand up to Hitler's war machine. During the Battle of Britain—the bombings of British cities, and especially the blitz of London—the citizens of England adopted their leader's tough-minded determination as they bonded with him when he visited them in the bombed-out areas. He also boosted their morale with his inspiring speeches over the radio. Churchill and Franklin Roosevelt would form a strong alliance and a close relationship that would unite the two countries in their pursuit of defeating Germany and Japan.

Field Marshal Bernard Montgomery

"Leadership is the capacity to and will to rally men and women to a common purpose and the character which inspires confidence."

Field Marshall Montgomery, known to the Allies as "Monty," led his British Eighth Army to victory in the desert at El Alamein in North Africa over General Erwin Rommel's German Afrika Korps in 1942. He then proceeded to lead them into Sicily and then to Italy in 1943. Second in command to General Eisenhower, Montgomery's difficult personality clashed with that of Eisenhower's and created friction between the two. Montgomery was part of the D-Day planning for Normandy, and once in Europe he led his British Twenty-First Army Group across northwestern Europe and eventually across the Rhine River.

3

HEADING TO THE GATES OF HELL

"The only thing necessary for the triumph of evil is for good people to do nothing."

—Sir Edmund Burke

The Holocaust

"Where books are burned, in the end people will be burned."
—Heinrich Heine, German Jewish poet

Book burning in Berlin by Nazi storm troopers

The Holocaust was the systematic, state-sponsored persecution and murder of approximately six million Jewish men, women, and children. These atrocities of imprisonment, labor, and extermination began in 1933 and did not end until 1945. The Germans believed they were "racially superior," and the Jews were an "inferior people" who posed a threat to the German nation. Hitler believed that the German Aryan race was superior to all others.

Along with the Jews, other groups who were considered undesirables were also persecuted. To rid Germany of the "vermin," they were sent to various concentration, labor, and extermination camps. Over 11,000,000 died in these camps due to illness, starvation, firing squads, or in the gas chambers.

Later in the war, Allied forces moved across Europe, and they encountered the camps. At most locations, they saw starving, sick children and adults, and stacks of dead and decomposing bodies. The Allies were finally able to liberate the camps, and thousands of lives were saved.

Dr. Josef Mengele

"The more we do to you, the less you seem to believe we are doing it."

Josef Mengele (C)

At Auschwitz, Josef Mengele was known as the "Angel of Death." He personally sent thousands of Jews to their death, and he specialized in experimenting on twins to see how their bodily systems would react to being injected by different germs and diseases. He escaped Germany as the war was ending and was never captured.

Eva Mozes Kor

Holocaust Survivor
Hometown: Portz, Romania
Career: Realtor and curator of CANDLES Holocaust Museum and Education Center

Eva (left) and Miriam Mozes (twins) in Romania after World War II

My twin sister Miriam and I were born on January 31, 1935, in the tiny village of Portz, Transylvania. Besides my parents, we had two older sisters, Edit and Aliz. Once the Hungarian government took over Transylvania in 1940, they spread and advocated hatred. They also rewarded hating Jews. It was a rule of the day to call us "dirty Jews," beat us up, and spit on us. It was not looked down on.

During the four years of the Hungarian occupation, from 1940 to 1944, we heard a lot of rumors that Jews were being taken to Germany and murdered, so our hope was we would never be taken to Germany. We had a huge battery-operated radio, since there was no electricity in our village. Daily my parents would listen to the news in German, and Hitler would yell, "I'm going to kill all the Jews." I would ask my parents, "Who is Hitler, and why does he want to kill all the Jews?"

My parents would say, "You don't have to worry about it. Hitler is far away, and he will never come to this little village." Guess what? They were wrong; he did come to that little village to pick up six Jews. We were the only Jews in Portz.

What is the reason so many people always hate somebody who is richer? They envy them. Not because they think it is wrong to be rich, but they would like to be the ones. We were the rich people in the village. Now they had been given an opportunity and an excuse to hate us and get even with us. And they were rewarded for this. Even though they were Romanian, which wasn't necessarily good to be under Hungarian occupation, it was definitely better than being a Jew.

Fear. As a child, it started almost immediately. My parents said just be a good student, help around the farm when you come home, and say your prayers at night, and God will help us. Well, I did all those things, and my parents said everything would be okay. In my childish mind I wondered, "How on earth will it be okay? Conditions are getting worse and worse. When on earth will they start getting better and better if it is going to be okay?"

When I was eight years old, I told my parents we should escape to Romania. Jews in Romania were kept in ghettos, but they were never permitted to be picked up and taken to the camps. I do not know if the Germans challenged the Rumanian government, but Rumania decided to stand strong against Hitler, as did the Hungarian government. The Hungarian Jews were the last Jews to be taken to Auschwitz as a mass deportation—437,000 Jews from Hungary were sent to death camps.

I knew that once we were taken away in the cattle cars, nothing good was going to happen at the end of our travels. We were in the cattle cars for four days without any food and water, so we were numb when we stepped off the cattle car. There was such a big commotion as we left the cattle trains. Nobody could understand where we were. All we knew was we were not taken to Hungary to a labor camp, but we were taken to be murdered. We could see the wooden barracks, tall barbed-wire fences, guards in guard towers, dogs, and Nazis. We didn't really see, until later, people walking to work. They all looked like human skeletons. We did not know what the huge chimneys and smell were.

How do you convey to people a place like Auschwitz? If anybody would have ever described a place like Auschwitz, you would think there is no possibility of a place like that existing on the face of this earth. It's impossible to be prepared emotionally for a place like Auschwitz, no matter how you try. The conditions were atrocious. There was very little food. There was filth, lice, and rats everywhere. There was nothing that resembled anything that had to do with life.

When they were going to put the number tattoo on me, I knew I was supposed to cooperate, but I was going to give them as much trouble as I possibly could. I said, "I will let you do whatever you want as long as you bring my mother here." They promised we could see her the next day, but I knew they were lying. They ripped us apart with such brutality and force. I could not do much about it, but I could give them as much trouble as a ten-year-old could. I watched it; they heated a pen, like a writing pen, with a needle at the end. They heated it over the flame of a lamp, and when it got hot they dipped it into ink and burned it into me dot by dot. I was A-7063, and it is blurred on my left arm because I struggled and fought with them. Auschwitz is the only camp that gave tattoos.

Dr. Josef Mengele was a doctor who conducted atrocious genetic experiments with children who were twins. My sister Miriam and I were part of his studies. There was no doubt he was in charge. Whatever Mengele said, it would happen. He treated us like we didn't really exist, by creating an air of fear. His experiments were for the sake of science and advancing the Nazi regime.

There were 1,500 sets of twins at Auschwitz, and our biggest problem was the unknown diseases and germs that we were injected with. It was very clear to us you had to comply with them taking blood, giving you injections, and doing measurements. You had to cooperate to stay alive. My main way of resisting was to keep Miriam and me alive. From the moment I saw a dead child in the latrine, it was a clear message that it could happen to Miriam and me. I made a silent promise to myself that I would do everything in my power for Miriam and me not to end up on a latrine floor like that little girl. I believed, somehow, we would survive and walk out of that death camp alive.

Sisters Eva (left) and Miriam holding hands as they leave Auschwitz

When he came to our barracks, the supervisor would yell, "Mengele is coming," and we would stand by our bunk beds like little soldiers. We were in fear, because of the fear the supervisors had of him. One time, Mengele saw that some of the children had died, and he started raging furiously. His voice was carrying such horror. He yelled at the supervisors, "Why did you let these children die?" This was repeated many times, and I was very confused by this. We soon understood that Mengele was doing selections, and he was deciding who was going to live and who was going to die. I wondered what the big deal was if another person died. As I understand it today, those children who died in the barracks were not supposed to die. They died as a result of the conditions in the camp. Those who were used in the experiments by Mengele never died in the barracks. They died somewhere else or were murdered.

One day in the laboratory, I was injected with something that made me very ill, and I now know the illness came from the injections. When Mengele looked at my fever chart, he immediately said to the other doctors, "Too bad she is so young; she has only two weeks to live." He never examined me, and they didn't run any tests. He had to know what disease I had. How else could he pass that judgment?

I made my second silent pledge which was to prove Mengele wrong, to survive, and be reunited with my sister. I was between life and death for the next two weeks. For the times I was in the hospital I received no food, no water, and no medication. I would crawl on the barracks floor to a faucet at the other end. As I was crawling, I would faint in and out of consciousness. After two weeks, my fever broke, and I immediately felt a lot stronger. I remained in the hospital for another three weeks. You had to have some luck to survive. But you had to have an unbelievable will to live. Dying in Auschwitz was a daily reality. Everybody was sick at one time or another. Those who gave up their fight to live were as good as dead.

Miriam had lost her desire to fight for her life. When I asked her what they had done to her, she said, "I cannot talk about it, and I will not talk about it," and we did not talk about it until 1985. Miriam told me that for the first two weeks after I had been taken away to the laboratory, she was kept in isolation, with Nazi doctors monitoring her twenty-four hours a day. They were waiting for something to happen to Miriam. She didn't know what it was; they didn't tell her. It was the same two weeks that Mengele said I would die. If I had died, Mengele would have given directions that Miriam be rushed to his lab. She would have been killed immediately with an injection to the heart. Mengele wanted identical twins used in germ experiments to die as close in time together as possible, so there wouldn't be any change in the tissues and organs in the body except the germ.

There are a lot of people in the world today who say the Holocaust didn't happen. That it's an invention of the Jews. I wish the Holocaust didn't happen. I can tell you one thing. I experienced it. I had parents. I had a mother and a father. I had sisters; I had uncles; I had grandparents; I had cousins, and I had aunts. They all disappeared from the face of this earth.

We must never forget, and we must never let it happen again. We must also learn how to forgive our worst enemy. When we do, it frees our soul and sets us free. When I was able to forgive the Nazis, I liberated myself; I empowered myself, and I healed myself. Forgiveness does not condone, excuse, forget, or remove the tragedy of the Holocaust. Instead, it liberates and empowers those who forgive. Once a victim is able to forgive, he or she is no longer a victim.

Bob Swift

Army: Corporal, 71st Infantry Division
Hometown: Fountain City, Indiana
Career: Pharmaceutical sales trainer and inventor

Swift (left) and the French children who took him to assist with delivering a baby (Courtesy Robert Swift)

I landed at Le Havre, France, about a month after D-Day. Some little kids saw my Red Cross armband and to them that meant doctor. They pointed to it and pulled at my arm for me to go with them. They took me to a house in a small town near La Havre. One little kid's mother was having a baby. Fortunately, there was a midwife there, and she knew more about having a baby than I did. All I did was say, "Oui, oui," and everything came out okay. It was a boy.

I was a medic in a triage unit with the 71st Infantry Division, Third Army in Europe. Before I entered the army I had no medical training. We served as the aid station at the front lines. We would pick up the wounded soldiers and stabilize them until we could get them to the field hospital. There had to be at least two of us together because we had to put the wounded guys on stretchers and remove them during battle.

We had two physicians. One was my commanding officer, who was an ob-gyn from New Jersey. He was a hell of a belly surgeon. Occasionally we had to do surgery before we transported them back to the hospital. There were times he would get so tired that I had to close up for him; I sewed them up.

As we traveled across Europe, we were to be stationed at the front. Our section would be given coordinates on where we were to go, and then we would move in that direction. One day my commanding officer, his jeep, and our three ambulances got lost. This was near Dachau, and as we were traveling, about fifteen to twenty Germans came out of the woods, and we were captured. Our ambulances were marked, and they knew we were medics. They did not really want us because at that point everybody knew the war was over. They didn't even go through our stuff because they were trying to get out of there.

The closest place they could get rid of us was, I think, Dachau. It was at a concentration camp, and the ten of us were locked alone into an old barracks. Because of the smell we knew there were bodies rotting nearby, but I didn't see any. It was not long until members of the 71st Infantry caught up with us and let us go.

As we moved across southern Germany, we helped out in at least six or seven small concentration camps, and some large ones, but since we were primarily a triage unit, we called field hospital personnel in as soon as possible. Some of the smaller camps just had shack buildings with no floors. These were camps where the people had been in forced labor camps and were no longer useful. They would send them to these small camps to die.

We were usually the first ones into some of these smaller camps. Most of these camps were fenced in and locked up. There were times when that they kissed our feet. It was unbelievable. Some were dead, and the people around them took their clothes, so they could have some. I lost my sense of smell for three years—strictly psychological. You just block it out. They always told us they were hungry. We broke up our rations and passed them out, and they ate everything. Once they took the cigarettes out of our rations and ate them. We had no idea at the time that when we gave them the food it would make them sick, and they would die within minutes. As a result, we learned not to give out our food.

At one camp, many were so starved they couldn't even stand up, and we lost a lot. Since we could not feed them, the only thing we could do was try and give them IVs. We were able to get quite a few IVs in. With some of them, their skin was so thin there just wasn't much there to insert an IV. There is one big vein that runs across the top of the foot, and it's the last vein you want to use because if you get an infection you lose the leg. We had to do this because it's better to lose a leg than your life. When we entered the camps, lice were everywhere, and we treated the people with DDT. We lined them up and sprayed them with a powder.

When the Germans were fleeing, my commanding officer learned from some German POWs that a British flyboy prisoner camp was in the area, so he decided to go and get them. He talked one of the tank commanders in our unit into going with him, and they returned with the twelve British flyers. A couple days later, after learning of this event, General Patton chewed out the tank commander and my captain for taking one of "his" tanks. My commanding officer replied, "General, it's your job to kill people, and it's my job to save them." Without hesitation, Patton said, "Carry on, Captain."

In war you have your job, and you do it. You're all brothers; you become a family. If your brother is hurt, you're going to take care of him. If your brother is in danger, you're going to do what you can to help him. It's a brotherhood. We knew how bad some of the things were in Germany, and we didn't want to live like that. We were willing to do whatever it took.

When the war started, we were unprepared. Before the war, I don't think we were keeping up with what was going on in the world. We didn't know what was going on with the total picture; we had no idea. We have to know what's going on in the world and pay attention, because at that time we weren't.

> *"There are a lot of people in the world today who say the Holocaust didn't happen."*
> —Eva Mozes Kor, Holocaust survivor

I survived.

I was hanged in Auschwitz.

Mom and I were shot; I survived.

At nineteen, I was gassed.

We were all killed in Auschwitz in 1944.

My friends on each side of me survived. I was shot and killed fleeing into Hungary.

The three of us survived, but my wife and youngest son died at Auschwitz.

4

THE IMPERIAL EMPIRE

Japan

"Tora! Tora! Tora!"
(The code signifying surprise had been achieved for the attack on Pearl Harbor)
—Mitsuo Fuchiada

To expand its territory, the Empire of Japan set its eyes on invading and taking over China in the 1920s; in 1931 it began this quest by taking over Manchuria. When the League of Nations called on Japan to halt its aggression against China, it countered by pulling out of the League of Nations. An armistice was signed in 1933 between the two countries, but Japanese and Chinese troops clashed in an incident in 1937, which caused Japan to invade northern China.

In 1940, Japan became a member of the Axis nations when it signed a Tripartite Pact with Germany and Italy, and vowed to provide aid to one another for ten years. As Japan continued its goal of taking over territories in the western Pacific and East Asia, it encountered stiff sanctions from the United States, which included stopping scrap-iron shipments, halting oil shipments, and freezing Japanese assets in the United States. From the Japanese perspective, these sanctions were an act of war.

On December 7, 1941, Japanese naval and air forces conducted a surprise attack on the American naval and air bases stationed on Oahu, Hawaii. The Japanese navy and ground forces began military escalation that expanded throughout the Pacific. Only the United States posed any threat to Japan's mission of controlling the Philippines, China, Burma, Malaya, Singapore, the Dutch East Indies, and the Aleutian and Solomon Islands.

The Japanese believed that the United States, which was involved in a war in Europe, would be willing to negotiate a peace agreement with them. As a result of this thinking, they underestimated the resolve of the American people.

Under the leadership of General Douglas MacArthur and Admiral Chester Nimitz, Allied army and naval forces began a series of "island-hopping" campaigns, securing victories in hard-fought battles at Midway, New Guinea, Guadalcanal, Tarawa, Mariana Islands, Leyte Gulf, the Philippines, Iwo Jima, and Okinawa.

After the atomic bombs were dropped on Hiroshima and Nagasaki, in August 1945, the Japanese emperor, Hirohito, agreed to an unconditional surrender, and the Allied forces began the occupation of Japan.

Emperor Hirohito

"We have resolved to endure the unendurable and suffer what is insufferable."

He was the emperor of Japan during the war. Although not directly leading the war effort, he supported Japan's involvement in the war. At the end of the war, when defeat was imminent, he gave his approval for the Japanese kamikaze pilots to fly suicide missions, crashing their planes into American ships. These attacks were done in the name of the emperor. He made the decision for Japan's unconditional surrender after the dropping of the atomic bombs. When he broadcast this news over the radio to the Japanese people, it was the first time the people had ever heard his voice.

Prime Minister Hideki Tojo

"It goes without saying that when survival is threatened, struggles erupt between peoples, and unfortunate wars between nations result."

Tojo, a tough militarist, sought to establish Japan's military supremacy as he served as army chief of staff, and war minister; in October 1941 he was appointed as prime minister of Japan. Tojo, nicknamed the "Razor," authorized the attack on Pearl Harbor. When Japan surrendered, he attempted suicide but failed. During the war crimes trials after the war, he was convicted as a war criminal and was hanged in 1948.

Admiral Isoroku Yamamoto

"I fear all that we have done is to awaken a sleeping giant and fill him with a terrible resolve."

Yamamoto was a naval attaché in Washington, D.C., from 1925 to 1927, and he was aware of the United States' industrial and military capabilities. Initially, he was opposed to going to war with the United States, but when war was inevitable, it was he who was the mastermind of the attack on Pearl Harbor. Yamamoto would go on to lead the Japanese navy to victories early in the war, but the navy did not recover its dominance after his defeat at Midway. In 1943, the United States decoded a Japanese message that included Yamamoto's personal flight schedule. As a result, the Americans planned a successful ambush, and his plane was shot down in the South Pacific.

5

Remember Pearl Harbor!

"Air raid on Pearl Harbor. This is no drill."

Telegram from commander in chief of the Pacific Fleet (CINCPAC)
to all ships in Hawaiian area, December 7, 1941

Pearl Harbor

"Yesterday, December 7, 1941, a date which will live in infamy, the United States of America was suddenly and deliberately attacked by naval and air forces of the Empire of Japan."
—Franklin D. Roosevelt

Early in the morning on December 7, 1941, Japan countered the economic and material sanctions levied against it by the United States when hundreds of Japanese aircraft conducted a surprise attack on the American naval fleet stationed at Pearl Harbor in Hawaii.

The two-wave air attack, with over 200 planes, was secretly launched from aircraft carriers in the Pacific. This swift and well-executed plan struck a devastating blow to the American fleet, which resulted in over 2,300 military personnel being killed, 188 aircraft destroyed, and 18 ships damaged or sunk. The surprise attack on Pearl Harbor destroyed and damaged many navy vessels, but the Japanese high command realized their mission was not complete. The high-value aircraft carriers, which they had wanted to destroy, were out at sea during the attack.

The news stunned the nation and left Americans asking one another the question "Where is Pearl Harbor?" The next day, Americans huddled around radios in living rooms, grocery stores, and school classrooms as President Franklin D. Roosevelt spoke those immortal words, "Yesterday, December 7, 1941 …" Three days after President Roosevelt declared war on Japan, Germany and Italy issued their own declaration of war against the United States. The United States was fully engaged in World War II.

With the country now at war, the navy and its sailors, who vowed to "Remember Pearl Harbor," sailed out into the oceans around the world. Many would never return home.

Crews putting out fire on the USS *Wes Virginia*

Harold Dove

Navy: Chief Yeoman, USS *Sacramento*
Hometown: Hillsborough, Indiana
Career: International Harvester and Chrysler Motors

Sailors attempt to rescue men in the capsized USS *Oklahoma*

I was on the USS *Sacramento*, a gunboat, when we were attacked at Pearl Harbor on December 7, 1941. It was a terrible and frightening sight, and one I will never forget! Our military people in Washington knew the Japanese were going to attack but did not know where or when. It was a complete surprise.

The Japanese bombers were after our big ships docked on Battleship Row. We were all scared because we didn't know if our ship would be hit, since we were docked not far from Battleship Row.

My ship was among the first to start firing, and we were credited with knocking down one of the first Japanese planes. Their planes flew so low and close we could see the Japanese pilots in their cockpits. I remember slinging heavy ammunition belts over each shoulder and climbing an iron ladder to get ammunition to our antiaircraft gunners. Men were running everywhere trying to help however they could. It was awful to see our ships exploding and men jumping into the water, which was covered with fire and oil.

During the attack, I saw the USS *Arizona* exploding into flames. It sank in nine minutes, and 1,117 sailors and Marines on board were killed. I also saw the USS *Oklahoma*, which was just across the channel from us, get hit by a torpedo. The *Oklahoma* rolled over, trapping a lot of its men inside, and there was no way they could escape. I will never forget their screams for help and hearing the pounding on the bulkhead hoping someone could get them out. Nearly all of them drowned.

A large naval base like Pearl Harbor should have been prepared for an attack, and none of the high command saw that we were. Many lives would have been saved, if we had been ready for the attack.

People ask me about heroes during the attack. To me, the real heroes are the 2,341 men who never made it home and the 1,100 who were injured.

President Franklin Delano Roosevelt

"The massed armed forces of common humanity are on the march. They are going forward to Europe and to the vast Pacific converging on our enemies, Berlin and Tokyo."

Franklin D. Roosevelt, known as FDR, was elected president in 1932 while the nation was in the depths of the Great Depression, and he would go on to be reelected three more times. He brought the nation together through his "Fireside Chats," which he used to explain the economic problems and how he intended to create jobs for families. His upbeat personality helped give the American people a sense of hope during the Great Depression. When the United States was attacked by Japan, he set lofty production goals for American industry, so the troops who were fighting on two fronts would have the necessary equipment to win the war. He continued to "chat" with the American people about the war's progress and encouraged patriotism and sacrifice from all Americans. The presidency, the Great Depression, and the war took a heavy toll on his health, and with the Allies on the verge of defeating Germany, Roosevelt died while in Warm Springs, Georgia.

Tom Petso

Army: Staff Sergeant, Hawaiian Division
Hometown: Martins Ferry, Ohio
Career: Lumber company owner

Around 7:55 a.m. on the beautiful, sunny, warm day of December 7, 1941, I was playing touch football with a group of my buddies who lived in Schofield Barracks. As we looked up we were stunned at what we heard and saw. A wave of Japanese planes was flying only about two hundred feet above the ground. It seemed like just minutes, as they shot up and bombed over one hundred of our fighter planes on the air base. Some of the soldiers later recalled that they were flying so low you could actually see the Jap pilots smiling at you.

As the attack took place, there was panic and confusion because we weren't armed or prepared. We ran to get our rifles and ammunition belts, and once we were back outside we started firing at the planes. A few guys took a BAR (Browning automatic rifle) on top of the barracks and fired at the planes. They were wide open and exposed to enemy fire, but they shot down two planes.

Since our fighter planes were obliterated, I heard that two Army Air Corps pilots took off for another airfield, where each one found a fighter plane. They were credited with shooting down eight Japanese planes. It is also ironic, and good fortune, that when the Japanese planes went to destroy our bomber base at Hickam Field, our bombers were not there. They were returning from training exercises in California; thus, our B-17 bombers were spared.

After the initial attack on Wheeler Field, the Japanese planes came in a second wave, bombing and strafing our ships, which were together on Battleship Row. From our location at the barracks, we helplessly stood by and watched the horror unfold before our eyes. Within minutes, our naval fleet was destroyed. We could see the burning, smoking, and sinking ships while men were trapped in oil-slick water with flames all around them. Others were in sinking ships and could not get out. It was an experience I will never forget. One of those killed was a boy I knew in high school. He was eating breakfast when a plane dropped a bomb on his mess hall.

Another thing I remember is part of Pearl Harbor history. I saw the two Japanese ambassadors who stopped at Pearl Harbor on their way to Washington, D.C. to meet with Secretary of State Cordell Hull. The entire division gave them a ceremonial welcome. Little did we know that the Japanese naval fleet and their aircraft carriers were headed east to Pearl Harbor.

6

THE HOME FRONT

*"In this year 1942, we shall produce 60,000 planes
... 45,000 tanks ... 20,000 antiaircraft guns ...
and 8,000,000 deadweight tons of shipping.*

*Next year, 1943, we shall produce 125,000 airplanes,
75,000 tanks ... 35,000 aircraft guns ...
and 10,000,000 tons of shipping.
We must raise our sight all along the production line.
Let no man say it cannot be done. It must be done."*

—Franklin D. Roosevelt

We Can Do It!

"There is one front and one battle where everyone, man, woman and child will be privileged to remain in action throughout the war."
—Franklin Delano Roosevelt

While not prepared for war, America, almost overnight, became a war machine like no other in history. Young men enlisted by the thousands to fight, and American people gave up luxuries to support the war effort. When the men left the workplace to join the military, millions of women filled their jobs in the workforce and helped make the military equipment and supplies for those fighting the war. In addition, families grew victory gardens to produce their own food, so the government would have more to send to the troops. Towns across America held scrap, rubber, and paper drives, and recycled these items to help make military equipment. American citizens also responded to the government policies of rationing gas, food, and other goods.

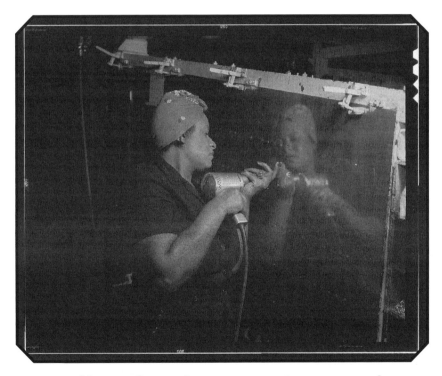

One of the many factory jobs was riveting equipment parts together, which earned women workers the nickname "Rosie the Riveter."

Families proudly displayed Blue Star banners in their windows indicating family members serving in the military. The blue star was changed to gold if a family member was killed.

Rose Rahanian Balogh

Home Front: Factory worker
Hometown: Detroit, Michigan
Career: Ford Motor Company

I was eighteen when I graduated from high school. During the war, I went to work in a factory in Dearborn, Michigan, and worked there for two years. Before the war it was a glass factory, but it was converted to assemble wings for B-24 bombers, and it was my job was to put rivets in the wings. I guess you could call me an original "Rosie the Riveter," since my name is Rose. We wore head scarves or nets for safety reasons. The factory was very clean but noisy. I worked eight-hour days five days a week, and mostly all women worked in my factory. I also participated in the monthly factory blood drives. At only eighteen, I understood the importance of the job we were doing.

Sally Beck

Home Front
Hometown: Indianapolis, Indiana
Career: College professor, clinical, social and learning psychology

A rubber salvage drive in Hazard County, Kentucky
(courtesy of the Bobby Davis Museum)

I was only ten years old when Pearl Harbor was bombed. Shortly after the war began, President Roosevelt called upon the American people to take part in the war effort. From the beginning, it became clear to civilians that the government would need large sums of money to support our military. The president encouraged all citizens to become involved, including children. I remember unwrapping chewing gum so the tinfoil could be taken to collection centers.

We grew victory gardens to help feed ourselves, since other food was needed to send overseas to feed our troops. Rubber, including tires, lightbulbs, sugar, cigarettes, butter, and even toothpaste were rationed. We turned in old lightbulbs and toothpaste tubes to get new ones. Gasoline was rationed. You had to have a special sticker on your car's windshield which indicated how much gasoline you were allowed. Anything that could be rationed or collected was used to support our troops.

People were asked to purchase war bonds by contributing $18.75. In ten years, when the war bond matured, it was worth $25. Even school children bought special government savings stamps by using their allowance or doing other small jobs. We could purchase them in our home rooms in school. When the coupon book totaled $18.75, we would buy a war bond. After the war, many people who had purchased war bonds were able to use the maturity value of their bonds to help purchase homes or cars, or to start small businesses. The bonds helped to provide a new beginning for many Americans.

Almost everyone did what was necessary and more. Everything we were asked to do or collect was to support the war. I don't remember any of our neighbors complaining about the sacrifices we made, when the war rationing began. It was an expectation and the patriotic thing to do.

One of my fond memories was when my mother saved enough sugar to make me chocolate fudge for my birthday, since she did not have enough to make a cake. She cooked it at night, and held a flashlight while she stirred the fudge. We taped down the window shades so the light could not be seen outdoors, but a neighborhood "watch warden" saw the light on and came to the door. He blew a loud whistle and knocked on the door. We were told that no visible lights were allowed, until the blackout was over. The fudge was completely overcooked, and we had to throw it out, burned pan and all. There was no more fudge until the war was over.

Another time, we had not eaten any meat for several weeks. Mother went to the grocery store to buy some, but the butcher said he had no meat. However, he did give her a large ham bone with a few ham scraps. Mother ground the ham scraps, added some other ingredients and made a ham loaf that was delicious. My mother, as many other women, could do a lot with very little.

Women's silk nylon hose were not worn, since they were used in the war effort to help make parachutes. As teenagers, we had dances but no nylon hose to wear. We would go to the dime store or drugstore and buy pancake makeup and use wet sponges to paint our legs. A friend would take a marking pen and draw a seam up the back of each leg. All the gals prayed for no rain during and after the dance.

Sometimes, for a joke, my girlfriends and I would go to a store and start a rumor that a shipment of hose would be coming in soon. Lines of women would form quickly, waiting for the hose that didn't come, since stores were not getting any shipments. Shoes were also a problem and had to last. If you wore out the soles, you had to cut out pieces of cardboard and line the inside of your shoes.

On one occasion, my daddy had to make a business trip to Louisville, Kentucky, and Mother and I joined him for the trip. On the way back, we had a flat tire. Fortunately, there was a service station close by. Daddy saw a stack of old tires and asked the attendant if we could have one to put on the car. Although he wasn't supposed to give tires to anyone, because they were to be collected and used for the war, he told us to go ahead and look for one. It must have been a funny sight to see the three of us climbing a stack of tires to find one that fit. Once daddy got the tire on the car, we could only travel about 22 miles per hour, since the tire was so worn. We didn't want to have another flat. It took several hours to get back to Indianapolis.

At the end of our church service, we always sang "America the Beautiful." Several years after the war, we sang that hymn one Sunday, and I broke out crying, but I didn't know why. The pastor told me it made me think of the past, when we sang the song during the war years.

Another church memory I have is the soldiers and sailors who were in town on Sundays. They would sit in the last three rows of pews, which were reserved for them. After the church service had ended, families would rush back to invite a serviceman home for Sunday dinner. Later we would take them to where they could catch a bus to return to their camp. We saved food stamps during the week, so we could have a special meal on Sunday and invite the servicemen or servicewomen to share dinner with us. Those were fond memories.

My family and I never felt the sacrifices we were making caused an undue burden. We did what we were supposed to do. The morale of families in our neighborhood was very high because we knew we were helping the war effort.

Brigitt Caito

Home Front
Hometown: Elkhart, Indiana
Career: Homemaker

Robert, Brigitt (center), and Alberta Reno

Brigitt Caito

My father, Corporal Robert V. Reno, was killed in action (KIA) on Easter Sunday, April 1, 1945. I was born on August 20, 1945, four months after his death. My brother was only ten months old, when my father was killed. We became but two of the over 183,000 World War II war orphans.

In January 1942, my father did his basic military police training at Fort Barrancas in Pensacola, Florida. Further training was done in 1944, at Fort Benning, Georgia, when he was assigned to the 71st Infantry Division.

In January 1945 his unit was sent to Le Havre, France, where they continued northeast through France and crossed the Rhine River. Outside of Frankfurt, Germany, the 71st Division's job was to protect the flanks of General Patton's Third Army, which was headed toward Berlin.

On that fateful Easter morning, the Seventy-First encountered the German 6th SS Mountain Nord Division, which was in a final defensive stand as the Allies were advancing through the heart of Germany. My father was killed on the first day of battle, being shot in the head. After heavy fighting for three days, his division was able to force the German 6th SS Mountain Division to retreat.

On April 14, 1945, my mother received a telegram informing her of his death. He remained buried in France for three years. His mother was persistent that his body be returned and buried in his hometown of Winchester, Indiana. She made the necessary arrangements for his body to be brought home in October 1948.

Growing up, Mother never talked about my father, nor about the circumstances of his death, to my brother and me. This was a fairly common practice at the time. People wanted to look forward, not look to the past. As a result, I did not have the opportunity to find out what kind of man he was. My brother and I lived surrounded by "a wall of silence," a silence that would haunt me most of my life. In a "Dick and Jane; mother and father; Sally, Spot, and Puff world," we could only live with the "if only" in our lives. At one point, I do remember my mother saying she was angry at my father for enlisting in the army. I know she mourned his loss, but her life was subjected to many changes. Dreams were shattered.

As war orphans, we see our fathers as forever young, forever perfect. They had such a short time on earth, not enough to be flawed; yet, our ideals and images of them were tempered by reality. I have a wounded child inside of me, and many of us live with unresolved grief and questions still unanswered. The solace we do have is in knowing our fathers made their ultimate sacrifice in a just war.

Death defined so much for us as World War II orphans. We are survivors, and our values and ethics are pronounced. Our fathers died that we might live in freedom. Their lives were cut short, but they are with us. Their lifeblood, shed in hundreds of battles, still runs in our veins today. Their lives and deaths made a difference.

We are finally finding each other in an organization called AWON—the American WWII Orphans Network, which was founded in 1992 and dedicated to our fathers and the service of their families.

Joyce Hodson

Home Front: American Women Volunteer Service (AWVS)
Hometown: Allentown, Pennsylvania
Career: Homemaker

After graduating from Allentown High School, I joined the American Women Volunteer Service, which was a branch of the United Service Organization (USO). The purpose of this volunteer group was to provide various kinds of support for our soldiers prior to and during the war. My first job was a "doughnut girl," and we served doughnuts and coffee to the troops at the train station as they traveled to their military camps.

In our neighborhood were several German families, and they were often looked upon with suspicion by other neighbors. The truth is these families were loyal to America. However, there was a German American Nazi organization called the Bund. Their job was to try to recruit young boys to become a part of the Hitler Youth Organization, which was pro Nazi. A neighbor boy discovered that his father was a member of the Bund and was a German spy. One day, two FBI agents arrested his father and took him away. The boy and his family never saw him again. Shortly after, the boy joined the army with some other neighborhood boys.

While working, I continued volunteering for the AWVS in a variety of capacities. I worked on the Rationing Board, sold war bonds and stamps, helped with the victory gardens, and planned dances and social events for the soldiers..

I also visited the burn hospital at Indiantown Gap, Pennsylvania, and it was very difficult to see so many disfigured faces and bodies. During my visits, I would talk with them, and since most of these soldiers were badly injured and unable to write letters, they would tell me what to write, and I would write the letters to send home to their families and wives. The soldiers seemed to be more concerned about the welfare of their families than their injuries. The courage of these soldiers touched my life. Throughout the four years of the war, I continued to write letters and send care packages to our soldiers overseas. While I did not know these men, I could tell from letters they sent to me that many were homesick, lonely, and afraid.

I became engaged to one of the neighborhood boys with whom I had graduated from high school. He wanted to get married before he went overseas, but I told him that I would wait for him, until he returned home. Unfortunately, one day after the invasion of Normandy, his bomber crashed while taking off to make bombing runs over France. I was heartbroken when I got the letter informing me of his death. Tragically, three of his four brothers were also killed in the war. His parents were devastated to lose four of their five sons. I will never understand how his parents endured this terrible tragedy.

During the war, I was proud to have served my country on the home front. I did not fight the battles, but, hopefully, I brought some comfort, support, and encouragement to those brave men who did. We can't repay the soldiers for their sacrifice and what they did for us.

Mrs. Marcella Jefferies

Home Front: Factory worker
Hometown: Lynn, Indiana
Career: Jewelry store sales

Poster recruiting women into the workforce

On my sixteenth birthday, Pearl Harbor was bombed. Some of my friends and I were riding in a car in downtown Greenville, Ohio, when we heard the news on the radio.

After high school, I began work in a newly opened factory in Richmond, Indiana, the Perfect Circle. It was designed to make piston rings for our ships. A year later, I worked in the Crosley factory, where we made jeeps for the war. Many women worked in the factories, and even as a teenager I understood the jobs we were doing were important. We worked five days a week, eight hours a day. Sometimes I worked the midnight to 8:00 a.m. shift. My girlfriend and I never thought about our safety, when waiting for a bus at that time of the morning. We didn't have much free time, but when we did, we would go to a movie or roller skating. My three brothers served during the war, and my high school boyfriend was killed.

Peggy Votaw (Doherty)

Home Front
Hometown: Huntington, Indiana
Career: Cofounder of Votaw Electric

C. A. Doherty

My brother, C. A., was my "hero" long before he enlisted in the army. He was ten years older than me, and as a child I adored him. My mother and father divorced when I was young, and, later, my dad was killed in an auto accident. From about the time I entered the 5th grade; C. A. took on the role of "dad" and became the head of our household.

Above all, he thought that I was good, and he expected me to make the right choices. He was an influence in every decision that I made. This included when it was time to cut off my long braids to get a more current hairstyle and expected dating morals. He didn't offer the dreaded "sex" talk, but he gave me very good reasons to protect my innate goodness and make wise choices about my conduct. I never wanted to disappoint C. A. and his faith in me.

When my brother left to serve his country during World War II, it left a very big hole in our family. I can still recall the day he left for basic training. A bus was to pick up the young recruits in front of Ellis's restaurant on Jefferson Street in downtown Huntington, Indiana. We went inside and ate something, but as we did, we all had huge lumps in our throats. When the bus arrived, and we had to hug good-bye, I remember hanging onto C. A. and crying. It must have been heartbreaking for him to have had to pry his "baby sister's" arms loose and board that bus with all the uncertainties of our futures.

With my brother in the army, my mother worked second shift at the Majestic defense plant in Huntington, where they manufactured bombs during the war. My older sister moved back in with us, along with her two-year-old daughter, when her husband left for the army. Not a day went by without one of us writing to C. A. or my brother-in-law. A front window of our small but adequate apartment displayed a card with two stars on it, showing that we had two people serving our country in the military. Our neighborhood, like all neighborhoods, had a volunteer air raid warden, who was identified by an armband. Even in our small community, we observed blackouts faithfully. There was a unified feeling of support for our men and for one another that helped us all get through the tough times.

Like most people, we were more than willing to sacrifice scarce food items in order for our troops to be fed. We traded at a small neighborhood grocery store, and the price of our groceries would be added to our tab. We paid our bill at the end of the week, on payday. Occasionally, a surprise scarce item would be secretly slipped into our grocery bag by our grocer. One time, we were very excited when a small can of pineapple showed up in our bag. We were always looking for better ways to ship cookies or other treats. One suggestion that we tried was dipping oranges in paraffin. The fudge that we mailed according to packaging instructions did reach him, but the fudge and foil were inseparable.

Before C. A. shipped out to Europe, he married his fiancée, Vi; she was young, very young. When C. A. had been overseas for many months, I remember Vi telling me, "Sometimes, I can barely remember how he looks." Still, she held fast to her memories and worked and prayed for him continuously. She moved to Huntington to stay close to our family. When C. A. went overseas, he was part of the 314th Infantry Regiment, with the 79th Division. He was a sergeant when his unit landed in France, but because of his actions during a battle at Cherbourg his commanding officer gave him a battlefield commission. As a mother myself, I can't imagine how my mother dealt with having her only son in constant danger. She went to bed at night not knowing where he was or how he was doing.

Life did go on, of course, and I spent much of the war years in high school. I went to proms and did all the other things girls in high school do. One difference compared to the prewar years was the emphasis on physical training for girls at our school. Obstacle courses were set up in the gym, and one of the classes I took was "riflery." During my senior year in high school, I was nominated for "Miss Modulus" which was the name of our school yearbook. Vi wrote to my brother and informed him of my nomination, and he sent me a document with the signatures of almost everyone in his unit voting for me. Ticket selling for a high school production was the deciding factor, and not even my brother's soldiers could help me win, so I became "runner-up Miss Modulus."

While C. A. was still overseas, Vi sent him a key to their first apartment, which he kept with him, as he looked forward to the day when he could open the door to that apartment and see his wife. When the war was over, and he could come home, C. A. didn't announce his arrival date. Instead, he arrived at his apartment and opened the door before the rest of us even knew he was back.

I remember where I was when I heard C. A. was back home. I was at the "Swing-In" which was a hangout inside the local YMCA. The teenagers went there after school and on Friday and Saturday nights to dance to jukebox music and hang out with our friends. My mother called me and said that he was home. I can't explain the joy and relief I felt. I practically ran home with my feet barely touching the brick sidewalk. The reunion was sweet. C. A. was shocked at how much I had grown up. His memory of me was the picture of a child, and now I was a young lady.

After the war, a couple of C. A.'s men who served under him while in France and Germany made a special visit to meet my mother. One of them said, "You don't understand, Mrs. Doherty. C. A.'s men would have died for him." The respect and admiration these men had for my brother showed that I had been right all along. He really was a "hero."

My brother was an inspiring and powerful presence in my life, and God placed another outstanding man in my life. I had the honor of being married to Jim Votaw for over fifty years. We didn't know each other in school, but I knew of him because he played basketball and football. I went to the games and cheered for the teams, but he didn't know I existed. He was a familiar face, one that I recognized from a distance.

Jim left high school during his senior to join the navy because he knew that he would soon be drafted into the army. He was sent to Pearl Harbor shortly after the attack and remained there for four years as a dental technician. Like many, he entered the war as a boy and came out as a man. Jim didn't know what the future out of the navy would be, but he had dreams, ambitions, and great hopes. At our 50th wedding anniversary party, through tears of gratitude, he told of how at nineteen years old he prayed and asked God for three things while in the navy. He wanted a good wife, a family, and a job. He told all who were at our party, "God has given me all the things I prayed for."

Many of our World War II veterans put the three or four years they had spent serving our country behind them and moved forward in their lives. Jim had the ability to see possibilities where others saw obstacles. He had an unlimited sense of God, and an almost unlimited sense of what an individual could accomplish, as always, with the help of God.

7

ISLAND-HOPPING IN THE PACIFIC

(courtesy Robert Albright)

Combat in the Pacific

"I Shall Return."
—General Douglas MacArthur

After Japan launched its surprise attack on Pearl Harbor on December 7, 1941, and severely damaged America's naval fleet, the United States declared war on Japan. America was not prepared for war, and President Roosevelt called upon the American people to make personal sacrifices. The country began to build the world's most powerful war machine ever assembled.

Japan achieved a long series of military successes beginning in December 1941 by capturing numerous islands and territories in the Pacific, including Guam, Wake, Malaya, Singapore, and the Philippines. These conquests provided the Japanese with strategic locations for their military and naval bases.

In June 1942, the turning point for the Allies fighting in the Pacific was a naval battle known as the Battle of Midway. The Japanese naval fleet sustained heavy losses and was turned back in late summer. The victory at Midway ended Japan's dominance of the seas, and American forces slowly gained naval and air supremacy in the Pacific.

With the bloody and hard-fought victory on the island of Guadalcanal, the eyes of the American people began to turn to the Pacific. Soon, mothers and fathers began reading about their sons in hard-fought battles on islands with names they had never heard before. Newspaper headlines filled front pages with the names of the Solomons, Marianas Islands, Marshalls Islands, Gilbert Islands, the Coral Sea, Peleliu, Pavuvu, New Britain, Cape Gloucester, Mindanao, Leyte, Luzon, New Guinea, Tinian, Tarawa, Iwo Jima, and Okinawa.

Each island provided its own obstacles, as some were filled with dense jungles with rough and steep terrain, further complicated by extreme heat and heavy rains. Other islands were dominated by bare, hard, jagged land that made it nearly impossible to find cover from the enemy, let alone dig a foxhole.

Late in 1944, American forces liberated the Philippines, and in 1945 won victories on the islands of Iwo Jima and Okinawa, suffering heavy losses during both battles. By capturing these two strategic islands, American and Allied forces were in position to prepare for a mainland invasion of Japan.

The Pacific Campaign lasted for over three years, with both the Japanese and Allies sustaining thousands of casualties. The men who traversed these islands and demonstrated selfless acts of bravery ensured that the names of the once unknown islands and the acts of heroism that occurred there would never be forgotten.

Les Cheesman

Army: Staff Sergeant, 43rd Infantry Division
Hometown: Terre Haute, Indiana
Career: Insurance agent

Cheesman in Terre Haute, Indiana, 1945

I was drafted at age eighteen but didn't report to boot camp until after I graduated from high school. I did my boot camp at Fort McClelland, and after that I was sent to Fort Ord, California, for further training. Next, I went to Camp Stoneman, which is north of San Francisco, California. I later shipped out with 124 other men to New Caledonia in the Pacific.

We served as replacements for the 43rd Infantry Division, after the original Guadalcanal battle. It was our job to "mop up" what was left of Japanese soldiers who were still on the island. The Japs liked to fight us at night by attacking or dropping bombs. We went out on patrols looking for the enemy. Oftentimes, we were engaged in firefights, and they would ambush us from the tall grasses. During five months of battle on Guadalcanal, we lost 22 of the 125 men in my unit. Later, we were assigned to protect Henderson Field, so our fighter pilots could land and conduct their missions. If a pilot hit an enemy ship or shot down an enemy plane, he would do a "victory roll" over the airfield.

After Guadalcanal, we landed in New Guinea in water that was up to our backpacks. Fortunately, the Japanese were not firing at us. They usually preferred to let our troops land and fight us when we got on the island. On New Guinea, the island natives were very helpful to us by carrying our ammunition and food supplies, and served as stretcher carriers for our wounded.

On one patrol, we were marching upstream in a river, and leaches attached to my leg. If you pulled them off, it would break the skin and bleed; it was painful. One of the guys told me to take a cigarette and burn them off with the lit end, and this worked. One day our cook asked if we wanted doughnuts, and of course we said yes. He told us to watch for the C-47 cargo planes and where they dropped the supplies. The doughnuts were inside waterproof mortar round containers, which floated.

When the supplies were dropped, we were on one side of the river, and the Japs were on the other side. We had been engaged in some firefights, but when the doughnuts landed in the water, the Japs ran for them, and so did we. We didn't shoot at one another. This was a funny sight because doughnuts floating in a river in the jungle caused a temporary cease-fire. We never did figure out how the Japanese knew there were doughnuts in the containers.

From New Guinea, we went to the Philippines, landing at Lingayen Gulf, on the island of Luzon. When we landed on Luzon, we were hit hard by Japanese artillery fire. They were positioned in old silver mines in the hills and were in a good position to fire on us, but we couldn't hit them. Everyday about 3:30 p.m., they would roll out a huge artillery gun, which had a long range, and would fire on our ships off the beach. At night the Japs would march through the hills holding lanterns and taunting us, since they knew we could not reach them. We had trouble getting the coordinates to call in a bombing attack.

One day, we saw one of our small Piper Cub scout planes trying to find the location of that large artillery gun, when all of a sudden a Japanese Zero fighter fired on it. The scout plane started going down in a spiral, and the Zero left. But then we saw the scout plane pull out of the dive. The pilot had "faked a hit" to get away from the Japanese fighter plane. The pilot finally got the coordinate location of their big gun, and our bombers were able to destroy the artillery gun and kill a lot of Japanese soldiers as well.

On one patrol, I was the platoon leader for 22 men. We were ambushed by some Japs, and eleven of my men were wounded, and eleven had combat fatigue, also called shell shock. The 11 who had shell shock were sent back to the States, because they were in no condition to fight anymore.

I often thought about how we fought the Japanese twenty-four hours a day. They fought us at night, and we fought them during the daytime.

On another occasion, my buddy and I were trying to rescue one of our guys who was wounded and in an open grassy field. A Japanese sniper in a tree had shot him and was trying to finish the job. My buddy said he would go around the side to draw his fire, and I was to shoot the sniper. I was finally able to shoot him. I then crawled out in the field and brought him back, so he could be taken to a field hospital. My buddy and I received the Silver Star and Bronze Star for Valor, respectively. However, after all of the fighting I experienced, I realized you don't fight for medals; you fight to save your buddies. A lot of guys died trying to save someone.

One of the dangerous things for an infantryman, besides getting shot at or stepping on land mines, was the possibility of getting hit by one of your own artillery shells. Although our artillery crews would try to fire about seventy-five yards in front of us, sometimes the shells fell short. These were called "short rounds." During a Japanese artillery barrage I was in a foxhole with my buddy when a shell exploded nearby. I sustained shrapnel in my head and shins. After two days in the hospital, I was released and was sent back to the front lines.

A few months later, I was hit by shell shrapnel again. The guy close by me was also hit and died. My wound was more serious this time, since my ribs were crushed, and a lung was collapsed. I had to be carried down the hill on a stretcher by six of our men in order to get me to a field hospital. The Japs prefered to wound us rather than kill us, because they knew we took care of our wounded and dead. When six guys were carrying you on a stretcher, that meant there were six fewer guys to fight them.

I was sent to a field hospital, where I was operated on by a surgeon from Richmond, Indiana. I believe God sent this surgeon to save my life. If he wasn't a chest surgeon, I'm not sure I would have survived. The next day when I woke up, the ward boy said the doctor had removed everything inside me and laid it on my stomach while he was performing the operation—not a pleasant thought. To this day, I still carry a piece of shrapnel in my lung.

Averitte Corley

Marine Corps: Corporal, 6th Replacement Heavy Artillery Antiaircraft (Provisional)
Hometown: Indianapolis, Indiana
Career: Police officer and US Postal Service

Montford Marines football team at Montford Point, North Carolina

At sixteen, I dropped out of high school after my sophomore year. I lied about my age and joined the Army Air Corps in March 1944. While in processing at Fort Benjamin Harrison, in Indianapolis, Indiana, I saw something that took me by surprise. There was a large group of Japanese soldiers who were training. I later learned that they were Japanese Americans who had enlisted and were part of the 100th Battalion, 442nd Regimental Combat Team. Later in the war, this division served with distinction in Italy and throughout Europe and became one of the war's most highly decorated units.

From Fort Harrison, I went to Keesler Field in Mississippi for basic training and was assigned to the 1169th Training Group. While at Kessler Field, I became friends with Jimmy Bivins, who became heavyweight boxing champion. I shined his shoes and hung around with him. Nobody messed with me.

After basic training, I was sent to Baer Field in Fort Wayne, Indiana, as a general duty soldier charged with helping load our big C-47 cargo planes. Baer Field was where the C-47 transport planes departed for the China-Burma-India Theater. I was scheduled to go to China-Burma-India but did not pass the physical requirements for pilot training. Somehow, it was discovered I was only sixteen, and I was sent home with an honorable discharge for the convenience of the government.

A few months later, when I was seventeen, I lied about my age again because I wanted to join the Marine Corps. I was standing with a navy group at the processing center, when a Marine sergeant, who was recruiting black Marines, told me I was going to be a Marine. I had seen the movie *Guadalcanal Diary* at the Indiana Theater in Indianapolis, and from then on I knew I wanted to become a Marine. My wish had come true. Prior to June 1942, there were no blacks in the Marines.

I became part of "this new military experiment" of training black Marines. For Marine Corps basic training, we were sent to Montford Point, North Carolina, in July 1945, which was a segregated training facility at Camp Lejeune, North Carolina.

Basic training was demanding and intensive for all Marines. We were treated more harshly by our black drill instructors (DIs) than the white ones. Our DIs wanted to make us better Marines, so we would be prepared to endure the racial and war-related challenges many of us would experience. Once you are trained as a Marine, you feel you can do anything.

We were the first black World War II Marines, and we had to measure up, being the first black fighters in the last branch of the military service to accept us. After boot camp, I was sent to the Marine Corps Communication School to become a telephone lineman and message center specialist.

Marines from Montford Point were being sent to the Pacific every week after their basic training. For liberty, we would often go to a small town called Jacksonville, North Carolina. We had to stay in the black community which was on the "other side" of the railroad tracks. The white people did not want us in their part of town. The bars and pool halls said, "Whites Only." If you went across the tracks, you might not come back. This was racism at its worst, and it was "the law of the land" in the South at this time.

When we were ready to board the buses to go to town, two lines were formed, one for the white Marines and one for the black Marines. The whites got on the bus first. If a bus was full of black Marines, we were expected to give up our seats. I know some of the white Marines were embarrassed, because many of these guys thought it wasn't right for us to be treated like this. We were all Marines, and many of the white Marines had begun to accept us. However, these were the social norms of the time, which reinforced the practice of segregation and discrimination against black soldiers. You didn't dare to rebel, or you could get in big trouble.

My first overseas assignment was with the 6th Replacement, and we were sent to Saipan and Guam in the Mariana Islands in the Pacific. Our job was to relieve elements of the 52nd Defense Battalion, which was a heavy antiaircraft artillery unit, and we were to guard 2,000 Japanese prisoners of war. There were only 250 to 300 of us. The prisoners were held in a large, fenced-in compound, and one of my jobs was to feed seven prisoners who were going to be hanged by the navy for war crimes. These Japanese soldiers had killed and cannibalized a family of Chamorro civilians. They were the biggest Japs I had ever seen, well over six feet tall, had red eyes, and wore only loincloths. Their appearance was menacing. At nineteen, I didn't like going into the compound to give them their food, even though guys were outside the fence with machine guns trained on them. I felt these seven prisoners could grab and kill me, since they had nothing to lose.

One day, leaflets were dropped telling us about an all island dance that was being hosted by a white Marine outfit on Mount Tapochau. Our unit went to the dance expecting that there would be some black Red Cross girls sent over from Guam. Well, there were no black Red Cross girls. A black sailor asked a white girl to dance, and she said to him, "How dare you ask a white woman to dance." We couldn't believe it, and the guy hauled off and hit her, knocking her to the floor, where she landed at the feet of the island commander. He ordered his aide to shoot the guy, who had already run out of the building and down the hill. We heard shots and ran outside thinking some Japanese may be shooting at us. It was the commander's aide shooting at the sailor, who got away.

When I got outside, I ended up standing right next to the white commander, so I was the first black he saw. He told an aide to take me to the brig, and the aide told him I had just come outside. He was told to take me to the brig anyway and hold me, until they found the guy who hit the nurse. When they found the guy, I was released, and all charges were expunged from my records. I thought, here I am, a black Marine who had to spend three days in solitary confinement because a black sailor hit a white woman.

After my release, my orders were to report to the 5th Service Command Headquarters on Guam. I didn't understand why I was the only black guy in the outfit. I was even promoted to sergeant and provided with a recon vehicle to drive to headquarters. Later, I thought this assignment and promotion was made so I wouldn't press charges against the white commander.

As Marines, both blacks and whites served in combat and various support and supply roles, but the army did not have many black soldiers in combat units. In the 7th Ammunition Company, serving on Pelelieu, some black Marines were assigned as stretcher (litter) carriers to bring the wounded white Marines back to camp for medical treatment. Because of their courage and efforts, some of the white wounded soldiers referred to them as the "Black Angels."

The military became a safe place for me and provided a sense of security that I did not have growing up. I liked the discipline and structure, which I had first learned in the Boy Scouts and from being in my high school ROTC.

In August 1947, at nineteen years old, I returned to the States. When I joined the Marines, I had no idea I would become a part of history. I am proud to be a Montford Point Marine. These were men of strength, pride, and character who overcame segregation and bigotry while working for a common goal.

Everett Hodgin

Army: Tech Sergeant, 38th Infantry Division
Hometown: Richmond, Indiana
Career: Self-employed auto supplier

Camp Shelby, Mississippi, July 1941

After entering the army in 1942, I was sent to Fort Harrison in Indianapolis for processing. From there, I went to Camp Shelby, Mississippi, for basic training, and then to Camp Polk in Louisiana, where we did our simulated jungle training. I will never forget when we got our orders saying we were shipping out to go overseas. Our captain said to our company, "Men, divide your group in half. This half over here will probably make it home. The other half probably won't." After about 30 days on the troop carrier, we landed at Leyte Gulf. Getting off the landing craft, my little finger got mashed when the gate went down. Later, I said to one of my buddies, "I hope this is the closest I come to getting a Purple Heart."

I was in the 113th Medical Battalion, and it was our job to get the medics and doctors the medical supplies they needed. I remember the wounded being brought back from the front lines, and the doctors performing surgery in MASH (Mobile Army Surgical Hospital) unit tents in the jungle. I often heard the screams of severely wounded soldiers who begged the doctors to end their lives. The dead bodies were also brought back to our area, and one time we unloaded 75 dead soldiers from trucks and stacked them in tents. The smell was awful.

We were in the jungles of New Guinea and it was very hot, and we often had heavy rains. There were lots of snakes, and we were told that many of them were poisonous. One night while I was in my cot, a snake crawled across my chest. Other guys found snakes in their foxholes and under their tents.

A funny thing I remember happening was when we loaded up in troop transport trucks one day to ride to headquarters. Our sergeant told us to put on our helmets, since we were riding in open trucks. One of the guys asked if we had to worry about Japanese snipers. It wasn't long until objects were hitting us on our helmets and landing in our truck. At first, we thought it might be hand grenades, but instead, it was coconuts. The coconuts were being thrown at us by monkeys in the trees. The Japs must have trained them.

The Japs were dug in the hills above us and would fire down at us. We dug foxholes to protect ourselves in case we came under heavy fire. Our captain made us have our rifles with us at all times. I thought this made no sense for those of us involved with the medical supply distribution. We were too busy to worry about a Japanese attack. I kept mine in the corner of the medical supply tent and never had to shoot it.

The closest I came to being killed was when a buddy asked me to go with him to headquarters. I told him, "No" because I had too much work to do. A few hours later, he was brought back dead in an ambulance. He had been shot by a Japanese sniper.

I will always remember when I saw General Douglas MacArthur, commander of the Pacific Theater. It was not under the best of circumstances as to how I saw him. I was on a one-day pass in Manila, Philippines, standing on a corner trading malaria tablets with a Filipino citizen for a chrome-plated .45 caliber pistol. I had my back to the street and didn't see MacArthur's black Packard coming down the street. His car stopped right by me, and his driver, a lieutenant colonel, go out of the car and came over to me. He said, "Soldier, you failed to salute your commanding general." I could see MacArthur sitting in the backseat. The lieutenant colonel took my dog tag information, my .45 pistol, and drove away. Two days later, posted on our camp bulletin board was a letter from headquarters saying I was confined to camp for 30 days for failing to salute MacArthur.

I severely injured my back unloading heavy crates of medical supplies from a truck. The handle straps on a 200 pound crate broke, and the crate landed on top of me. I was on my back in a tent for 30 days and could not move. Later, I contracted a serious case of malaria, and I lost about 50 pounds. After serving over two years in the Pacific, I was finally sent home to an army hospital in Kentucky, where I remained for six weeks.

My first son was born while I was in New Guinea, and I did not see him until he was fifteen months old. Overall, I enjoyed the army, the discipline and the teamwork we learned, and the lifelong friendships I made.

William Jefferies

Marine Corps: Corporal, 2nd Division
Hometown: Cambridge City, Indiana
Career: Driver for Dietzen Bakery Company

I tried to join the Marines at seventeen, but I was two pounds underweight. The recruiting sergeant told me to eat lots of bananas and drink water for a week. I returned a week later and had gained three pounds. My mother signed the enlistment papers, since I was underage.

Our first landing was on the beaches of the Tarawa Atoll in the Gilbert Islands, in November 1943. We lost many men as the Japs were firing down on us from the hills. We captured the island in 76 days, but our causalities were around 3,000 Marines dead and wounded. Tarawa was one of the bloodiest battles in the Pacific.

In June 1944, we went to Saipan. I was in charge of a rocket launching unit (bazookas), and our job was to knock out enemy tanks. During one battle, I saw my platoon leader and commanding officer killed by Japanese machine gun fire. When we were firing on a Japanese tank, one of my men was killed, and another one was seriously injured. I will never forget the deaths of our officers and my men.

The Japanese often attacked us at night with their tanks and infantry. During their nighttime attacks, they would often scream, "Banzai," which was a Japanese battle cry. They did this to try to scare us. It didn't work! One morning, they attacked us at three o'clock. By midmorning, after nearly ten hours of nonstop fighting, we had destroyed 27 of their tanks. Some of our men were killed in their foxholes as the Jap tanks rolled over them. One time, I ran to where heavy fighting was happening, and I saw a Japanese officer getting ready to kill one of my buddies with his sword. I ran between them, blocked his sword with my rifle, knocked him down, and shot him.

Another time my bazooka section knocked out four Japanese tanks. When we finally ran out of ammunition, I ran back to get more, and a wounded Jap soldier on the ground tried to shoot me. I don't know how, but I shot him on the run. Weeks later, we were on another patrol, and some Japanese were dug in and firing at us. We saw gunfire coming from a village house, so we started to set up our bazooka to take them out. A bullet hit my buddy in the chest and went through my dungaree jacket. He was sent to a hospital in Guadalcanal, and I never saw him again until after the war. We both thought each other had been killed.

We were sent to Okinawa, and on April 1, 1945 (April Fools' Day), we did a "fake invasion" on one side of the island. Our job was to act as diversionary troops and draw Japanese fire, while other Marines carried out the actual invasion on the other side.

In over two years in the Pacific, we killed thousands of Japanese soldiers, thousands more than they killed of us. However, I saw so many of our guys killed and wounded.

After Okinawa, we went to Tinian Island and captured a strategic airfield from the Japanese. It wasn't long until our B-29 bombers were able to land on the island. In August 1945, the Enola Gay flew from Tinian to drop the atomic bombs on Japan.

I received the Silver Star for my actions in combat. I never felt I really deserved this. I was just doing my job, as were the other guys.

Harry Macy

Army: Captain, 1st Cavalry Division
Hometown: Hudson, Michigan
Career: Physicist

A kamikaze crashes near the USS *White Plains* during
the Battle of Leyte Gulf

I was stationed at Fort Lewis, Washington, with the 61st Field Artillery, when I heard about the bombing of Pearl Harbor. We immediately went on full alert because of the possibility that the Japanese would attack along our West Coast.

From Fort Lewis, I went to New Guinea, where we were fighting the Japanese in the Pacific. My unit was headed to the Philippines, but I was ordered to board the aircraft carrier USS *White Plains*. My job was to install a radio reconnaissance system for the carrier, so we could communicate with our recon planes. We were part of the naval fleet assembled at Leyte Gulf.

While in the San Bernardino Strait at Leyte Gulf, we came under heavy fire from five to six Japanese battleships. At first, we thought they were our ships, but we quickly realized it was the Japanese shooting at us. We had several close calls. Our cruisers and destroyers retaliated, and the Japanese ships retreated. Soon after their retreat, kamikaze suicide planes began attacking us and the other ships. One kamikaze crashed into a carrier (*St. Lo*) less than two hundred yards away from our ship. The ship exploded immediately and sank within twenty minutes. We picked up as many survivors as we could, but the guys on the lower decks of that ship never had a chance.

I saw a kamikaze headed toward our carrier. I radioed the captain, and he was able to turn the ship just enough, and the plane overshot our landing deck. It exploded near the side of the ship, before it hit the water. We found pieces of the plane and the pilot on the deck. Two of our fighter pilots were able to get off the carrier and attack one of the Japanese ships. One of the pilots made a direct attack on the ship, but he was shot down and killed. The other pilot made some successful hits.

If the atomic bomb had not been dropped, and we had to do a mainland invasion of Japan, the loss of lives on both sides would have been horrendous. The Japanese were entrenched in the hills with thousands of troops; they were fortified with numerous kinds of heavy artillery equipment, and they had over one hundred Japanese fighter planes and kamikazes ready to attack.

I remember how the Japanese abandoned their dead, and we never did. Throughout all of my combat experiences, the Lord was good to me. I returned home without a scratch.

Joe McAndrews

Army: Private First Class, 32nd Infantry Division
Hometown: Indianapolis, Indiana
Career: Sales representative for the Catholic Church Extension Magazine

General Douglas MacArthur wades ashore on the
island of Leyte, returning to the Philippines, in October 1944

I first landed at Saidor in Papua, New Guinea, where we set up our outpost. There was a mountain we had to ascend, and when we got to the top, we could see some Japanese troops in the valley below. We had to cross the Mot River, where a battle was taking place. Because we couldn't swim across with our weapons and packs, our platoon leader took a rope and swam across the river, and secured it on the other side. We attached it on our side, and the men were able to cross the river using the rope. Somewhere along the way, I broke my glasses, and I could not see well without them. I was sent back to our base camp, where I had to wait a month until my parents could mail the prescription. I thought I had it made, since I did not have to be in combat. I had heard the Japanese military was brutal in the treatment of their prisoners, and I wasn't anxious to be taken prisoner.

Our next landing was at Leyte Gulf in the Philippines, prior to the big naval battles. I was there when McArthur landed for his promised return to the Philippines. From a distance, I could see him and his crew coming ashore.

As of then, I had experienced no combat action, but that changed when I was chosen to be a lead scout. My squad's job was to secure a lookout post on top of Lanan Point in the Philippines and to keep the Allied fleet informed of what the Japanese fleet was doing. As my squad approached the top of the mountain, I saw three Japanese machine-gun bunkers ahead of us. I was able to get close enough to throw a grenade in each one.

We came across a platoon of Japanese soldiers, and I began shooting at them. In what seemed like a matter of seconds I saw a flash. I had been shot in the hip. There was another burst of fire, and my right elbow was shattered. On the ground, I looked around and saw a Japanese soldier about thirty feet from me. I held up my hands and said, "You've already shot me twice. You don't need to shoot me again." He lowered his rifle and pointed it toward the ground. He could have easily killed me. I don't know if he understood English, but he saw how badly I was injured.

I started running down the hill, and the first person I saw was a soldier I knew from Evansville, Indiana, and I yelled at him to get down. When I got closer, I saw him leaning on his rifle. He was dead from a head wound. Soon after, a lieutenant tripped me and pulled me to safety behind a tree stump. The medics were able to give me some assistance, but I kept trying to push the bones back inside my arm so they would not flap around. My squad carried me on a stretcher for eight days through rough terrain. When they stumbled over rocks or roots, it caused terrible pain in my hip. By the time they were able to get me to a medical unit, gangrene had infected my arm, and the surgeon had to amputate it.

After I was shot, I never thought about dying. My thought was, "I'm going home." I was flown back to the States and had various surgeries before going home to Indianapolis. My parents knew I had been seriously injured, but they did not know I had lost my arm. When I returned home and knocked on my front door, my mother opened it, and we hugged each other and cried. It was a very emotional experience. From my war experience, I realized freedom is not achieved without war. Freedom isn't free. We must protect it.

General of the Army Douglas MacArthur

"Liberty knows nothing but victory."

MacArthur was the supreme commander of the Allied Forces in the Pacific Theater. When his men were losing the battle in the Philippines in December 1941 and January 1942, he was ordered by President Roosevelt to leave and break through to Australia. Upon his arrival in Australia he spoke the now-famous words, "I shall return." Later in the war, when the Philippines campaign began, MacArthur and American forces landed at Leyte to begin the liberation of the Philippines as they continued their march across the Pacific to defeat Japanese forces. After Japan surrendered, MacArthur supervised the official surrender ceremony of the Japanese aboard the USS *Missouri* in Tokyo Bay.

Roy Nicoloff

Marine Corps: Corporal, 1st Division
Hometown: Indianapolis, Indiana
Career: Newspaper and radio advertising; automobile sales

I tried to enlist at seventeen, while still in high school, but the recruiter told me I didn't weigh enough at 123 pounds. He told me to go home and eat a lot of bananas, drink water, and come back later. After high school, I was drafted in August 1943 but decided to join the Marines. In September, I did my basic training in San Diego, California, and later, I was sent to machine-gun training school in Camp Elliott, California.

I was given no leave before I was shipped out in January 1944 as part of the 422nd Replacement Battalion. Our first stop was at our base in Hilo, Hawaii. We helped build a military camp on top of a mountain and practiced for later beach landings.

While on Oahu, I witnessed a terrible accident, when four of our LSTs (Landing Ship Tank) exploded in Honolulu Harbor, killing over 250 men. The boats were loaded with ammunition, and it was thought that a navy man was repairing one of the boats with a welding torch and sparked the explosion.

We loaded our supplies and sailed to the Marianas Islands, where our first landing was on the on Saipan. Prior to landing, our ships had shelled the island for nearly ten days. I had a scary experience while boarding the Higgins boat that took us to the island. While descending the cargo net on the side of the ship, my foot slipped, and I ended up hanging upside down on the net. A guy on the Higgins boat wedged his rifle between the boat and the ship, so I wouldn't be crushed. Finally, I fell into the boat with a thud.

Thirty thousand Japanese soldiers were on Saipan when the 2nd and 4th Marine Divisions went ashore. Our unit landed in the second wave, and during our time on the island, we experienced heavy fighting. Although we suffered many casualties, we were able to wipe out a large number of the Japanese force. One evening I was on guard duty in my foxhole. Foxholes were dug so two men could occupy one foxhole. One slept, while the other took guard duty. I heard a noise that sounded like someone was crawling in the sand close to us. I knew the Japs attacked at night, so I leaned back with my carbine pointed up toward the top of the foxhole. As some sand spilled over the side, I was ready to fire, when I saw the intruder was a large sand crab. At least he didn't have a rifle and a bayonet.

The 4th Marine Division was finally able to capture the airstrip on the island and turned it over to the army. At night the Japanese would attack and recapture the airstrip, and the Marines would have to recapture it the next day. Marines were trained to move fast, and the army moved at a slower pace to lessen the number of causalities. As a result, when we were advancing up a hill, the army was moving much slower behind us, leaving a large gap between our units. This allowed the Japs to get behind us and attack us from the rear.

As we continued to advance, we encountered a large sugarcane field. The stalks were about six feet tall and reminded me of corn rows. The Japs hid in the fields and fired at us, so our tanks would move forward, clearing a path for us. We heared some of the Japs running away. We looked for feet between the rows. If the feet and lower legs weren't green, we shot it. The Marines' clothing was green, and the Japanese uniforms were tan.

I saw many dead Japanese soldiers rotting in the hot sun. They must have been there for several days, since some of the bodies were bloated. The stench was awful. The terrain on the island was very rugged, consisting of hills, valleys, and ravines. The Japs would hide in the ravines and attack us when we got close. We used specially trained doberman pinscher dogs to flush them out of their locations. Those dogs were amazing.

Mount Tapochau was the highest point on the island, and the Japs were entrenched in the hills and caves. When we were able to get close enough, our flamethrower guys would burn them out of their caves. You could hear their screams, when hit with the fire. One day, heading down the mountain, one of our replacement companies was headed up. I yelled, "Anybody from Indiana?"

A guy responded, "I am." I told him I was from Indianapolis, and he said he was from Crawfordsville. On the way back to the States, we met again on our troop ship. When we arrived in Indianapolis, I walked him to the bus depot. After the war, I tried to find him but was never able to locate him.

Prior to leaving Saipan, a Jap sniper shot me in my helmet, grazing my head. It started bleeding profusely, and I yelled for a medic. He came over, looked at me, and said it was just a scratch. I learned that most head wounds bleed a lot. If the bullet had hit me below my helmet, I would have been dead. We secured Saipan in mid-July of 1944. The fighting had been brutal. I witnessed a terrible thing, when it was obvious we were going to capture the island. I saw Japanese women throwing their babies over a tall cliff into the ocean below. They jumped off the cliff as well. This later became known as "Suicide Cliff." The Japanese soldiers had told the civilians on the island not to get captured because the Americans would torture and kill them. It was all a part of their propaganda. Once we knew the island was secure, we sent Jeeps fitted with loudspeakers to inform the civilians that if they surrendered, no harm would come to them. Those who did not commit suicide were treated well, and many of them helped us by providing various kinds of information.

Our next land invasion was at Tinian Island, the island from which our bomber the Enola Gay flew to drop the atomic bomb on Hiroshima in August 1945. We experienced little resistance, since most of the Japanese troops had loaded onto barges and went to fight at Saipan. On Tinian, one of our guys had fired his rifle, and a bullet fragment ricocheted and struck me and got lodged in my shoulder. Another time, I was grazed by a bullet, and the medic asked if I wanted him to fill out the paperwork for a Purple Heart. I told him no, because I knew if my mother got a telegram from the War Department saying I had been wounded, she would worry that it was serious.

In February 1945, prior to our March landing on Okinawa, I received my "Dear John letter" from my high school sweetheart. I was just one of many serving in the military who received such letters.

The 1st, 6th, and 8th Marine Divisions made the Okinawa landing on April 1, 1945. Our division, the 2nd, was assigned to remain on our ships. We were to conduct the "fake invasion" at the south end of the island. Our Higgins boats, loaded with rockets, moved around the back of our ships and ended up in a formation facing the beach. The boats were unmanned, and the Japanese fired on the boats, which exploded. While staying offshore, we were under constant kamikaze attacks, and many of our boats were hit, killing many helpless Marines. During the first ten days of the landing at Okinawa, we had more casualties than the other two divisions that had landed.

On April 14, we headed back to Saipan while the land battle raged on. Okinawa came to be called the "bloodiest battle in the Pacific." The battle lasted for days before the island was secured. We saw no further action, until after the atomic bomb was dropped on August 6, 1945.

We were sent to Nagasaki, Japan, on September 18, 1945, where the second bomb had been dropped on August 9. In places, we walked through ash as high as eight inches deep. At that time, none of us knew of the effects of the lingering radioactive fallout still in the air. I had seen a lot of dead and wounded Japanese soldiers. One of the most terrible things I saw during our occupation was the numerous civilians who were still alive with huge burns and blisters on their bodies. I saw one little boy who had the flesh burned off of his arm with his bones exposed. People forget that the people of Hiroshima and Nagasaki were warned, prior to the bombs being dropped.

As Allied Occupation Forces in Nagasaki, Japan, our job was to find Japanese weapons and ammunitions. The weapons and ammunition were loaded on barges and dumped at sea.

On December 1, 1945, I left Sasebo, Japan, transferred to the 5th Marine Division, and headed home to "the good old USA," landing in San Diego on December 5.

Carl F. Scott

Marine Corps: Corporal, 1st Division
Hometown: Elwood, Indiana
Career: Agricultural education; Indiana Department of Education; Ivy Tech chancellor

Appearing in *Leatherneck Magazine*, Scott is seated on the left side holding the Browning Automatic Rifle (BAR)
(courtesy of Carl Scott)

I graduated from high school in 1942. My dad was a farmer, and at the time you could receive a farm exemption from the draft, because farming was considered an essential operation. I did not accept this because my buddies and others were joining the military, and I felt it was my duty to join. I tried to join the Army Air Corps, but when I took my test at Purdue University, I failed it. I talked my best friend since fourth grade into joining the Marines with me.

During the war, I found out that three other Elwood boys were serving in the Pacific. Two graduated with me, and the other was in the class behind me. Before the war ended, two of the three I knew were killed. I thought it strange that four boys from the same small Indiana town were serving in the same areas of the Pacific.

After enlisting, my best friend and I started basic training in San Diego, California, in February 1943. I was assigned to the 20th Replacement Battalion and was sent to Melbourne, Australia. During the 30 day trip across the ocean, I was seasick most of the time. As a Midwestern farm boy, I had not previously been on the ocean. Upon my arrival at Melbourne, I was attached to the 7th Regiment.

In September 1943, my unit landed at Oral Bay, New Guinea. The island had already been secured by the army, so in late December 1943, our next stop was at Cape Gloucester, New Britain, which was a Japanese-controlled island. After landing in our LCI (Landing Craft Infantry), we waded ashore with no enemy resistance. Our first mission was Target Hill 440. I was a Browning Automatic Rifleman (BAR), which exposed me to enemy fire. The beach was narrow, and we moved forward through wide, deep swamps. There were large craters, which were created by our bombing, that were filled with water. Some of the guys fell into the holes and would have drowned had we not been able to pull them out.

Our second night on the island, the Japs attacked and tried to retake Hill 440. For some reason we did not understand, a gap of nearly 200 feet was left between A Company and B Company. This left only eight of us to defend the gap. Fortunately, the Japanese either did not notice, or chose not to attack the gap, and directed their attack on the beach, where many of our troops were located. A lot of our guys on the beach were killed during this assault.

Besides the firefights we encountered, the conditions were terrible with extreme heat of over one hundred degrees, mud, rain, and mosquitoes. On the third day, we took Hill 150, and all three of our scouts were killed. The Japanese even shot our wounded lying on stretchers and the stretcher carriers. My lieutenant, another guy, and I were talking, when my lieutenant was shot in the back by a sniper and killed. This was the first death of someone close to me that I saw. The sniper killed eight of our other men before he was killed. We also captured Hills 150 and 660 and experienced heavy firefights to do so. We had captured four hills within a few days.

One incident occurred that was rather funny. A guy was relieving himself, when all of a sudden; a Jap soldier came out from the jungle and started chasing him with his bayonet. He was running and trying to pull up his pants, when our sergeant shot and killed the Jap.

During the battle on Cape Gloucester, only eight of us survived from our platoon of 40 men. I contracted malaria while on the Cape and had a temperature of 105 degrees. I became so delirious I came out of my tent and announced I was walking back to the United States. After a few days, I was back on the front lines.

In April 1944, we moved to Pavuvu on Russell Island, where there was no Japanese resistance. Our biggest problems were large sand crabs and huge rats, which would try to get in our beds. While on Pavuvu, we built roads, and did our practice landings on Guadalcanal.

It was September 15 when we landed at Peleliu. This battle became one of the bloodiest battles in the Pacific, as far as size per square yard. It was even questioned whether this was a strategic island for us to capture. We headed to shore in amtracs on the third wave. When we got to the beach area, many of our fellow Marines were already dead or wounded. The amtracs, upon landing on the beach, hit mines, causing horrific explosions. Later, I heard that I was one of only 13 survivors out of our company of 200 men.

Once on the island, I was no longer a BAR gunner. I now was assigned to be a "runner," and I delivered messages between commanders in the field. As runners we were often exposed to enemy fire, and during the intense fighting I could see and hear bullets whiz by and land near my feet as I was running. One night, the Japanese launched a banzai attack, and a Japanese officer used his sword to kill one of our guys. On another occasion, I was prepared to deliver a message, and another runner said he would do it. He was shot and killed.

One of the strangest things happened to me while I was on patrol walking along a beach. I heard someone say, "Don't step there." I looked down and saw an enemy mine exposed in the sand. I turned around to see who had warned me, and no one was around. Some guys called these incidents, "Angels looking over us." Within a few days we were sent to relieve the unit, under the command of the famous Marine Colonel Chesty Puller.

The Japs were dug into caves; some were five stories deep. We were getting ready to advance toward the caves, but before we left I asked my lieutenant if I could go back and briefly see my buddy. When I returned to my platoon, they had already advanced. After I caught up with them, I found my lieutenant severely injured, and many of my platoon members were also wounded or killed. This was hard for me to deal with because I should have been there with them. I have been told this is called "survivor's guilt." I still think about it. In my company on Peleliu, over 200 were injured. One out of thirteen survived. The island was a death trap.

On April 1, 1945, our LSTs (Landing Ship Tanks) were in the first wave at Okinawa. We experienced little resistance during the first month. When we relieved the 27th Army Division, we became engaged in some heavy firefights taking hill by hill. To clear the caves from which the Japanese were shooting, our guys threw satchel bombs inside the caves, and our tanks used flamethrowers, followed by our Marine flamethrowers.

After we had nearly secured the island, some new replacements were sent to join our unit. One guy was 24 years old with four kids and a wife. I wondered why they would send a guy with four kids and a wife into combat. During one of our patrols, our platoon came under fire, and we ran to the left to take cover. Unfortunately, he must have panicked, and he ran directly into enemy fire and was killed. Also, I found out that one of my Elwood buddies was killed on Okinawa. When he and 15 other Marines took cover inside a cave, they were killed because the cave had been booby-trapped.

While on Okinawa, I was wounded when a bullet went through my helmet, causing fragments from the helmet to embed in my shoulder. A few days later my shoulder became badly infected, and I was sent to a fleet hospital on Guam. While recuperating on Guam, my buddies and I were playing basketball, and some other Marines asked to play. One of the new players asked if any of us knew the name of a certain Marine officer. I said I knew him, and I told the new player that the Marine officer was the worst officer I ever had. The new player said, "He's my brother."

Edgar Whitcomb

Army Air Corps: Second Lieutenant, 19th Bomb Group
Hometown: Hayden, Indiana
Career: Politician, former governor of Indiana

Americans surrendering at Corregidor in May 1942

My story begins in 1939, when I was a student at Indiana University. I decided to drop out of college to enlist in the military in 1940. I was assigned to navigation school in Coral Gables, Florida.

In August 1941, I drove from Florida to Albuquerque, New Mexico, where I was assigned as a navigator to a B-17 crew. After flying to San Francisco, we flew across the Pacific, landing at Clark Field in the Philippines. At that time, our crew was part of the largest mass flight in aviation history. The Japanese had not yet attacked Pearl Harbor, but war was on the horizon for the United States. None of us had any idea of the dangers we would be facing. When we received word Pearl Harbor had been bombed, we did not know the damage that had been done to our fleet. However, it was strange that we did not receive orders to bomb the Japanese bases, because we thought the Japs did not know we were there.

On the same day Pearl Harbor was attacked, the Japanese knew we were on Clark Field and hit us hard and fast with their heavy bombers. I jumped in a trench, as the ground around me shook with terrible explosions. The bombers were followed by fighter planes, which hit us with strafing attacks. Our planes were destroyed, so most of our fighter planes could not even get off the ground. At times, their planes were flying so low I could see the pilots' faces. We were trapped on Clark Field with no place to go and not knowing if help was on the way. It would be a matter of weeks before the Japs overran us. It was April 9, 1942, when we moved to Cabcaban Field, after being on Bataan for over 100 days, with little food and water.

Along with some others, I escaped from Bataan in a small boat. Due to our escape, we were not part of one of the most notorious marches of the century, the sixty-five-mile "Bataan Death March," where hundreds of American and Filipino soldiers either died or were killed. We finally made it to Corregidor, the most heavily fortified island in the war. What we were about to experience made Bataan look like a Sunday school picnic. We endured constant shelling while waiting for the Japanese to attack us with their ground troops. May 5, 1942, the Japs attacked and finally overran us. At noon the next day, General Wainwright surrendered, and we became prisoners of war. Our days consisted of hard labor in the blistering sun. People began to die in increasing numbers, and I began to wonder if any of us would survive.

While some of us began talking about escaping once again, a buddy approached me with an escape plan. I was hesitant at first, but I knew I did not want to stay in this hell hole. On the night of May 22, 1942, as we prepared to swim back toward Bataan, we found some flotation-like devices at the water's edge, which had probably washed ashore from a ship. I think the Lord must have put them there for us.

After experiencing some stormy and rough seas, we eventually became separated, but located one another later. We finally made it to Bataan, after swimming three miles overnight. We hid in some bushes when we got ashore and waited for early morning, before we began our walk through the jungles and small villages. Many of the natives were helpful to us and provided food and water. At one time, we even thought about eating a dead monkey. One day, a villager who was a Japanese sympathizer turned us in to the Japanese. We were taken to Fort Santiago in Manila, one of the most notorious and dreaded Japanese prison camps. Only one out of ten prisoners survived.

I was taken to be interrogated and was beaten with a lead pipe across my back. I gave them a fictitious name, and would not tell them what they wanted to know. I have no idea why they transferred me to a civilian encampment, other than the Japanese had too many prisoners at Fort Santiago. Within a few days, I was moved to a civilian internment camp in Saint Tomas, Manila. After being sent to another civilian camp, I was eventually transferred to Shanghai, China, to a civilian internment camp. After fourteen months in the Shanghai camp, with some assistance and deceptive measures, I boarded a repatriation ship and sailed to Manila. Leaving Manila, a Swedish ship, the Grispholm, sailed to Goa, India. In India, there was an exchange with Japanese diplomats, and I was sent on the Gripsholm back to the United States.

Upon my return, I was looked at with suspicion, and I was interrogated by our own military personnel. I think they thought I might have been a spy, since I had used two different names to escape. After they learned who I was, I was assigned to the Pentagon. I asked to return to the

Pacific and join a bomber crew, but my request was initially denied. Instead, I was assigned to serve as a navigator on planes that flew military and diplomatic personnel to various locations in Europe and North Africa. On one of my flights, the first lady, Eleanor Roosevelt, was aboard.

After a few months, I received orders to report to a B-25 bomber crew in the Pacific. I was able to participate in bombing attacks against the Japanese. In July 1945, we were sent to Okinawa to prepare for the mainland invasion of Japan. A week after the atomic bomb was dropped, a commanding general asked me to be his navigator, so he could go to Clark Field. This was the very field where over three years earlier the Japanese bombers had rained death and destruction upon us, which resulted in the long journey of my "escape from Corregidor."

I returned to the United States in December 1945, after nearly two years of either trying to avoid capture or serving as a POW.

8

GUADALCANAL

The Canal

"There is no question that Japan's doom was Guadalcanal."
—Rear Admiral Raizo Tanaka, Japan

On August 7, 1942, the Marine Corps would write another chapter to its illustrious history as the names Tenaru River, Henderson Field, and Bloody Ridge would become synonymous with the battle that would simply become known as "The Canal."

The landings at Guadalcanal and other small islands in the Solomons were the first amphibious invasions in the Pacific. The Marines were quickly introduced to the tenacious Japanese fighter. Two days after the landings, the American navy suffered a devastating defeat at the Battle of Savo Island, which cost the navy three cruisers and 1,023 sailors. The navy left the waters around Guadalcanal, and 16,000 Marines were stranded on Guadalcanal and in the Solomons with just over a month's food supply and a few days of ammunition.

The survival of the Marines depended on being able to defend and hold on to Henderson Field and not let it fall into Japanese hands. In the air and on the sea, Japan had the upper hand, but their land forces were not high in numbers. However, the Marines quickly learned that the Japanese soldier was willing to give his life without a second thought, and he was a formidable foe. During the day, the Japanese would retreat into their caves and let the Marines search for them and attack in the day. When the day turned to night, the Japanese would venture out and move quietly through the dense jungle and attack the American lines, and attack they did. Their banzai assaults would come in continuous waves trying to drive the Americans back to the coastline. And during these banzai assaults, the Japanese soon learned that the American Marine was just as determined, just as brave, and just as tenacious a fighter as they were.

The Japanese bombers had full control of the skies and could provide air support for their troops. Finally, on August 20, 31 planes landed at Henderson, and four days later the American pilots, nicknamed the "Cactus Air Force," stunned the Japanese Zeros. They shot down six Japanese fighters and ten bombers. Joining the attack were American carrier planes, and they destroyed ninety planes and sank a light carrier, a destroyer, and a cruiser. From there on out, the Japanese bombing raids that had gone uncontested would now be met by the deadly American fighter pilots.

On land, hard, brutal fighting continued by both the Japanese and the Americans. Individual and unit heroics occurred in small pockets of the jungle throughout the six-month-long battle. On Guadalcanal, the Marine Corps saw its first enlisted man become the recipient of the Medal of Honor when Sergeant John Basilone almost single-handedly destroyed a Japanese regiment at an area known as Coffin Corner.

Both sides had kept sending more men into this small, jungle-filled island, and by the beginning of January 1943, there were nearly 50,000 Americans, which included more Marine divisions and army troops. The Japanese had 25,000 soldiers on the island. From the beginning, it was a difficult task as the Marines took the land battle to the Japanese, and then they were cut off and surrounded with minimal rations. The outlook appeared bleak for the Marines, but once again, as they have done throughout the history of the Corps, they rallied and relied on one another to gain the victory.

After six months of battle, the fighting subsided when 12,000 Japanese soldiers were able to be secretly evacuated off the island. From fighting and disease, 23,000 Japanese soldiers died. This included 600 of their fighter pilots. On the island of Guadalcanal, the Marines, army, and aviation units lost 1,598. The joint effort of all elements of this campaign helped give the Americans a crucial land victory over the Japanese.

Dr. Gadi Lawton

Marine Corps: First Lieutenant, 1st Division
Hometown: Indianapolis, Indiana
Career: Dentist

Lawton with his wife Julia Ann, February 1944

I was born in Orlando, Florida, in 1919. One Sunday after church, we had orange and grapefruit salad for lunch. After lunch my brother and I went to play, and mom and dad sat there at the table. We were a fun family, but they stayed sitting there at the table looking serious. After a while, we went back over to the table and asked what was wrong. My dad pointed to some money on the table. It was thirty-five cents. He said, "Well, that's all we have." I know what it is to be poor, and that wasn't any fun.

My brother and I were both fortunate to get football scholarships. My scholarship was from Stetson University in Florida. I was set to graduate in 1941, when the government instituted the draft. I signed up because it was the law. I had a lot of patriotism, and I wanted to enlist. I chose the Marines because the Marines had never drafted anyone. Everyone who goes into the Marines is a volunteer. When I graduated from Stetson in June, the war was on in Europe, and we knew it was going to happen sometime. I went to boot camp, at Parris Island, South Carolina. It had not been used since World War I. The buildings were a mess, so we were in two-man tents. I was as green as could be. A corporal stepped up to the door of the bus and yelled in, and I was scared pea green. He then said, "Men, give your hearts to the Lord, because your butts belong to the government." Welcome to the Marine Corps. The rifles we were issued were 1903 Springfield rifles, single shot, bolt action. We carried those weapons clear through Guadalcanal. America was totally unprepared for the war.

Marine Corps boot camp is something every young man should have. You will learn more in boot camp in three months than you will have learned in your entire life. You learn responsibility, you learn discipline, and you learn to accept things that normally you would have complained about. It is tough. They are trying to teach you discipline, and when you're told to do something, do it quickly. Discipline is part of the Marines. When you're given an order to jump, you ask, "How high?" on the way up. My definition of discipline is, "Giving up something small now, for a greater reward later on."

After Parris Island, I went to Quantico, Virginia. When we got off the bus, I saw a big ol' master sergeant standing there, and he had only one little campaign ribbon on his uniform. Our sergeant took the group over to him and said, "Sergeant Truesdale, here are your recruits." The sergeant saluted and Sergeant Truesdale returned the salute with his left hand and not his right. I had never seen that in my life. Then I noticed that Sergeant Truesdale did not have a right arm. I learned that several years earlier, while on patrol in Nicaragua, a rifle grenade fell from its carrier. It ignited, and he picked it up and threw it, but not quite in time. His action saved many lives. The one little ribbon on his uniform was for the Congressional Medal of Honor. I learned to never judge anyone by the ribbons they had on their uniform.

I was there a short time. Because I had a college degree, they sent me to Officer Candidate School. I had been there three weeks when, on a sunny Sunday afternoon, someone came and said, "Pearl Harbor has been bombed." I didn't even know where it was. I had never heard of it. We knew we were going to war. When I was finished with my schools, they made me a platoon leader and assigned me to the 5th Marine (Regiment), 1st Division.

I went to the South Pacific through the Panama Canal. The Battles of Midway and Coral Sea had already occurred. Our navy had very limited resources. We crossed the Pacific with no escorts, and our Liberty ship had no guns. Four days out we hit a storm with eighty-foot waves, and the storm lasted a few days. Fortunately we made it to New Zealand. We hadn't been there very long, and the coast watchers notified us that the Japanese were almost done with the landing strip on Guadalcanal. If the Japanese had the airstrip, they could bomb Australia, New Zealand, and New Guinea. They would have owned the Pacific if we had not stopped them.

Our landing date was to be August 7, 1942. Twenty miles from Guadalcanal are the tiny islands of Tulagi, Gavoutu, and Tanambogo. The group I was with landed at Tulagi. We got ashore, and for about three hours there was heavy fighting. We walked on, and thought we had taken the island. Actually, the Japanese had retreated into caves, and at midnight they came out, and the battle started again. They came out screaming, "Banzi!" It was a nightlong battle, and casualties were heavy. Come daylight, they were gone again. They never fought in daylight unless we were attacking them. The evening of the eighth, at midnight, the Jap navy sailed around Savo Island and fired down on the troopships. Our supply ships took off, and we had hardly unloaded any supplies. We came there with a sixteen-day supply of food and a twenty-day supply of ammunition. The Japanese had sunk many of our ships, and the rest of our ships sailed away. We stayed another five months.

The Japanese on the island hid in caves. We did not have any flamethrowers or other equipment to get the Japanese out of the caves. One of my men threw a hand grenade into the cave. Once you throw a hand grenade, it explodes within seven seconds. After he threw it into the cave after the grenade came flying back out and exploded. My Marine then took another grenade, pulled the pin, and held it for three and a half seconds before he tossed it back into the cave. It did not come back this time.

About the tenth day, my company was on the tiny beach of Tulagi at night. One of our guys, Private Vandiver, yelled out to someone to halt. He yelled it again, and the guy muttered something in Japanese. He said it once more, "Halt, or I'll shoot." The guy said something again in Japanese, and Vandiver shot. The bullet went over my head. I heard it hit the Japanese soldier. When the guy fell, he was so close to me that I reached out and touched him.

One night after a major Japanese counterattack on Guadalcanal, they moved the Marines from the two other islands, to Guadalcanal. When I arrived on the island, I had no idea what to do. A guy came walking up and shined a little red light on his collar. He was a full colonel, and he said, "I am your new regimental commander. Your first regimental commander has already been shot. Who's in charge here?"
I replied, "I am, sir."
"What are you doing?" he asked.
"Well, nothing." That was the wrong answer.
He said, "Any idiot can do nothing. I expect more than that from a Marine officer." That night I grew up. I became an officer and a leader worthy of the name on that very black night on Guadalcanal. I knew I was responsible for what I did, and I had to answer for it. I always had a plan from that night on. About three weeks later, he appointed me company commander of F Company.

By September 13, the enemy had landed on both sides of us. They built a trail through the jungle called the East-West Trail that surrounded our six-mile area. They brought their ships and shelled us every night with their sixteen-inch shells. It was terrifying. Every noon the Japanese flew over with their bombers and bombed us. They could come as low as they wanted because we had no planes. Every day we ran shorter and shorter of food. I was 195 pounds when I arrived, and when I left I weighed 129 pounds. It was a long, tough campaign.

By sending out patrols each day to that East-West Trail, we tried to keep track of where they were and what they were doing. Our patrols got ambushed. We decided, and very accurately, that the Japanese were going to come down a ridge; we called it Bloody Ridge. The ridge runs parallel to the ocean, and behind it is Henderson Field. The East-West Trail connected to the ridge. It was bare on top but slopped off into deep jungle. Our colonel set up strong emplacements, and the Japanese attacked at midnight. F Company was set up in reserve.

When you're in reserve, you miss the terror of the initial banzai attack, but as the battle develops, the reserve gets sent to where the fighting is the heaviest. The Japanese were beginning to break through, but it was almost daylight. We were ordered up to the ridge but were held back to see if they would retreat. They did. We moved out along the ridge, and when it was my time to go over the ridge, a boy from E Company was going over at the same time. We jumped up and ran across the ridge trying to take cover when a sniper shot rang out. The bullet went through his head, and he dropped dead. Why he was chosen? I have no idea.

When we got up on top of the ridge, the next night, the fighting continued. When it ended, there were over 2,200 dead Japanese in and around Bloody Ridge. The next day or two, we stayed there to ensure it was over. On July 15, the navy brought us supplies, but they were ambushed by a squadron of submarines. The ships turned around and left. They did return and tried to get us some supplies, but it was tough.

About two weeks later, the 7th Regiment was able to join us, and we got a little more ammunition and supplies. Now we went after the Japanese, and we finally got some fighter planes. We couldn't wait for the next day at noon, when their bombers came after us. Since they came unprotected, our boys blasted them out of the sky, and every noon after that we watched the aerial fights. We saw the planes fighting, and they were about ten feet apart. There was a Marine aviator named Joe Foss. I saw him on the tail of a Zero, and he shot him down. When Foss turned up, he was right under the belly of another Zero, and bang, bang, bang, down it went. He completed his arc, and he was on the tail of another Zero. In a short time he shot down five enemy planes. He was awarded the Congressional Medal of Honor.

In October, we started out for the enemy toward the Matanikau River. My company was given the ridge to walk along to protect the flank of the main body. We patrolled this several times. We knew the enemy was on the other side of the river, and our commander decided to cross it. We went down the ridge and came down the river, and we were the first in line. Paul Moore's platoon was the first in line, and I told Paul to approach this like a beachhead. He was to send five men to the other side, so it would be safe for the rest of us to cross. When he got across, the enemy opened fire, and all five were wounded. We started firing over Paul's platoon to drive them back and protect the boys who were wounded. Paul walked across five times and brought a boy back every time. Bullets were flying everywhere and never touched him. He was the bravest man I ever knew.

A little while later, we were told to cross again. It was the end of October, and that night the engineers built floating bridges. Then next morning we crossed. We got across fine and in about a day or two, the main body was stopped at the beach. I was told to go down the ridge and find a place to cut off the enemy. I saw a clear spot, so we started down. We were behind the enemy group that cut off our main body. We knew there were more Japanese on the other side, so I divided them up. Half faced east and half faced west. One of my boys found some cable wires, and this was the connection between the two enemy units. I swallowed hard, and told him to cut the wires. As soon as he cut the wires, guys came with their heads down looking for the wires. My boys got some of them, but others got away. Soon, forces from two sides came in on us, and we were trapped in the trap that we had set.

I was walking along one of the lines when I saw a bush moving. There was no wind, and I knew somebody was behind it. Out stepped an enemy soldier. We looked each other eyeball to eyeball. I grabbed my pistol, and he grabbed his rifle. I shot first. Killing a man is the last thing you want to engage in. I can still see that boy's face, and I know his parents had no idea where he was or how he died. I think about him so many times. I was happy that I had killed an enemy, but then I realized I had killed a man. All the training in the world does not prepare you for killing.

We held them off and wiped out their outfit. The next day higher headquarters sent another company down the ridge to relieve us. We pulled ourselves back onto the ridge, thinking we would get a little rest. We had just gotten out, when I got called and was told that tomorrow our unit would be the third element to surround the rest of the Japanese. We were on the west; another of our units was on the east, and the ocean was out there. I was told to spread out my men, go down the hill, and wipe them out. At the crack of dawn, we started down that hill, and they were looking for us. We left at 5:00 a.m., and by 8:00 a.m., we got to the bottom of the hill. We had not done any good. They were shooting us up pretty good. I saw Paul Moore move to a position, and an enemy burst hit him right in the chest and went clear through his body. He went down like a ton of bricks. I thought, "I have to crawl over there and tell him good-bye."

A navy corpsman said, "I'm crawling with you. I'll see if I can help him." When we got to him, Paul was barely alive. The corpsman put a huge patch on him and was holding as hard as he could to stop the bleeding. How it missed his heart, I'll never know, but it did. I saw a boy about to move in the line of fire that got Paul. I half raised and said, "Don't go over there." As I did, a bullet came across my chest and went clear through my left shoulder. The corpsman said, "I can't help you; I'm trying to keep Paul from bleeding to death." He gave me some sulfur and said, "Sprinkle a little on it, and do the best you can." The medics were some of the bravest men I knew.

My wound was not serious, so I crawled through the undergrowth on my belly like a snake. On the flank, someone was bringing up a 37mm artillery piece on wheels. We dragged the artillery piece to its position, and we emptied all the ammunition we had, and, sure enough, we knocked out their machine guns. We started the slow process of driving them into the water. Those that we didn't kill jumped into the ocean and tried to swim away. Some tried to run away, but they were met by the outfit that relieved us. None of the Japanese lived. When I was back at the hospital, I had to do the worst job a company commander has to do. I wrote to the parents of those killed, and told them, "Your boy is not coming home." Hardest job ever.

My faith in God was what helped me most during the war. I was often afraid, but I was never paralyzed by fear. I would pray, "Lord, help me," but I did not pray to keep me alive.

9

MARINES STORM ASHORE ON IWO

Iwo Jima

"Of the Marines I saw on Iwo Jima, uncommon valor was a common virtue."
—Admiral Chester Nimitz

The Battle of Iwo Jima took place on a very small Pacific Island full of underground tunnels and caves occupied by the Japanese force. Despite its size, five miles long and two and a half miles wide, it had significant tactical importance to the Allies and to the Japanese. The Allies needed to capture and secure two airfields to stop the Japanese fighter planes from attacking the Allied planes on bombing missions. Once the island was secured, the airfields could be used as emergency landing strips for American bombers.

On the first day of the landing, February 19, 1945, the Marines experienced heavy casualties while Japanese troops and snipers pinned down the Marines' advance for several hours. The thirty-six-day battle was one of the most intense and bloody battles of the war in the Pacific. On March 16, 1945, the island was officially declared secured. The Americans suffered 26,000 casualties, which included 6,800 killed in action. After the fighting, there were only 1,083 Japanese soldiers of the original 20,000 defenders.

Four days after the battle began a group of five Marines and one navy corpsman planted the American flag on the top of Mount Suribachi. The event was captured by war photographer Joe Rosenthal, and the historic photo was an instant morale booster to the American people as it appeared in newspapers across the country. However, the now historic photo actually captured the second flag-raising that day on Mount Suribachi. Earlier, with a smaller flag, Marines raised the first American flag, which was greeted with cheers by Marines and sailors aboard ships. This small flag was replaced by the larger second flag.

The battle on Iwo Jima demonstrated to the Allies how fanatical the Japanese army was to protect its occupied territories, and, for many, surrender was not an option. They considered it an honor to die in war by enemy fire or by suicide.

6th Fleet going ashore on Iwo Jima

James Baize

Navy: Boatswain Mate Second Class, USS *Highlands*
Hometown: Indianapolis, Indiana
Career: Chief plant engineer at General Motors Corp.

Baize's LCVP AP 119-13 (left) is floating near the shore after taking a direct hit

I went to Great Lakes boot camp, and I wanted to get on an aircraft carrier. However, I ended up being a coxswain for a LCVP (Landing Craft Vehicle Personnel). I was aboard the USS *Freemont*, and I transported Marines onto Saipan, Tinian, and Guam. On Saipan I made three trips in and out, and five on Tinian, but there was not a lot of fire there. The Japanese were not prepared on Tinian like they were on Iwo.

On January 17, 1945, while on the USS *Highlands*, we were briefed about the upcoming invasion of Iwo Jima. We knew we were going to invade a small island, because we had been rehearsing maneuvers for an invasion, but we were not sure where. They had been talking about assembling for the invasion of Tokyo, so we didn't know for sure where we were heading. We bypassed Kruk, which is a small island, and we were called to general quarters. This was rare because no one was shooting at us. Our commander told us we were heading to an island called Iwo Jima, and it had been bombed for over 30 consecutive days. There was no sign of life left on the island. He said the island still had to be taken because the distance between Saipan and Guam was 1,500 miles, and Iwo was 700 miles. We needed it for our bombers.

Iwo Jima was four miles long and two miles wide. On Mount Suribachi, we bombed it for 30 to 40 days. We did not realize that for four years the Japanese were digging all those tunnels and had 1,421 pillboxes along the ridge. With nothing standing, there was no place to hide for the Marines. The airfield was all blown to hell; you couldn't get anything on or out. Inside Suribachi were seventeen miles of tunnels, and they had the commissary, barracks, and their hospital. With 20,000 Japanese and 70,000 Americans, that's 90,000; with eight square miles that's 11,000 men in combat per square mile.

The night of the eighteenth we were all briefed as to what time we were to man the boat station and embark. We went onto Iwo Jima on February 19. I had two gunners in the turrets on the LCVP, and I had a bowman to watch on the ramps. I was the coxswain driving boat APA 119-13. There were 25 LCVPs (Landing Craft Vehicle Personnel) on the *Highlands*.

First, we lowered the LCVPs over the side into the water, then cargo nets were dropped down, and 38 Marines loaded up. Once we were ready, we headed out and rendezvoused with eleven other LCVPs. This formed a wave. Once each wave was ready, we got the signal from the boat leader, and we headed to the beach. When we were going in, the water was very choppy because of all the landing craft.

We were on the second wave headed to Red Beach I, and the Japanese were just pounding that beach. The first wave on all the beaches was about 50 LCVPs, and at my landing area at Red Beach I, there were twelve. We landed around 2,200 men on the beach in the first hour and a half, and with the body parts and other broached boats, that didn't leave a whole lot of room. Two boats had broached and did not go in straight, so this took up spaces to land. As some of the LCVPs were backing up, I saw an opening and thought I could make it. We got within about twenty yards of the beach, and that's when I took a direct hit. I lost 38 Marines and three crewmen—Sammy, Eddie, and Jimmy. My crew and I had been together for about three and a half months.

I was thrown out of the boat when it got hit, and I lay on the beach for about forty-five minutes. I had a life jacket on; my helmet was gone, and my shoes were gone. I remember looking up and looking for my crew, but nobody was around. A Marine named Jack pulled me out of the surf, and he got a navy corpsman to fix me up. I didn't have a lot of time to think. I was thinking about trying to get on another boat to get off the island, but Jack told me it was a waste of time. He said I would be killed by the time I got to the area to find a boat. He told me to stay with him, and he got hold of some stuff from a dead Marine, an M-I rifle, a poncho, a canteen, and a helmet. He showed me how to load an M-I, so I fought with the 24th Marines (Regiment), 4th Division.

It was chaos. Machine-gun and mortar fire was all around us. Guys were fighting everywhere, but it was not until three days later that we joined up with Jack's unit. There was a ridge of pillboxes, and as we moved out and up the beach, they were shooting down on us. The pillboxes were right there in front of us, and Jack took out three pillboxes with grenades. You tried to wait until night, so when you saw them fire you would know to go and clear it out. However, because of the tunnels they would refill it immediately.

A couple of times I fought hand-to-hand combat. I knew nothing about a bayonet, and Jack told me you had to shove it in, rip it to the side, and then fire. I only had to do this once. That was at night, and he was trying to come in on us. They came through at night because they figured Marines wouldn't fight at night. So they would come and attack at night with three to four together. This was a different thing for a navy guy to fight in combat. We had very little rations and water. Jack got some rations off of dead comrades, but we had very little. We had some hardtack. We had very little water, and there were no wells or water on the island. So the water you had is what you carried in, or what you took off of dead comrades.

The morning of the twenty-third, Jack and I were at the foothills of Suribachi, and we looked up, and they were raising the flag. There was some cheering and the thought that we must have pretty much taken the island, but of course we fought for another thirty days. About a half hour later, I saw them taking that flag down. They got a larger flag, and they raised that flag. Joe Rosenthal was taking the photos of the second flag-raising, and they were sent to the Associated Press. They said that photo would sell a lot of war bonds in the United States.

I was not in a foxhole. If you dug down, it was hotter than hell, and it stunk just like rotten eggs. It smelled like sulfur; it was horrible. At night, you tried to lay as flat as you could with your rifle, with your eyes open as much as you could. There was no rest, and no way to sleep. There was some fire at night, but not a whole lot of mortar fire.

No tents or hospitals were put up. The medics that were trying to get these guys off the beach to the hospital ships were having a hell of a time. The Japs were even blasting the boys lying on the stretchers. They were killing them just as fast as they could do it. There was no mercy just because a man was on a stretcher. No way! And a Red Cross flag didn't mean anything. The Japs were there to stay and there to win. They made vows, and their goal was kill ten Americans—if they had to charge with bayonets, if they had to charge with grenades, or any way they could do it—before they died. It was a bloodbath.

We had a lot of brave guys. I don't know how they did it. They held their guts together and still kept charging. They were great heroes. I saw this kid who had taken on some lead and was holding his gut. He was trying to move forward, and he had about half of his side hanging out and was holding his side. He still had his rifle pointing out, and he kept on going. It was about seventy-five yards from the water's edge to the ridge, and they were trying to get over that without being picked off. The Japs were clipping them off as soon as they came. Those were brave kids.

On the night of January 26, the battalion leader said we were going to take the airfield. About seven of us were crossing on the south edge of the airfield, when the navy came through and dropped flares. It lit that place up, and the Japs just opened up. The Japs were about fifteen hundred yards from us and just cut Jack down. I knew he was gone, and I dove into a mortar hole. I never knew Jack's last name. It was Jack and Jim. I had gotten hit by artillery shrapnel in the knee and in the back of the neck. A piece almost went into the back of my lower brain. I don't know what happened to the others, and I don't know how long I was in that hole. When I came to, I was on a hospital ship at Iwo.

First of all, we knew that we were going to win. The action that the U.S. government took in training these kids, I think, was the key to it. Discipline helped us win the war. Most of these boys were from families that worked on farms; they carried paper routes, worked at grocery stores, and worked in gardens, and we had parents who controlled their children. These were kids who worked and who had discipline. When they went into the service and a chief boatswain's mate told you to go to attention, you went to attention. And when he told you to pick up that bag and put it on your back, or told you to do fifty push-ups, by golly you did.

We were actually fighting for our country—the love of our country. We knew that if we did not win this war, our country was gone. Parents, grandparents, all those kids were fighting for the love of their country. This generation sacrificed their food supply and their gasoline for their cars; they used retread tires on their cars, and were willing to work long hours night and day, on the farm or producing goods—anything for the war effort. They believed what their government was telling them.

When I drove my LCVP to the beach at Iwo, I was seventeen-years-old. I turned seventeen on November 18, 1944, just three months before the invasion. For 54 years the men in my own unit had thought I was deceased. They knew my LCVP was hit, but it was not until I went to my unit's reunion that they found out I had survived.

10

BLOODIEST BATTLE
IN THE PACIFIC

Okinawa

"The Japanese fought to win—it was savage, brutal, inhumane, exhausting, and dirty business."
—Corporal Eugene Sledge

The Battle of Okinawa began on April 4, 1945, and lasted for nearly two months. It is often referred to as the "bloodiest battle in the Pacific," due to the American and Japanese lives lost and wounded. Okinawa was a strategic island for the Americans and for the Japanese, and it was part of a three-part plan the United States had for winning the war in the Far East.

Okinawa contained what was left of Japan's crucial merchant fleet, which carried Japanese supplies. The Americans also wanted to capture the four airfields in order to launch bombing raids on Japan's industrial complexes. A major obstacle for the Americans was that they had not been able to obtain much intelligence about the island.

It was originally thought that the Japanese had only about 65,000 troops stationed on the island, but the actual number was over 130,000 soldiers and nearly a half million civilians. The Americans landed 180,000 troops. The Japanese commander had been ordered to hold the island at all costs.

As on Iwo Jima, U.S. naval forces heavily bombarded the island prior to the assault. The navy experienced resistance from Japanese fighters and kamikazes. Out of nearly two hundred kamikaze planes, 169 were destroyed; however, those that did get through did heavy damage to the American fleet, especially the aircraft carriers.

The real battle for Okinawa occurred in the south end of the island, where the Japanese had established the Machinato and Shuri Lines, their last bastions of defense. The Japanese forces strongly resisted before the Marines and soldiers were able to secure the island on July 2, three months after the initial landing. American forces experienced heavy casualties, including the land invasion and the loss of 21 warships and heavy damage to 66 others.

In the Pacific, Okinawa was one of more than 100 D-Days. When the invasions of the islands had ceased, Marines and GIs had gone ashore on islands that contained brutal terrain and unimaginable conditions that could only be described as "hell on earth." To their buddies and their missions, they were always faithful—Semper Fi!

Robert Albright

Army: Sergeant, 3231 Photo Detachment
Hometown: Indianapolis, Indiana
Career: Medical illustrator and designer for Eli Lilly

Albright (right) taking photographs
of Japanese POWs
(Courtesy Robert Albright)

After graduating from high school in 1941, I immediately signed up for the navy V-5 Program, because I wanted to be a pilot. I was sent to the Great Lakes Naval Training Center in Chicago, where I took a battery of exams. I was to report to the University of Iowa for preflight training. A week prior to being sent for training, the navy informed us that our unit was not needed. We were honorably discharged. I was very disappointed.

Within a few months after my discharge, I was drafted by the army and assigned to the Signal Corps to become a code breaker and cryptologist. I told those in charge I didn't want to do this, because I wanted to be a pilot. Someone finally listened to me, and I was sent to preflight training at Mississippi State College. My flight training was at Kelley Field in San Antonio, Texas. Once again, my flight class was eliminated, and I was placed on detached service. The rest of my unit was sent overseas.

I received my orders and reported to Paramount Studios in New York City. This was an unbelievable experience for a nineteen-year-old boy who was recently out of high school. At Paramount, a group of us learned how to operate movie cameras and do still photography. One day I was late to work, and I found out that ten of the guys I had been training with for combat photography were being sent as photographers for the Normandy invasion. I later found out they were sent in a day prior to the invasion, landing in rubber rafts at night. Their job was to photograph the D-Day landing. Seven out of the ten were killed by the Germans before the invasion had begun. I often wonder had I been on time that day, if I would have been sent with them.

After my training, I went for additional training in Kodak, Hawaii, where the Eastman Kodak Company was located. My first overseas assignment was in the Philippines as a photographic specialist with the 24th Headquarters Operation. My assignment was "top secret," since I was to document film and still photography to be used as part of the evidence in the Japanese War Crimes Tribunals. I wore a pass around my neck personally signed by Admiral Nimitz and General MacArthur that read, "This soldier is permitted access to all areas. No one is to interfere with him in the performance of his duties."

As part of the third wave invasion of Okinawa in 1945, my job was to take film and pictures of what was occurring during the battle and later occupation. I came to know the famous war correspondent Ernie Pyle, who was also from Indiana. I remember him being a very intelligent, kind, and helpful person to the other war correspondents and photographers. On the day he was killed at Ie Shima, I was supposed to be part of his group; however, I was given another assignment to take some pictures of the Japanese two-man submarines. After the bombing of Pearl Harbor, the American public was not informed that three of these two-man subs had made it to Pearl Harbor, and two of them did some untold damage to our fleet.

There were times when I was shot at while taking pictures, but I faced nowhere near the dangers that our combat troops did. One day, I was told to take a jeep up to Sugar Loaf Hill, and another soldier accompanied me. I was to take pictures from as many angles as possible so our commanders could discover a way through the Japanese defenses. This had been a strategic location, where intense fighting had taken place. The Marines would capture it during the day, and the Japanese would retake it during the night.

One time, we went too far and found ourselves behind enemy lines. I heard a Japanese patrol approaching, and I hurriedly got into my jeep and took off down the mountain. As I came down from the mountain, I could see yellow objects protruding from the sand on the beach. The beach was covered with land mines. The tide had washed away some of the sand so the mines were visible. If the mines had still been covered by sand, it is likely I would have hit one. I carefully negotiated my jeep through the field and returned safely to my unit. I was told the photographs I brought back were extremely vital.

At certain times each day, the Japanese would roll out these huge guns from a cave and shell our ships off the coast. The guns would then be rolled back inside the cave, and a large steel door would close, concealing the weapon. I watched a Seabee repel down from the top of the cave and weld the door seam shut while exposing himself to possible enemy fire from a Japanese soldier or sniper.

Another time on Okinawa, I flew in a scout plane to take some aerial pictures. I witnessed something that day I will never forget. I saw Japanese women committing suicide by jumping off the side of a big cliff into the ocean below. Some jumped off with their children in their arms, and others just threw their children over the cliff. It was part of their honor code, or they did not want to surrender to us.

After we captured the island, I was taking three Japanese women to look through some of the burial caves located in the sides of the hills and mountains. While looking in one cave, a Japanese soldier came out with his hands above his head holding a camera in his hand. He was also a combat photographer. I think he thought I might shoot him. He gave his camera to me, and I escorted him back to our base camp, although we had been given orders to take no prisoners. I don't know what happened to him.

After the Japanese surrender in September 1945, I went to Seoul, Korea. My assignment was to provide more film and photo documentation to be used for the planned war crime trials. A group of Japanese soldiers, who had recently surrendered, was assigned to be my escort and protector. I thought this was strange, since just a few days prior to their surrender they were trying to kill us. I wasn't sure how safe I would be as they accompanied me to various locations with their rifles and fixed bayonets.

I filmed and photographed surviving Allied soldiers of the Bataan Death March who had not been relocated by the Japanese. What I witnessed, I couldn't believe, and it is something you don't want to remember. I thought, "How could a person treat another person like this?" It was part of the reality of war. I also took pictures in the prison camps where they had been held. I cannot begin to describe the horrendous conditions and torture devices I saw.

During the war, I had three different cameras. One was literally shot out of my hands; one was broken while I was jumping into a foxhole when we were under enemy fire, and the other one just wore out.

I was discharged from Seoul and sent back to the States in early 1946. Years later, I was told by the Indiana Historical Society that they thought I was the first and only World War II combat photographer from Indiana.

Ernie Pyle

The lives of the soldiers were humanized by the stories that appeared in the newspaper column written by war correspondent Ernie Pyle, who was raised in Dana, Indiana. Pyle was the voice of the men in the trenches, and he conveyed their hardships, struggles, and emotions with the readers back on the home front. After finishing his tour in the European Theater and a brief rest in the States, Pyle left for the Pacific Theater to report on the action there. While on the island of Ie Shima, Pyle was killed by a Japanese sniper. His death was mourned by his fellow countrymen, but especially by those serving in the military.

Louis Balogh

Marine Corps: Tech Sergeant, Air Group 14
Hometown: Vandergriff, Pennsylvania
Career: Department supervisor, Ford Motor Company

A downed Japanese plane on Okinawa
(courtesy Robert Albright)

I enlisted in the Marine Corps and then volunteered to go overseas after my stateside training was completed. My two brothers also served in the war. One was in the army, and the other was in the Army Air Corps.

We shipped out from Hawaii early in 1945. The seas were rough, and many of us were seasick from time to time. The ship had to take a zigzag course, which helped to avoid enemy submarines. After about 30 days, we landed at Leyte Gulf in the Philippines. A week later, we headed to Okinawa but had to wait seven days in our ships before we could go ashore. This was a scary time, because we were "sitting ducks." Japanese fighter and kamikaze planes attacked our ships, and we did not have fighter protection. One of the ships close by was hit by a kamikaze and was severely damaged.

When we finally headed to the Okinawa beachhead, I was part of a group of ten LSTs carrying men and equipment. My LST was carrying gasoline. I was concerned that if we got hit, our LST would explode, and we would all be killed. We had not yet captured the island, and heavy fighting was still taking place inland. We constantly heard the artillery from our ships shelling the island. It is a noise you don't forget.

After landing, my job was to supervise the setup of our base camp with tents and equipment, and the construction of two large Quonset huts. We were on the island about three months before the two atomic bombs were dropped. In October, a huge typhoon hit the island. The winds were up to 190 miles per hour, destroying our tents and equipment. We took cover in caves which the Japanese used to bury their civilian dead. I saw the storm pick up one of our

B-24 bombers and throw it inland. Many of our ships were damaged or sunk. I knew my brother was on one of the army ships, and I was concerned about his welfare. After the typhoon was over, I went to the large hospital tent to see if he was alive. I was able to find him and saw that he had suffered serious head and facial wounds. We remained on Okinawa through November 1945.

At one point, I had lost my dog tags, so I got a piece of metal from a downed Japanese plane and made my own dog tags. It was important to have your dog tags in case you were wounded or killed, because they had your name, rank, serial number, and blood type inscribed.

While on Okinawa, our unit did not experience combat. Our worst enemy was the major typhoon. The guys who had it tough were the army and Marine infantry groups who were doing the fighting.

In December 1945, we departed from Okinawa and were sent as an occupation force to a Japanese naval base. On the way to Japan, our boats had Marine sharpshooters stationed on the ship. It was their job to shoot the floating mines the Japanese had set. I was asked to set up guard duties. I asked the lieutenant why we needed to do this, since the entire base had been destroyed by our troops. His response was, "Do it anyway." Like many occupation troops in Japan after the bombs were dropped, we did not know we were exposed to the radioactive fallout.

Eddie Mode

Navy: Seabee attached to Marine Air Group 31, 1st Marine Division.
Hometown: Muncie, Indiana
Career: Restaurant and nightclub owner

Mode (right) on Okinawa, Japan

When I was fifteen, I was a newspaper boy, and we were called in to the newspaper office early on Sunday, December 7, 1941. The manager told us the paper was running a special edition announcing the Japanese bombing of Pearl Harbor. I was one of those newsboys who went around selling papers and saying, "Extra-Extra Read All About it. *Japs bomb Pearl Harbor!*"

I joined the navy when I was seventeen, and was a Seabee attached to Marine Air Group 31, 1st Division. I was aboard the USS *Florence Nightingale*.

We landed on Okinawa three days after the initial landing, which was on Easter Sunday, April 1, 1945. We went ashore in an LCVP, and I remember that several of our LCVPs were close to the one carrying the ammunition. Our drivers stayed as far away as possible from that boat because if it got hit we would probably have been blown up. It wasn't long until that boat was all alone.

When we first landed, we thought it would be a "piece of cake" because we experienced no opposition. However, it wasn't long until Japanese machine-gunners began firing on us from caves in the hills. The Japanese made pillboxes out of civilian burial tombs dug into the sides of the mountains. When we landed on Okinawa, I was a seventeen-year-old kid. It scared the "shit out of me."

The reality of war hit me quickly as the fighting was going on. When I saw dead American and Japanese soldiers, my thought was, "How many more of us will end up like this?" I remember seeing a dead Japanese soldier in a foxhole with no head. Many of our guys would dig two or three foxholes, because when they would fire at the Japanese, the Japanese could see where the shooting was coming from and would return fire to that location. After our guys fired, they would quickly move to another foxhole.

Our unit was assigned to build an airstrip on the island, so our planes could take off and land. We were told by the Army Corps of Engineers that it couldn't be done because that area was too marshy. We built it in two weeks! While building the airstrip, we were often under fire.

While on the island, I remember coming across two enemy foxholes. The bodies were "burned to a crisp" because our flamethrowers burned them out. Another time, one of our guys was on night guard duty in his foxhole. This was a scary duty because it was so dark you couldn't see in front of you, and the Japanese would often attack at night. He heard a noise and went crazy standing up and shooting his machine gun in a volley of bursts. We found out it was a goat moving in the bushes. The guy was so "shell shocked" that he had to be taken back to the States.

By the middle of June the battle was officially over, but hostilities were still occurring. Japanese fighter planes would get past our fighter cover and attack our camp and our ships. Even after atomic bombs had been dropped, we were attacked by Japanese planes. On August 12, 1945, three days after the second atomic bomb, some Japanese attacked the USS *Pennsylvania*, docked in Buckner Bay, with an aerial torpedo. It caused a major explosion. I was driving a truck at the time, and heavy shrapnel from the ship flew right over me. Another close call happened when I was working in one of our power generator buildings. A buddy relieved me, and shortly after, the building was hit by enemy fire, and he was killed.

In October, the biggest typhoon in Japan's history hit the island. Our camps were completely destroyed, and most of us took cover in the burial caves, which had previously been the Japanese machine-gun pillboxes. Some of our ships were flipped over, and others were heavily damaged, due to the over 150 miles per hour winds and rain torrents. In November, we departed Okinawa.

Fred Wood

Marine Corps: Captain, 324th Fighter Squadron
Hometown: Indianapolis, Indiana
Career: Distributor for McKee Bakeries

A Corsair fires rockets at a Japanese location on Okinawa

I earned my pilot wings at our air base in Corpus Christi, Texas, Naval Air Station. We shipped out to Hawaii and on to Midway Island, after the Battle of Midway had ended. We were sent to Okinawa while fighting was still taking place on the southern end of the island. I flew the Corsair FU4, and our fighter squadron's job was to do bombing and strafing runs on Japanese positions. We also dropped deadly napalm firebombs, and we flew cover missions for our bombers and provided protective cover for our early-warning ships. These ships kept our navy informed of any incoming enemy planes.

We were on Okinawa for about three months. While on the island, our squadron was assigned a bombing run to some location in Japan. We never got to our target because we were caught in a bad storm. Many of our pilots got separated and lost from the group. We had to drop our bombs on another Japanese island while heading back to our base.

On one of our sorties, one of our pilots had engine failure and had to ditch his plane in the ocean. He did a "textbook landing" and safely got out of his plane and into his life raft. We radioed one of our ships and circled above him until our fuel was running low. The ship picked him up about two hours later. He told us that it was the longest two hours of his life.

I remember when our flight leader told us he was going to fly low out of formation to see if he could draw any enemy antiaircraft fire. We thought he was crazy and were glad he didn't tell one of us to do it.

During the time I was on Okinawa, our infantry finally captured the island after heavy casualties on both sides. However, the Japs got the worst of it. Since I was an escort pilot, I was fortunate not to have to engage the enemy in air combat or be worried about antiaircraft flak. We had control of the air, at this time.

On August 6, 1945, the first atomic bomb was dropped on Japan. We knew the war would soon be over. President Truman made a difficult but right decision in ordering the atomic bombs to be dropped. If this had not been done, it was estimated that over a million lives, on both sides, would have been lost, if we had had to invade Japan.

Unfortunately, war is about killing, trying to kill the enemy before he kills you. That's what we were trained to do. It is not a pleasant experience.

11

VICTORY AT SEA!

Anchors Aweigh

"Fight—Let's Go! Join the Navy"
U.S. Navy recruiting poster

On September 3, 1939, twenty-seven months before the day of infamy at Pearl Harbor, the United States Navy joined with the Royal Navy and the Royal Canadian Navy. As a result, England would not stand alone against the German U-boat infested waters of the North Atlantic. The North Atlantic would become the longest lasting battle of World War II, and it would provide President Roosevelt with tragic prewar events at sea, which helped open the isolationist eyes of many Americans.

In the North Atlantic, 38 Americans were the first to die at the hands of Germany, when a German U-boat sank a British cruise liner. As a result, Roosevelt directed the U.S. Navy to sink any foreign vessel that posed a threat to the eastern shoreline of the United States. The Lend-Lease Act provided supplies to England, but before this act was passed in Congress, Roosevelt had already been utilizing the navy to transport supplies and equipment, and to provide protection for convoys bound for England. The consequence was that Americans began losing their lives in a war they had not yet entered.

After the attack on Pearl Harbor, the Japanese navy was running free throughout the Pacific and was adding to its conquests. Japan had defeated British forces in Hong Kong, Singapore, and Malaya, and won at the Battle of Java Sea. In spring 1942, Japan's naval force was in control of the New Guinea and Solomon Islands region in the South Pacific, but the tide started to change and shift toward Admiral Nimitz's sailors because of two successive victories for the United States.

At the battles of Coral Sea and Midway, naval airpower was delivered into the fray by the great aircraft carriers, which served as land bases for the aircraft. In both contests, combat raged between fighter pilots from both sides, as they sought to destroy one another's carriers and ships.

The American Navy and its fliers prevailed at Coral Sea, but what did not occur in this naval battle were ships engaging ships. When the mighty aircraft carriers came within striking distance, they unleashed their pilots to fight in the skies above and attack the ships below. The victory went to the American Navy, but 543 men, along with 66 planes, were lost, as well as the carrier USS *Lexington*.

On June 4, 1942, Japan launched a massive sea and air armada against Midway. The Japanese forces were superior to those of the U.S. Navy, as it had 190 ships, compared to less than 40 for the U.S. Navy. American fighter pilots based at Midway and those from the navy carriers were outnumbered as well, but the pilots threw caution to the wind and attacked with an unshakable determination to control the skies and knock out the attacking Japanese fleet. What the Japanese planners did not realize was that their codes had been cracked, and its plans were in the hands of the American admirals. This allowed the United States to devise a plan that would offset Japan's advantage in numbers.

As the attack raged on, many American planes were shot from the skies, but this did not deter the remaining pilots. They continued their aggressive attacks and inflicted heavy damage on Japan's fleet. At Midway, the Japanese navy lost four aircraft carriers, one heavy cruiser, 322 planes, and 3,500 sailors. The United States lost one carrier, one destroyer, and 307 men. The navy delivered a crushing blow to the Japanese navy, from which it would never recover. Control of the Pacific was now in the hands of the U.S. Navy.

While naval battles such as Midway, the Philippine Sea, and Leyte Gulf grabbed the headlines, victories could not have been achieved without the sailors who operated the landing crafts, ran the boiler rooms, provided fresh water to troops, and manned the decks through long, dark nights. It was the navy that protected, transported, and delivered Marines and infantrymen to far-off beaches, as they fought the war on the ground. The brave sailors who sailed into harm's way, achieved "victory at sea" for America.

Dick Beck

Navy: Electrician's Mate-Fireman First Class
Hometown: Madison, Wisconsin
Career: College professor of civil engineering

I enlisted when I was seventeen after graduating from high school. I did my basic training, boot camp, at the Great Lakes Naval Training Base in Illinois, and then went to Bainbridge, Maryland, for electrician's mate school. In September 1945, I was sent to Subic Bay and Manila Harbor in the Philippines. This was one month after the atomic bomb was dropped.

The trip from Bainbridge, Maryland, to San Francisco, California, aboard a troop train was an experience. In Chicago, we stopped next to a cattle train for two or three hours. The smell was awful, and there was no way getting away from it. After leaving Chicago, we were crossing the salt flats in Utah when the train broke down. The heat was sweltering, and if you left the train, there was a good chance you would step on some snakes. After several hours, we continued on to San Francisco.

The next trip was from San Francisco to Subic Bay aboard a Kaiser troop ship. The ship was full of young men who had never been aboard a ship. We were ordered to remain below deck so enemy spies could not see us and report troop movements. As you sail under the Golden Gate Bridge, there are large ground swells that raise and lower the ship. Needless to say, nearly all of the young, mostly Midwestern boys got very seasick. Since we were below deck, they were vomiting all over the place. If a guy was in an upper bunk, and you were below him, you "got hit." The smell was awful, and the cleanup was worse.

When we arrived at Subic Bay, I was assigned to the YW108, a yard water tanker. The water tankers provided fresh water to ships, so the men could shower. It was a real treat, if a ship's crew could get a freshwater shower. The guys we had to watch out for were the PT boat crews. As soon as they were tied up to our ship, they would come roaring aboard heading to the showers. We would duck behind something, so we wouldn't get trampled. It was great being part of the supply support system because we not only got freshwater showers, but we were also able to get the best food from our fellow food supply ship.

I was an electrician's mate, and I was responsible for maintaining the electrical system for our ship. I was only nineteen and felt overwhelmed to see all that was involved. I wasn't sure my training had prepared me for this, and I thought, "What if I mess up, and the ship loses its electrical power, and we can't provide the water needed for our other ships?" Fortunately, our problems were minor, and I was able to handle them.

I often thought it was amazing that we won the war with so many young boys doing the work. There were so many seventeen- and eighteen-year-old boys just out of high school who had to learn many different and complex jobs in all branches of the military. Sometimes they received little training, and they had to learn their jobs fast. Overall, everyone did an outstanding job, and we all did whatever we had to do to help win the war.

Fleet Admiral Chester Nimitz

"They fought together as brothers-in-arms. They died together, and now they sleep side by side. To them we have a solemn obligation."

After the disaster at Pearl Harbor, Nimitz was appointed commander of the Pacific Fleet and held that position until the war's end. Nimitz was an outstanding strategist, and under his leadership the navy went on the offensive in the Pacific after the attack on Pearl Harbor. Nimitz, however, often disagreed with his army counterpart, General MacArthur, over how operations should be conducted in the Pacific Theater. To ease the tension that had arisen, President Roosevelt intervened and assigned Nimitz as commander of the Central Pacific, and MacArthur was commander of the Southwest Pacific. Nimitz played a key role in the battles of Midway, Tarawa, the Marianas, Iwo Jima, and Okinawa.

James Bowman

Navy: Signalman, Senior First Class Petty Officer
Hometown: Amboy, Indiana
Career: Career military

Prior to graduating from high school, I tried to enlist in the navy, but I was turned down due to flat feet and being too short, and I didn't weigh enough. The recruiter told me to go home, finish high school, and try again later. When I graduated, I worked a while on a dairy farm, but this did not satisfy my search for adventure. So, I tried once again to join the navy. Since I was only seventeen, my mother had to sign the enlistment papers. I enlisted on May 19, 1941.

My boot camp was at Great Lakes Naval Training Center near Chicago. Before leaving boot camp, we were given tests to determine our next assignment. I was assigned to the Visual Signalman School in Toledo, Ohio. We worked hard to learn Morse code, semaphore, the names of the various signal corps flags, and the meaning of flag hoists. After training, my first assignment was the Armed Guard Center on Goat Island between Oakland and San Francisco, California. During my entire time in the navy, once I left signal school, I was in the Armed Guard and was assigned to merchant ships. My main job was relaying messages between our ships. I also assisted or manned a weapon on the flying wing, if necessary.

On December 7, 1941, the day Pearl Harbor was bombed, I was in San Francisco, California, and boarded the SS *Philipa*, a merchant ship that was primarily a freighter. Our departure was delayed for a week due to the outbreak of the war. Our ship was in the first convoy that left the West Coast at the start of World War II. When we arrived in Hawaii, I saw the smoking battleships of our Pacific Fleet partially submerged in a sea of oil and floating debris. The devastation at Pearl Harbor and Hickam Field made me realize what war was like.

My second assignment was to the SS *Steel Engineer*. We formed up another convoy and headed to Christmas Island, just north of the equator. We followed the equator to Lima, Peru, and landed at the seaport town of Callo, Peru. We then headed back to the Gulf of Mexico through the Panama Canal. When we left San Francisco for the second time, we were on our own without destroyer escorts. This left us exposed to enemy ships and submarines. While we were busy passing messages, our escort vessels were dropping depth charges on an enemy submarine.

After returning to New York Harbor, we sailed throughout the Caribbean and arrived in Curacao, Venezuela, on October 7, 1942. The ship was loaded with oil and gasoline heading for Freetown, British West Africa. The next day, one of our tankers was sunk by a Japanese submarine. Since many of our ships had been sunk in the area, this part of the Caribbean became known as "Torpedo Alley."

The voyages were often for months at a time, and "cabin fever" was a problem among the men. At times, there were some pretty violent fights. Conditions were cramped and hot, and we often ran short of fresh water and had to shower in saltwater. Even though we used a special kind of soap, it was hard to get clean using saltwater.

In January 1943, we were back again in New York Harbor. By the end of January, we were once again leading convoys back and forth between the East Coast and Europe. To get a convoy organized and under way in submarine-infested waters was always a challenge. Each convoy had fifty or more ships that performed various functions.

During one trip, I was on the bridge and saw a light flashing on a ship. I called our commodore, and we were both looking at the light with our binoculars when, all of a sudden, there was a huge explosion. A German sub had sighted in on one of our ships and blew it out of the water. The German submarines would sometimes form a wolf pack, a group of subs, and attack our convoys in force.

Subsequent trips to the Mediterranean took us to Algiers, Tunis, Palermo, and Naples, as we followed on the heels of our conquering Allied forces. In Palermo and Naples, Italy, we were bombed and strafed in the harbors. We had a few casualties, and those who were wounded received the Purple Heart, which General Patton personally distributed to them during his visit to the hospital. After returning to Norfolk, Virginia, we flew out of New York and landed in Belfast, Ireland, and once again headed to Naples, Italy. I do not know how many trips I took crossing the Atlantic or passing through the Straits of Gibraltar. I also lost track of the number of different ships I sailed on from 1941 to 1945. I know there were at least 21, some U.S. and some foreign.

I was proud to have served in the Armed Guard, sailing throughout the war on merchant ships with merchant seamen. We would never have been able to win the war, if not for the ships that transported troops and supplies all over the world. The mariners were not military and were not trained to man the ship's guns, but they often did. Their duty was extremely hazardous. Many people do not know that the mariners suffered a greater percentage of war-related deaths than all of the other military services.

I returned home in late fall 1945, docking in San Diego, California, after nearly four years of duty at sea.

Howard Caldwell

Navy: Petty Officer Second Class, USS *Shoveler*
Hometown: Indianapolis, Indiana
Career: Broadcast journalist and news anchor

USS *Shoveler*

I was drafted after completing my high school courses in the fall semester of 1943. I chose to receive my diploma in the June commencement ceremonies with my classmates. Since I was already in the navy by February 1944, my parents attended the commencement and accepted my diploma for me.

I was sent to the Great Lakes Naval Training Center north of Chicago, Illinois, for boot camp. Other special training took place in Mississippi and Wisconsin, and in Norfolk, Virginia. Eventually, I became a radio operator and was assigned to a new minesweeper, the USS *Shoveler*.

We had a crew of one hundred or so men, and I liked the small ship atmosphere. In September 1945, after the atomic bombs had been dropped, we headed to Okinawa. The ship pitched and rolled on the ocean for several days, since we were on the edge of a hurricane. By October, we landed at our home base, the Japanese Naval Station at Sasebo.

Our assignment, with the Japanese navy, was to clear and destroy the remaining water mines placed in the area during the war. Sweep assignments were conducted in waters around the southern islands of Kyushu, Japan. My duties were in the radio shack. I never had a hands-on part in the sweeps.

I knew we worked with other minesweepers by dropping cutters in the water, which would cause the mines to surface. When a mine surfaced, our 20mm and 40mm guns were used to fire at and explode them. When the mines exploded, they shot straight up in the air, accompanied by a horrendous sound. There was always the chance that your ship could hit or be hit by an undetected mine. The results would be devastating.

While at Sasebo, we found ourselves side by side the USS *Minivet*, another minesweeper. Since we were docked so close together, we talked back and forth and got to know several of the other crew members. The rumor was that our ship was going to return to the States in a few months. Several members of the *Minivet* crew were approaching discharge eligibility and were assigned to our ship. The men on our ship who had longer to serve replaced them. The decision came down for us to head for Guam (so much for going back to the States). We departed in December 1945, and crew members of both ships waved good-bye to one another. Little did we know that it would be our last look at the *Minivet*.

The *Minivet* was assigned to direct a shallow mine sweep that was not considered vital to the American Occupation Forces. In such situations, sweep action was designated a Japanese responsibility; however, four other American minesweepers, including the *Minivet*, were involved in the sweep. The Japanese were to conduct the mine sweeps, since they were the ones who had placed the mines. As the Japanese swept for mines, the American sweepers were supposed to remain on the edge of the water mine areas. This practice was supposed to be in effect during the *Minivet*'s last mission.

The minesweepers came across a line of floating mines, and the *Minivet*, whose view was obscured, crossed the mine line. About three hundred yards beyond the line, an explosion rocked the ship. The ship had struck a mine apparently left in the path of the Japanese sweepers. The *Minivet* capsized within three to four minutes, killing about one third of its crew. It was the first American minesweeper sunk since V-J (Victory in Japan) Day. When the loss of the *Minivet* became known to the American people, many were angered. An editorial in the Indianapolis News headlined, "The job of clearing mines should be the loser's job" (referring to the Japanese). By the end of the war, over 20,000 water mines were destroyed by American minesweepers.

We left Okinawa on Christmas Eve 1945, heading toward Guam. A few days later, we learned of the *Minivet* tragedy. This hit us hard, because we knew many of the thirty-one crew members who died. It was a tragedy that should not have happened, if proper protocol had been followed.

On March 1, 1946, a group of us was transferred to another minesweeper, the USS *Embattle*. We thought we were going back to the States. Wrong again. Instead, we were sent to the Philippines but not for minesweeper duty. In June, we docked in Shanghai, China, along with nine other U.S. minesweepers. We were told to turn our ships over to the Nationalist Chinese government, which was fighting Communist forces. As crew members, we had to teach the Nationalist Chinese how to operate our ships—not an easy task.

We finally headed back home from Tokyo, Japan, in late summer 1946. On the way back, we spotted a water mine in the Pacific Ocean. Our gun crews fired at it, but it didn't explode. After several tries, we determined it was a "dud." I couldn't help thinking of those thirty-one *Minivet* crew members who lost their lives in their final months of service. On that fateful day, had that mine been a "dud," like the one we encountered, those men would probably be alive.

Charles Maurer

Navy: Photographer's Mate Second Class, USS *Antietam*
Hometown: Teaneck, New Jersey
Career: Movie theater manager

(Courtesy of Charles Maurer)

One day, while still in high school, a priest visited our classroom. He told us that two of our classmates, who had dropped out of school, were killed in the war. One was a merchant marine who died when his ship was sunk, and the other student was killed in France. After telling us about their deaths, he held up a 20mm shell and said, "This is what you will be facing in war." He got our attention.

After graduating from high school, I enlisted in the navy at seventeen. Most of the 15 boys in my class joined some branch of the military service. I wanted to join the navy because my father had been in the navy. I thought about being a pilot or going to gunnery school but found out I was color blind and could not be admitted to either program. My real interest was photography, since I was the photographer for our school newspaper and also earned my photography merit badge in the Boy Scouts. My scouting experiences helped me when I was in the military. I learned about patriotism, duty, honor, and country, and had developed self-discipline and the ability to persevere. Eventually, I achieved Eagle Scout rank.

I was sent to Pensacola, Florida, to be a combat photographer, and then on to Norfolk, Virginia, to be trained in aerial photography. Later, I was sent to MIT in Boston to the War School, where I was one of the first to be trained in three-dimensional photography. This was the newest photographic technology at the time. We were trained to take pictures from planes to determine the topography of the land in order to locate mountains, valleys, and rivers. Maps were made, and these were used to help our pilots.

I served aboard the aircraft carrier USS *Antietam*, which had 3,000 men and over 100 planes. There were four squadrons of planes—fighter bombers, dive bombers, torpedo bombers, and fighter planes. My job as the photographer's mate was to take pictures and film of our planes when they were doing their training for takeoff and landings. I was assigned to the VB89 Dive Bomb Squadron and was the only one on board who could process the film once it was taken. I took the film to the ready room, and officers studied it to see what caused some of our planes to crash on takeoffs and landings.

Plane crashing off of the USS *Antietam*
(Courtesy of Charles Maurer)

Sometimes pilots crashed into the ocean, and other times they crashed on the carrier deck. We were able to rescue many of the downed pilots because we had two destroyers flanking both sides of our carrier serving as rescue ships. I do know that at least seven of our pilots died while crash-landing on the deck.

When I flew to take aerial photos, I would sit behind the pilot in the backseat of the cockpit. We would fly at about ten thousand feet, and when you looked down on a clear day, the aircraft carrier looked like a postage stamp. Landing a plane on a carrier is a very difficult job because the plane's landing speed is around 100 miles per hour, and the ship is moving about 30 miles per hour. It takes a lot of skills and practice, and there is little margin for error. It's dangerous being on the deck of a carrier, and one day a terrible tragedy occurred during training. We were having gunnery practice, shooting at radio-controlled smaller planes that were flying toward the ship. One of the five-inch shells misfired and exploded, killing several sailors and damaging planes.

When the atomic bombs were dropped, we were in Pearl Harbor with other ships preparing to head to the Pacific to be part of the invasion of Japan. When we left Pearl the war was over, and one day as we were close to Midway Island we learned that the bombs ended the war. We were told the Japanese had surrendered, and the war was over; we were one happy crew. Our carrier continued on to the Yellow Sea in China to help the Marines, who were returning the defeated Japanese soldiers to their homeland.

When we were in the Yellow Sea in China conducting training exercises, one of our pilots landed with a badly damaged wing, but there were no bullet holes. We asked him what happened, but he only told us he wasn't sure. When I opened his gun camera magazine to get the film, it was missing. Later, he told me the whole story. While he was out on his mission, he was "showing off," and he flew too close to a Chinese junk boat, and his wing hit the boat's mast. The Chinese on the boat were waving at him. When he started to get too close, they all jumped overboard. I know he was embarrassed, so I never told anyone.

Something many people don't know is that we lost more pilots and airmen in training exercises than airmen killed in the war. Another thing that amazed me was how the navy could take seventeen- and eighteen-year-old boys and train them to do complex jobs in a short time.

Fleet Admiral William "Bull" Halsey, Jr.

"There are no extraordinary heroes; there are extraordinary circumstances to which ordinary men respond with extraordinary courage.

In April 1942, Halsey was commander of Task Force 16, which launched Jimmy Doolittle and his B-25s in a surprise attack on Tokyo, Japan. His naval forces were victorious in the naval engagement at Guadalcanal in November 1942, and in 1944 Admiral Nimitz transferred him to the Central Pacific to assume command of the Third Fleet as it prepared for action in the Philippines. At the Battle of Leyte Gulf, he and his fleet left the San Bernardino Strait to attack a fleet of Japanese carriers. When Halsey left, the strait was exposed and open to Japanese battleships. The Japanese plan was to lure Halsey out of the strait, so enemy battleships could take on components of the Seventh Fleet, which were outnumbered. However, the valiant stand of the American ships in the San Bernardino Strait repulsed the Japanese attack. While this was occurring, Halsey and his 64 ships attacked the Japanese aircraft carriers and sank or damaged what was left of Japan's carriers and eliminated its naval airpower.

Richard E. "Dick" Miller, Jr.

Navy: Electrician First Class, USS *Appalachian*.
Hometown: Arnett, Oklahoma
Career: Electrician

USS *Appalachian*

I was working in the oil fields of Oklahoma and enlisted in the navy in May 1942. After processing and swearing in, I was sent to the Great Lakes Naval Training Center for my basic training. I requested to be sent to electrician's school and was transferred to Morehead State Teachers College in Morehead, Kentucky, for my training.

In November 1942, I was assigned to the USS *Ariel* in Norfolk, Virginia. From there, we headed to Guantanamo Bay, Cuba, and dropped off ammunition. We traveled to various islands and locations, including the West Indies—Saint Thomas, Trinidad, and Aruba. After arriving in Aruba, my job was to route our oil tanker ships to the Pacific. At the time, Aruba was the largest oil refinery in the world, producing aviation fuel for our planes. I was also assigned on a ship to escort sub chasers and PT boats out of Aruba. We escorted them for about fifty miles, and then they were on their own.

After six months, in October 1943, I went to New York and was assigned to a new ship, the USS *Appalachian*. The ship was still under construction, and while it was being built, crew members had to learn how to operate and repair the ship. We worked seven days a week.

On January 13, 1944, we headed to Pearl Harbor, Hawaii. The following day, we put to sea again, headed for our first combat mission, Kwajalein Atoll in the Marshall Islands. Our specific area targets were the islands of Roi and Namur. This was our first of four invasions in the Pacific. As a communications ship, we were always one of the lead ships in the convoy.

On March 16, 1944, Admiral "Bull" Halsey, commander in the South Pacific, made an informal inspection of our ship. At the end of March, we headed back to Pearl Harbor to get supplies. On April 16 we headed back to Guadalcanal's Koli Point. Here, we spent a week training and preparing for the forthcoming assault on the Marianas. After several months of sorties to various locations in the Pacific, the Guam attack, our second invasion, came on July 14. Our job was to supervise preassault bombardment for our battleships and destroyers. When troops went ashore on June 21, it was the *Appalachian*'s commissioning flag that became the first American flag to fly over Guam since enemy capture. This was a very inspiring sight.

We returned to Pearl Harbor in late August and performed training exercises on Maui, preparing for an assault on Yap. The assault was canceled, and we proceeded to Manus Island in the Admiralties in mid-September. On October 3, 1944, we dropped anchor in Seeadler Harbor and reported for duty with the Seventh Fleet. The *Appalachian* was one of the lead ships in the assault on Leyte Island in the Philippines, October 20, 1944. We encountered mine-infested waters without mishap. The *Appalachian* and other ships sent out towering clouds of smoke to annoy the Jap pilots. General MacArthur, the army commander in chief of the Pacific, was aboard the USS *Nashville* and joined our convoy. Leyte was our third invasion, and we became a part of history in helping MacArthur to fulfill his promise regarding the Philippines: "I shall return!"

After the Leyte invasion, we returned to San Francisco for a few days, and then we returned to the Pacific for the Luzon invasion in the Philippines. As part of a reinforcement group carrying the 25th Division (army) for the Luzon invasion, we arrived safely in Lingayen Gulf on January 11, 1945. During our ten-day stay, we endured two air attacks but came away undamaged. Luzon was our fourth and final invasion.

In all, I was in the Pacific for a little over two years. I was aboard the *Appalachian* for thirteen months, and she earned four battle stars. We returned to dock in San Francisco in late December 1945. When people ask me about the war, I tell them we knew who our enemy was, and we knew who was going to win.

Ed Moss

Navy: Machinist Mate Second Class, USS *Neosho*
Hometown: Brooklyn, New York
Career: Chemical engineer in chemo-electronics industry

Moss (left) and fellow sailor while in Hawaii

I was just sitting down to Sunday dinner when the news came over our radio that Pearl Harbor had been bombed. Needless to say, the family was shocked. The next day at high school we all returned to our homerooms to listen to President Roosevelt's speech, which was played over the loudspeaker system.

When I was seventeen, I enlisted in the navy. After completing boot camp, I was sent to Purdue University to train as an electrician. I served aboard the USS *Neosho*, a refueling-at-sea tanker for the Third and Fifth Fleets in the Pacific Theater. I was excited and truly looked forward to the experience, but I was also a little frightened because I knew what could happen.

When I arrived on the *Neosho*, my chief engineer told me, "I have too many electricians; you are now a machinist's mate." My job on the tanker was below deck in the engine room. It was noisy, and all of the action was above deck. The sound of the guns firing above was louder in the engine room than up on deck because of the vibrating metal in the room. I did many jobs down in the engine room, but my main task was to maintain and repair the myriad of pumps aboard ship. Steamships, regardless of the type of fuel they burn, depend on pumps. We depended on pumps to store and move various fuels, pump water throughout the ship, clear the bilges of excess fluids, pump fuel to our engines, and especially to pump huge volumes of fuel during refueling-at-sea operations. In those days, most pumps were powered by steam, and some by self-contained diesel motors.

The function of the *Neosho* can best be described by the nickname given to us by other sailors, "floating gas station." Our mission was, and still is for the modern navy tankers, to make it possible for "fighting ships" to stay at sea for extended periods of time and to be able to resupply them with fuel and other critical supplies, even in the heat of battle. We had the technology and the technique to pass fuel between ships while sailing at speeds up to thirteen knots. Neither the Japanese nor the Germans had that capability, which meant that it was easier for us to "rule the seas." We carried over a million gallons of combined aviation, diesel, and "black oil" fuel.

When we were about 200 miles from Okinawa, we were hit by a kamikaze. We were hit on the fantail, which is the rearmost part of the ship. Luckily, it did not start a fire or do any critical damage. We arrived at Okinawa three days after the land invasion, and we supported and supplied the ships that were stationed off of the island.

We left Okinawa a few days after it was secured. We were on our way to the Sea of Japan to join the rest of the fleet for what was to be the invasion of the Japanese Islands. One day, the captain came on the intercom and announced that a "new and powerful weapon" had just been dropped on Hiroshima with tens of thousands of casualties. Our engineering officer told us that it might mean the end of the war, and we would not have to make an assault on mainland Japan.

We were still heading for the Sea of Japan when again the captain came on the intercom and told us the Japanese were surrendering. All hell broke loose on board. To celebrate, the captain opened up the liquor cabinet, and "all hands" were issued a two-ounce shot of whiskey, even those of us who were still underage. On August 5, 1945, we steamed into Tokyo Bay and anchored about a third of a mile from the USS *Missouri*, where General MacArthur was accepting the official Japanese surrender.

When we got our first liberty back in the United States, most guys headed for the nearest bar. I, and two other buddies, headed for the nearest grocery store. We bought a pound of fresh tomatoes and a quart of milk each. When the store owner found out we were just back from overseas, he refused to take any money from us and gave it to us free. We then went outside, sat down on the curbstone, and devoured our milk and tomatoes.

The life lesson I learned from the war was that I served my country for a purpose greater than myself.

Bob Petzel

Navy: Ship's Cook Second Class, PT Boat Squadron 31
Hometown: Bluffton, Indiana
Career: Teacher and principal

Petzel at the helm of his PT Boat, 1944

There were 14 crew members on our PT boat, and I was our ship's cook. Our squadron saw action in the Solomon Islands, New Guinea, the Philippines, and Okinawa. The PT boats held four torpedoes and were designed to make quick attacks on ships. Our boat was also manned with two twin .50 caliber machine-gun turrets and a 37mm on the bow. The boats patrolled in groups of three. When we were not engaged in any activity and had some time to relax, many of the crew members would play cards, roll dice, smoke, play jokes on each other, write letters, or read.

While patrolling, we had to look out for floating mines. They could only be seen visually, and one time, I looked over the bow and saw one near our boat. I yelled to the skipper, and he was able to steer our boat so we didn't hit it. Besides patrolling the shorelines of the Japanese islands, we also picked up Japanese soldiers who were trying to escape in different kinds of small boats. We would take them back to our base, where the army took care of them and sent them to POW camps.

We were the first PT boat squadron into Okinawa. Our job was to patrol for Japanese soldiers who were on ships trying to get to the islands to provide reinforcements. One time, while we were patrolling around the south end of Okinawa close to the beach, one of the guys told an officer we needed to watch out for coral reefs. The officer told us not to worry. Sure enough, we hit a reef, tearing off all three of our propellers and rudders. Our ship listed on its side, and we had to wait for the evening tides to come in, so another boat could come and rescue us. Another big problem we had while patrolling off the coast of Okinawa was typhoons, and we had two while I was there. Fortunately, we survived with little damage.

In late 1945, we were in Okinawa preparing and training for the mainland invasion of Japan, when President Truman ordered the dropping of the atomic bombs. We were all excited because we knew the war would soon be over, and we would not have to invade Japan. I respect President Truman for having the guts to drop the bombs and end the war.

In the military, you had a job to do, and you did it. I learned how to endure difficult conditions and situations. We were well-trained and dedicated to our jobs, and we depended on each other. The greatest influence the war had on me was that I developed an appreciation for the privilege of serving our country.

Ken Rash

Navy: Motor Machinist Mate First Class, Submarine Service
Hometown: Franklin, Indiana
Career: Banking

Ken Rash (left)

USS *Barbero* heading out to sea

I dropped out of high school my junior year to join the navy. I had noticed recruiting posters of a sailor in uniform with a pretty girl hanging on his arm. I thought, "Boy, this is for me." I enlisted on December 4, 1941, three days before the bombing of Pearl Harbor. My basic training (boot camp) was at the Great Lakes Naval Training Station in Illinois.

I was originally assigned to the aircraft carrier *Wasp*, but one day I was walking on the base and an old World War I navy chief stopped me and asked on what ship I would be serving. I told him the *Wasp*, and he told me not to get on an aircraft carrier because they were too large with too many men. Soon after this, I went to the dental clinic to see about a bad tooth. The dentist pulled my tooth, and I had to stay overnight, which caused me to miss my draft to the USS *Wasp*. While I was waiting for new orders, a recruiter came looking for volunteers for the Submarine Service. I volunteered and was sent to New London, Connecticut, for my sub training. I think the old navy chief must have been an "angel." I never saw him again, and a few months later, the USS *Wasp* was sunk by a Japanese sub. I lost some of my friends on the *Wasp*.

Submarine Service training is very intensive because you have to pass difficult scholastic, psychological, and swimming-related physical tests. One of the tests requires swimming up a one-hundred-foot water tower using a breathing device called a "Momsen lung." For another test, you are put in a pressure tank, and they let in fifty pounds of pressure. If your ears or nose bleed, or if you panic, you are out of the Submarine Service.

In May 1942, I was sent to Pearl Harbor and received my first submarine assignment to the USS *Plunger*. The *Plunger* had lots of "firsts" to her credit. She was the first to take radar to sea and the first in the Sea of Japan. I was trained as a motor machinist mate, and it was my job to see that the engine control rooms were functioning properly. The conditions were hot, noisy, and crowded, and the oil smell from the engines was terrible.

We were sent to the Pacific and conducted war patrols in the Indian Ocean, Southwest Pacific, Sea of Japan, and the Philippines. During our patrols, we sank supply and troop ships. Near Guadalcanal, while submerged in only fifty-five feet of water, we ran aground, damaging our sound head and hull on a coral reef. Because of the damages, we were ordered back to Brisbane, Australia, to make repairs.

On one of our patrols, we took part in an attack on the Japanese naval and air base at Truk, Caroline Islands. This base was like our Pearl Harbor, since it was their largest naval base. While on another patrol, a depth charge caused damage to our engine room, and it began to flood. If an engine room floods, and you lose power, you sink in "the iron coffin." In sub school, they told us to think about it this way, "If you don't eventually surface, you will have a $5 million coffin."

During my time on the USS *Plunger*, I made five war patrols and qualified for my "Dolphin Pin," which means you manned every station on the submarine and passed the required tests. This is the highest honor for submariner qualification.

After my service on the USS *Plunger*, I returned to the States and was assigned to a newer submarine, the USS *Barbero*. The crew consisted of 72 sailors and seven officers, and we completed two more combat patrols in the Pacific. I enjoyed serving on a submarine, but at times you experienced sheer panic, when enemy destroyers were unloading depth charges over you. On one of our runs, there were 55 documented depth charges dropped over or near us, with each containing 600 to 900 pounds of TNT, causing us to shake violently. The noise from the explosions was deafening, and it sounded like you were in a steel drum and someone was hitting it with a sledgehammer. I remember praying, "God, let me live through this, and I won't go on another war patrol again." In fact, there were many times when I prayed.

Submarines traveled in wolf packs of three subs. The pack was usually named after the ranking commander of the patrol. Wolf packs provided security and enabled the pack to make a more destructive attack on enemy ships, since each submarine carried 24 torpedoes. On the newer subs, there were six torpedo tubes on the front of the sub and four at the back. Before returning to base, the intent was to fire all of your torpedoes at enemy ships. When all 24 torpedoes were fired, it was called a "clean sweep."

Another scary experience happened while we were patrolling in the Lombok Strait in Indonesia. We were hit by a Japanese aerial bomb that damaged our reduction gear, which affected the speed of our sub. The sub began an immediate steep down angle nosedive, and I thought we were going to sink and be killed. The *Barbero* could submerge to depths of about four hundred feet. The damage knocked us out of the war, and we returned to the States. I was proud to have served as a member of the "Silent Service." The two submarines on which I served were involved in seven war patrols, and we earned seven war patrol commendations.

During World War II, the U.S. Navy had 273 submarines that patrolled against the enemy. Although the Submarine Service comprised less than 1.6 percent of the total U.S. Navy strength, we caused more than half of Japan's sea losses, 54.6 percent. Sinking these ships resulted in the loss of nearly a half million Japanese lives and thousands of tons of enemy ships. However, this success was made at the heaviest relative cost of any branch of the U.S. military during World War II. The Submarine Service lost one out of every five submarines. Fifty-two were sunk or "missing presumed lost." One out of every seven submariners died.

The submarine was my home, faith, pride, and weapon. My submarine service ranged from boredom to stark terror. As submariners, we had to contend with forces of the sea, the enemy, depth charges, mines, unintentional American aircraft attacks, and our own torpedoes, which could reverse direction. It was dangerous duty, but I considered it an honor to serve.

Walter Umbarger

Navy: Petty Officer Second Class, USS *Lowndes*
Hometown: Bargersville, Indiana
Career: Owner of Umbarger and Sons Feed and Grain Elevator

Umbarger is in the back row center.

USS *Lowndes*

I was married in 1942 and was drafted in 1943. A year before, I tried to enter, but the doctor said I had pneumonia scars on my lungs, and they would not let me join. But the second time around, I was able to get in. When it was time to enter, a busload of us went to Indianapolis to this armory. I went from table to table answering questions, and I remember asking for the army. I never even had any thoughts about the navy. I got to the last table, and the guy said, "So, you want the army?"
I said, "Yes, sir."
He looked at me, and marked on my paper, navy. He then said, "You are in the navy, son. If you don't like it, you can go talk to the chaplain."

I did my boot camp at the Great Lakes Naval Training Center in Chicago, Illinois. After boot camp, I went to Northwestern University for radio school. All I knew about a radio was how to turn it on and off. I was not very good at mechanics.

When I graduated out of radio school, my first ship assignment was on the USS *Lowndes* which was based in Astoria, Oregon. It was commissioned in September 1944, and I was part of the original crew. Our ship was an attack transport ship, which carried 1,500 Marines, landing vehicles and supplies, and equipment for the land invasions. My job was working in the radio communications room, and I was the only non-commissioned officer in the radio division. We usually worked four hours on and four hours off; however, if we were preparing for combat operations, the hours were much longer. Prior to and during one of the invasions, I worked for 36 consecutive hours.

As radio operators, we typed out coded messages from headquarters; they were prioritized, and the supervisor sent them to the officers to be decoded. I was always interested in Morse code, and learning it in the navy became a challenge to me; I ate it up. In high school I learned to type and could type sixty words a minute. I got pretty good at recording the messages, and I enjoyed it. Sometimes, I wore a different headphone on each ear, so I could monitor two frequencies at the same time, which was often challenging. Later, my assignment was as a supervisor, and I had to monitor the other men to see that they were recording the messages correctly. This work can be tense, stressful work, and difficult to learn, but I found the work interesting, and it was important.

Life at sea was terrible at first, but you learned to adjust to the food, crowded conditions, and boredom. I really liked peanut butter, so before we shipped out, one of the last things I bought was a whole case of peanut butter. I carried it about a mile to the ship, and then I had to worry about where I was going to store it. I did share it with some of the boys. We looked forward to mail and packages from home. One time I got back to my bunk, and I had about ten from the mail. One of the packages was a box of anchovies, and I still like anchovies today.

In February 1945, we arrived at Iwo Jima and participated in the invasion. From our ship, twenty-five or thirty Marines loaded into each of the smaller landing crafts and headed for the beach. For these Marines, it was about their third or fourth invasion, and they just had a blank, gaunt look; their faces were gray, and it was just like they knew they were going to die, and every one of them looked the same. It was terrible, really. They had just been through so much. So many were killed there on Iwo.

The *Lowndes* also sent in a beach party of around 40 men, and they helped evacuate the wounded, tried to repair landing craft, and kept the beach clear. The only guys we lost from our ship were pharmacist's mates (medics) who had gone ashore with the beach party. Two of them were killed, and three were wounded.

Once the landing crafts were able to drop off their men, they returned to the ship, awaiting further instructions. When the landing crafts returned to the beaches, they picked up any wounded and dead. We had heard that in some places, our dead Marines were stacked three feet high. During the landings, we lost eight of our landing crafts, which were hit by Japanese artillery fire, killing nearly everyone on board. It was a terrible experience. The wounded were brought back to our ship's medical facilities, and then they were transferred to various field or base hospitals for more treatment.

During the invasion, our position was off the right front bow of the *Indianapolis*. They sat there and pounded away at Suribachi for hours. It was tremendous. The *Indianapolis* was the ship that delivered components of the atomic bomb to Tinian, and it was later sunk by a Japanese submarine.

At the end of February, we left Iwo and headed on to Saipan and Guam to take on new supplies and get more fuel. We also picked up more Marines, and the next thing we knew we were going to Okinawa. Our group was to do "feint" (fake) beach landings on one side of the island to make the Japanese think that this was the main land invasion point. The real invasion was taking place on the other side of the island, so we did not actually land any Marines during the feint.

During our missions, the captain of our ship was very closed mouth. He kept everything to himself, so we found out what was going on mostly by word of mouth. However, we got some news from the head cook because the captain liked to talk once in a while, and we had some warrant officers who were very good at talking.

We were in San Francisco when word got out the war had ended. That town was bedlam in a half hour, and you could not walk through the streets; the people went wild. Some windows were broken, and cars were turned over. After that, we headed back to sea. It was disheartening when we found out that we were headed back to the Pacific.

I was glad that I had a chance to serve, since many of my friends had enlisted after Pearl Harbor. I think I would have been embarrassed to face those who went overseas if I had not been able to serve. There was never any doubt in my mind that we would win the war.

12

CHINA-BURMA-INDIA

The CBI

"There were at this time absolutely no amenities of life. It was a dread and dismal place.
—Eric Sevareid, journalist

In the far tucked away region known as the China-India-Burma Theater, or the CBI, Allied forces were operating in harrowing conditions against the Japanese. The terrain of the CBI ranged from mighty rivers in each country, to dusty plains and tea plantations in India, the daunting Himalaya Mountains, and the dense jungles of Burma. These terrain features, along with the Japanese forces, served as an admirable adversary for the American, British, and Chinese forces.

Lieutenant General Joseph "Vinegar Joe" Stillwell, the senior American military commander in the CBI, was highly regarded as an effective trainer of troops and military tactician. He was given the daunting task of training and preparing Chinese soldiers for combat, supervising the distribution of Lend-Lease supplies to China, and supporting the Chinese in their ongoing fight against the Japanese. By keeping the Chinese supplied and fighting the Japanese, it helped ensure the Japanese forces would not be diverted to battles in the Pacific. Stillwell had to accomplish his mission even though his theater of war was not the priority like Europe and the Pacific.

In 1942, Japanese forces pushed the Allies out of Burma and shut down the Burma Road, which was the overland supply route for Allied supplies into China. To counter the closing of the Burma Road, the U.S. Air Transport Command (ATC) was created, and a 500 aerial supply line was established from Assam, India, to Kunming, China. The daring American crews encountered brutal storms and high winds as they flew over the fifteen-hundred-foot Santsung Range in the Himalayas, which became known as "The Hump." The route's treacherous conditions and enemy planes resulted in a loss of 600 planes and 1,000 men.

While the ATC was delivering supplies from the air, a new overland supply route was under construction. American engineers began work on the Ledo Road, which was a 500 mile route that originated in Assam, India, and linked up with the Burma Road in northern Burma. Once the 600 mile Burma Road was repaired and the two roads were connected, supplies were delivered to Kunming, China.

Combat operations in the CBI saw Merrill's Marauders, named after Major General Frank Merrill, conduct guerilla-style warfare against the effective Japanese jungle fighters. The Marauders continuously conducted these raids and played an important role in helping secure the overland supply route to China. In the air, Major General Claire L. Chennault founded the famed Flying Tigers. The brave pilots, with their shark-faced fighter planes, became well known for victories over the Japanese Zeroes. Greatly outnumbered and flying obsolete P-40s, Chennault instructed his pilots to "use your speed and diving power to make a pass, shoot, and break away." At the conclusion of the war, the Flying Tigers had lost 573 planes, but these tough-minded pilots shot down 1,200 Japanese planes and played an important role in the CBI.

The jungles, mountains, rivers, and Japanese soldiers in the CBI were all tough obstacles to overcome. However, just as stubborn as the jungles, just as rugged as the Himalayas, just as mighty as the rivers, and just as tough as the enemy, were the soldiers and airmen of "Vinegar Joe" and "Old Leather Face" Chennault.

Dan Gates

Army: Corporal, 23rd Signal Construction Battalion
Hometown: Indianapolis, Indiana
Career: Manager for Indiana Bell Telephone Company and real estate agent

The Ledo-Burma Road in the CBI Theater

I served in the China-Burma-India Theater as a telephone lineman and dispatcher. My job was to see that the telephone lines remained operational on the 1,100 mile Burma Road. The Burma Road was constructed by our army engineers and construction crews. The workers included 15,000 soldiers, 60 percent of whom were black. Over one 1,000 men died during the construction, which took just over two years to build. It was an amazing engineering accomplishment. The two-lane narrow dirt road stretched from India to China through dense jungles and steep mountains, including the Himalayas, the highest mountain range in the world.

One time I was driving a jeep taking the executive officer to a location somewhere on the Burma Road. While we were driving, the road was so high that when we looked down from the side of the road we saw below us one of our C-46 transport planes flying above the clouds.

The purpose of the road was to provide fuel, ammunition, and supplies to the Chinese army, who were our allies fighting the Japanese. Because we could keep them supplied, the Chinese were able to keep 1,000,000 Japanese troops from attacking our soldiers and Marines in the various Pacific battle locations.

I remember a couple of humorous incidents. Once, two of our guys were riding in their jeep along a stretch of the Burma Road, and they came upon a huge Bengal tiger standing in the center of the road. They stopped immediately. One of the guys pulled his gun and shot it. They quickly turned the jeep around and took off, thinking the tiger was only wounded and might be chasing them. When they looked back they saw the tiger was dead. Another time, a large gorilla wandered into our base camp and walked through the door of my barracks. We all jumped up and ran through the bamboo walls to get away. The gorilla was just looking for food and not people.

E. Jerry Morehead

Air Corps: Tech Sergeant
Hometown: Indianapolis, Indiana
Career: Sales manager

A Piper Cub plane similar to the one flown by Morehead

I joined the Indiana National Guard while still in high school. Upon graduation, I enlisted in the Army Air Corps, because I wanted to be a pilot. After taking my exams, I was sent to Kelley Field in San Antonio, Texas, for preflight training, and from there I went to Plano, Texas, for primary flight training. However, I washed out of flight school.

The United States was assisting the Chinese, who were fighting the Japanese in the China, Burma, and India areas. We had about three thousand U.S. troops on the ground, while the rest were mostly Chinese, Australian, and other troops. This became known as the China-Burma-India (CBI) Theater, which is sometimes a forgotten part of World War II. Pilots were needed to fly supplies and equipment, tow gliders and do bombing runs on the Japanese. Although I had washed out of pilot training, I was granted permission to fly the L-1 and L-5 Piper Cub medical evacuation and rescue planes.

Our group of 500 British and American planes consisted of bombers, fighters, transport planes, gliders, and search and rescue. We were part of a top-secret mission and were not permitted to open our orders until we had been in the air for fifteen minutes. Our destination was to be Karachi, India, via South America and Egypt. Karachi was near Ledo, India, which was the starting point of the 1,000 mile Burma Road, one of the greatest engineering feats of the entire war.

My job was to fly the specially fitted Piper Cubs to pick up wounded and injured soldiers along the Burma Road and in the jungle fighting areas. The plane could fly at speeds of only 90 to 100 miles per hour, which made me a "sitting" duck if I ran into a Japanese Zero fighter plane. Fortunately, I did not see any, and I guess they did not see me. Depending upon the size of our plane, we could transport between two to eleven injured at a time. We flew them to our surgical MASH outfits in Myitkyina, Burma, which is close to the Chinese border. The doctors would perform over one hundred operations a day.

I had the privilege of flying the commanding general of the CBI Theater, "Vinegar Joe" Stillwell, to a jungle post in Burma. He was brash but an outstanding general. During the flight, the engine noise was so loud that we were not able to talk with one another. When we landed at our destination, there was a terrible storm, and he told me to stay overnight and return the next morning. While he went to some safe headquarters building, I had to dig a foxhole and sleep in the rain. During the night, I kept hearing gunfire, and I thought it was the Japanese coming toward us. In the morning, I learned it had been two Chinese forces firing at each other, thinking they were shooting at the Japanese.

Since we had to fly low when flying our missions, the Japanese would often shoot at us with their rifles and machine guns. During my flights I had only one bullet go through my plane. Perhaps my most frightening experience was when the colonel had sent three of us to fly over a location to see what Japanese movement was going on. Upon our return, we looked down and saw these huge bomb craters and explosions. We looked up and saw one of our B-25 bombers flying about five-hundred feet above us. Obviously, the pilot did not see us. If his bombs had not already been dropped, we would probably have been hit by one. God must have had his hand on me.

I helped evacuate those wounded soldiers who were part of Merrill's Marauders. I later learned that some of those that we couldn't evacuate were used by the Japanese for bayonet practice. Another special memory I have was when I was in China and saw our famous "Flying Tigers" fighter squadron. There was a funny thing I remember when we were at our base in India. At night, you could look across the river and, because of the base lights; you could see hundreds of eyes staring at you. It was an eerie sight. Those eyes belonged to monkeys.

On my last mission, I was returning to our airfield with an injured native. My landing instructions were not clear, and to avoid a collision with another one of our planes, I ended up doing a nosedive crash on the runway. My passenger must not have been hurt too badly, because he ran off and left me in the plane. When I was removed from the plane, I had a broken back. I was sent to the hospital in Ledo, India, where I stayed for two months encased in a full-body cast. I remember it being so hot, over 100 degrees, and there was only one fan in the hospital. Luckily for me, it was beside my bed. One of the generals sent orders to get all of the fans in the hotels in Calcutta and have them used for the patients in the hospital.

I was lying in my bed one day, when I looked up and saw a familiar face walking in. I couldn't believe it! It was one of my best friends from high school. We had been separated after our initial assignments, and I had been writing his mother throughout the war. She wrote him and told him what had happened to me and where I was. He "hitchhiked" a plane and flew 600 miles to visit me. Friendship doesn't get much better than that.

In September 1943, after my recovery, I was sent to Billings Hospital at Fort Benjamin Harrison in Indianapolis, Indiana, my hometown.

Robert Weaver

Army Air Corps: Sergeant, 14th Air Force
Hometown: Saint Joseph, Illinois
Career: Postal Service

P-47 Thunderbolt

On Sunday, December 7, 1941, I was working at my parents' household fixing some plumbing. I went to the Saint Joseph Oil Company to buy a part, and some men were talking about Pearl Harbor. I did not know where Pearl Harbor was located. I went home, and my parents had the news on the radio, and there were a lot of broadcasts about what had taken place there. It was a depressing announcement for everyone, and it just put the whole country in a defensive mood.

I was always interested in airplanes, so I went to Chanute Airbase in Illinois to enlist. I took some tests and qualified for airplane mechanics school and was sworn in on January 8, 1942. I ended up in the 93rd Fighter Squadron, and we trained at what is now Edwards Airbase. We completed our training toward the end of summer in 1942; the pilots left and went to England. Our unit was at full strength, and we thought we would go to England also, but this did not happen.

We loaded up and traveled across the country, going through southern Illinois, Indiana, and Ohio, and ended up in Newport News, Virginia. We stayed there for a day or two, and then one evening after chow an announcement was made that we were going to board a ship. We were restricted to quarters and did not load up on the GI trucks until after midnight. We couldn't tell where we were going, but we finally saw our ship, unloaded the trucks, and marched up to board it. We didn't get to our bunks until around 2:30 a.m.

Once out to sea, our commander told us we were going on an invasion of North Africa. Our mission was to land at Port Lyautey in Morocco and march seven miles to a French airport. They told us there probably wouldn't be resistance from the French. We were aboard the ship for three weeks preparing for the invasion, called Operation Torch.

The invasion was at predawn on a Sunday morning. I saw the small landing boats going in and out, and we were about a mile out. We were standing at the side looking over, and we began to see a splash here and a splash there. At first, we didn't know what it was, but then realized the French were shelling us. The ship's horn was sounded for everybody to get to their stations. Quickly, our ship peeled around and went out about three or four miles. Navy fighter planes from the carriers went in to take out an artillery position on a hill, and the planes were also protecting the troops already on the beaches. We saw cruisers come by and shoot their broadsides at the artillery position. We went in after dark on the second night, and headed up a river and got off at a dock near the airport. The airport runway had been bombed, and there were no friendly airplanes for us to work on.

After President Roosevelt visited Casablanca, they moved us by train to Algeria, which is next to Tunisia, and we set up camps there. I was south of Constantine, while some crews were closer to the border of Tunisia. One day we were alerted that the Germans were making a push against the Americans at Kasserine Pass. We were about 45 miles back. We thought we might have to retreat, but our forces held and shut them off.

Once we moved out of Constantine, we moved close to the Mediterranean Sea near Bone, Algeria. We moved by troop convoy with trucks and our other equipment. Our planes started patrolling and flying as escorts for the shipping lanes that led into the different ports in the Mediterranean.

From then on, my crew and I traveled in the back of a truck to several different points in Tunisia. We were in Bizerte, Sfax, Mareth, and Tripoli. We worked on airplanes doing major mechanical work. There was so much dust that some of the engines would not work. We had to change at least four engines in P-39s.

After about a year and a half, it was late winter, we received word that we were moving out of North Africa, so we started packing our equipment except for the P-39s which we left behind. My unit moved to Karachi, India, (now in Pakistan) which was part of the China-Burma-India Theater. We flew from Tunis to Tripoli, and on to Cairo, where we stayed overnight. The next day we flew over the pyramids, Jerusalem, the Dead Sea, and the Jordan River.

For the first three to four months we were stationed at Karachi, where I was a crew chief for the P-47 Thunderbolt, which could go up to higher altitudes. The P-47s were brought into Karachi aboard ships without their propellers. We put the propellers on, cleaned the salt from off them, and got them ready for the pilots. Every morning before dawn we did a preflight inspection around the plane, started it up and ran it, and checked all the plane's controls. While we were in India, the equipment we had to maintain the planes was much better than what we had in North Africa.

Once the pilots arrived at Karachi and were trained on the planes, we, the 93rd Squadron, moved 80 miles north of Calcutta to Gash Kara. They had already established some B-29 bomber bases close to Calcutta, India, and we were already flying missions into occupied China where the Japanese were. We had a squadron stationed on the other side of the Chinese border where our P-47s escorted B-29s during bombing runs against the Japs along the coastal areas. Our unit also picked up planes and escorted them into China and back. Up near Assam, in northeast India, is where they flew the "Hump." It took a while to get planes over the Hump, which is the Himalaya Mountains. I ended up being in India for about fifteen months.

13

Italian Campaign

Italy

"My dear Duce, it's no longer any good. Italy has gone to bits ... The soldiers don't want to fight anymore."
—King Victor Emmanuel III, Italy

When World War II erupted, Italy did not immediately enter the conflict, but instead waited until June 1940 to declare war on Great Britain and France. Mussolini's declaration of war came after Germany had all but defeated France; then he crossed the French-Italian border and committed his Italian troops. The Italian military was not as strong or effective as Germany's and suffered defeats in Greece, Albania, and North Africa.

When the Allies invaded and captured Sicily, Mussolini's Fascist government began to crumble. Shortly after Sicily was invaded, the king of Italy, Victor Emmanuel III, asserted his power and arrested and imprisoned Mussolini and replaced him with Marshal Pietro Badoglio. During a daring mission, German commandos rescued Mussolini and established him as leader of a puppet regime in northern Italy.

With Mussolini no longer recognized as the leader in Italy, the newly formed government did not align itself with Germany but instead signed an armistice with the Allies on September 3, 1943. The German military asserted itself and established a military government that controlled northern and central Italy with its forces.

On September 3, 1943, the British landed at Calabria, and six days later, American troops under General Mark Clark went ashore at Salerno. For the Allied troops, this became a hard-fought campaign, which would stretch northward to Anzio, Rome, the Apennine Mountains, and into the Po Valley. The German forces in Italy surrendered on May 2, 1945, giving control of the Italian Peninsula to the Allies.

Earl Anderson

Army Air Corps: Second Lieutenant, 15th Air Force
Hometown: LaGrange, Illinois
Career: General Motors Administrative Division

During the war, I was the pilot of B-24 bombers and flew 50 missions over northern Italy, France, Germany, and the Balkans with the 721st Squadron, 450th Bomb Group. During the D-Day invasion of Normandy, France, we flew one of the diversionary missions. Exactly one week later, June 13, 1944, I was flying my 50th and final mission over Munich, Germany. We were taking heavy flak from German antiaircraft guns, and an 88mm shell hit underneath the nose of our plane. It took out two engines and caused mechanical problems, and, as a result, we descended rapidly from twenty-two thousand to eight thousand feet. I told the crew to prepare to parachute from the plane.

I had to help my copilot get out of the cockpit because he was wounded. The entire crew was able to bail out, and they landed in different rural areas near Munich. On the way down, I saw a group of civilians with pitchforks and other weapons that were going to capture or kill us. Fortunately, after my copilot and I landed, we were able to hide in some bushes.

A short while later, a German soldier on patrol captured us. We became German prisoners of war (POW). At a camp in Frankfurt, Germany, we were processed, interrogated, and spent a week in solitary confinement. Later, we were marched to the Stalag Luft III, which was a POW camp for airmen. About 10,000 American and British airmen were imprisoned here. This was the camp where several months earlier some British prisoners had tunneled out and escaped. Many years after the war, the events of this escape were depicted in the movie, *The Great Escape*.

When we were POWs, we were not abused and were treated fairly well. At times, food became scarce, and in our fourteen-bunk barracks, we had to learn how to save and share food with one another. Our barracks were wooden buildings about sixty feet long and forty feet wide with double wooden bunk beds, and a single light bulb hanging from the middle of the ceiling. A secret group of POWs would bribe some of the German guards for food.

In January 1945, the Germans knew the Russian army was advancing on the Eastern front. The Germans gave us thirty minutes to get out, and then they force-marched us into wooded areas. We spent three days there—some of it in blizzard conditions. This was the worst and coldest blizzard in German history.

We were then marched to a train, where we were put in cattle cars. The inside of the cars were so crowded it was hard to find a place to sit or stand. Many of the men in these railcars were sick and very weak. The train took us to a POW camp in Moosburg, Germany. This was a terrible place since we had very little food and no toilet facilities. Some of my fellow prisoners managed to smuggle in radio parts and assembled a radio. They finally contacted Allied troops close by, and we were told to be prepared for liberation at 10:30 a.m. the next day. At 10:30 a.m. the following day, we were liberated by the 14th Armored Division.

The Germans gave little resistance and surrendered. A short while later, General Patton arrived astride the cannon of a Sherman tank. He explored the camp, and when he came out of one of the barracks, a soldier said he had tears in his eyes. I can tell you that Patton was a brilliant military leader and a compassionate man who truly cared about his troops.

After being liberated, we walked to Munich. Along the way, we walked by the notorious Dachau prison camp, where hundreds of thousands of Jews were killed earlier in the war. The camp was liberated the same day.

I will always remember being shot down and becoming a POW, the many forced marches by our captors, our liberation, and seeing General Patton. But the memory that stands out the most was a very emotional experience. Shortly after the Germans surrendered, U.S. Army tanks and trucks came rolling into the camp. I was not far from the front gate, and I saw the German swastika flag being taken down by our troops, and the American flag was raised. I still become emotional thinking about this experience.

Doug Horth

Army: Sergeant, 10th Mountain Division
Hometown: Youngstown, Ohio
Career: Railroad construction

Horth (L) with friends Dave "Mac" Frimodig and Dave Dupee

I was a member of the 10th Mountain Division and was a ski trooper. Our extensive mountain training took place in Colorado, and when we finished we were very well prepared. Our orders sent us to the Alps of northern Italy, where we met up with the U.S. Fifth Army. Our job was to advance on the German army and end the fighting in Italy. During the twelve weeks of combat in the mountains, our division lost almost 1,000 men, and over 4,000 more were wounded.

My first experience in combat was at Mount della Torraccia in the Apennine Mountains. This was my baptism by fire, and it's something I'll never forget. Advancing into enemy fire is scary because you know the enemy is trying to kill you before you kill him. Your adrenaline and your training keep you moving forward.

My platoon was assigned to move up a hill and secure the ridge. We were experiencing heavy enemy fire as we moved forward. It was during this action that I saw our lieutenant on the ground. He had been shot and was dead. He was an excellent officer and a good man. We were told in training we could not stop and help one of our men if he went down because our weapon was needed up front. I wanted to stop and say something to him, but I didn't. Still, these many years after the war, I ask myself, "Why didn't I stop to say, 'I'm sorry, sir. Thank you and good-bye.'"

In the military, you have a job to do and you do it. We were well-trained, and I learned how to endure difficult conditions and situations. Teamwork was important, and our main concern was surviving, so we had to depend on each other. The cold was unbelievable in the mountains, and we were in thirty-below-zero temperatures with no tents. War is terrible, not just the killing but also the sights, sounds, and smells you experience. During combat, I witnessed no act of cowardice by our men.

Carl Kleinknecht

Army Air Corps: Tech Sergeant, 15th Air Force
Hometown: Richmond, Indiana
Career: Electrical supply business

B-17 Flying Fortresses on a bombing run

After my graduation from high school in 1935, I worked until I was drafted in July 1941. I was sent for basic training to Fort Eustis, Virginia.

After only ten days of flight training, I was assigned as a radio operator on a B-17 bomber. I was sent to an air base near Foggia, Italy, in March 1944. For several months, we flew bombing missions to northern Italy, Yugoslavia, Romania, southern France and southern Germany.
On the morning of July 18, our mission target was a large German air base with over two hundred fighters.

The air base was called Hemminge Airdrome. The Hemminge mission was one of the highest priority counter air targets. Seventy-one B-17s were on this mission, but 44 were called back due to bad weather over the Adriatic Sea. The other 27 bombers, which included our plane, flew north over land, where the weather was clear. Shortly before we arrived at the target, an estimated 75 German fighter planes attacked us. They attacked in waves of five and six fighters at a time, and because of the bad weather, our usual fighter escort planes did not arrive as planned to protect us. During the course of this fierce air battle, 14 of our 27 B-17 bombers were shot down, and our 483rd Bombardment Group accounted for 53 downed enemy aircraft. Our bomb strike was very successful, resulting in heavy damage to the German airdrome. The Germans were dealt a moral and physical blow, due to the heavy damage inflicted by our bomb group.

While we were firing our guns, one of their shells hit our plane, which started a fire in our oxygen supply located in the radio room. My face was burned, but thanks to my helmet and flight suit, I was not severely injured. Our intercom was disabled, so I rushed to the rear of the plane and told the rest of the crew to bail out. Unfortunately, our ball turret gunner was already dead. I bailed out.

As I floated earthward, I saw a German fighter plane approach. He could have easily killed me, but he flew away. After the war, I would have liked to have met that good fellow. I landed on the edge of some woods and hid my parachute and myself. A while later, I heard voices and barking dogs in the distance. Fortunately, they did not locate me. In training, we were told to hide during the day and travel at night. I was hoping to reach Switzerland, but I learned later that Americans that crossed over into Switzerland were turned over to the Germans.

Since I didn't have much food, I drank water from clear streams. After about a week, I was becoming weaker. One evening at dusk, I was walking along a country road, and a man on a bicycle came over the hill. He was apparently an air raid warden. He could tell I was an American, because of my flight uniform. He came to me, took my arm, and started leading me away. After a short walk, I broke away from him and ran into a field of tall grass. I knew people and dogs were looking for me, but they did not find me.

After two weeks, I had become very weak, and my shoes and clothes were soaked from rain, and my ankles were bleeding. I was relieved when two farmers came out of the woods with pitchforks and captured me. They took me to one of their homes, where I was fed, able to bathe, and treated nicely. Finally, a policeman came and took me to jail.

After a couple of days in jail, I was taken to a German POW camp in what is now eastern Poland. As prisoners, we were transported by a train that was crowded with civilians and soldiers. At the camp, the conditions were very crowded and unsanitary. We were allowed a one-minute shower once a week. The British were kept on one side of the barracks, and the

Americans were kept on the other side. The British received Red Cross parcels of food, which included smuggled radio parts. Eventually, a radio transmitter was assembled, and we could pick up news from the BBC.

In early January 1945, the Russians were advancing in our direction, so the Germans evacuated the camp, and we were forced to walk in groups of about 50 men with German guards. We marched westward, and during the march we slept in barns and fields. The Germans did give us food. We crossed the Elbe River, and later we turned around and crossed the Elbe again, because the Germans knew the British were coming from that direction. On May 2, 1945, the British liberated us, and on May 7, 1945, the Germans surrendered.

The worst part of the entire POW ordeal was that I did not know what was going to happen from day to day. We experienced a lack of food, living in the same clothes for ten months, and not being able to keep clean. I was never physically mistreated by the Germans. I returned to the States in June 1945.

George Okamoto

Army: Private First Class, 34th Infantry Division
Hometown: Santa Anna, California
Career: Advertising and cartoonist

My parents were first-generation Japanese. My father came to the United States in the 1890s, but my mother did not come until 1915. I was born in Seattle, Washington, the second oldest of seven brothers and three sisters. My youngest brother was born in the internment camp in Poston, Arizona.

When we heard about the Japanese bombing of Pearl Harbor, my brothers and I were returning home with our father, after helping him with his landscape business. An American friend of mine saw us and said, "Get the hell out of here, Japs." We didn't understand why he said this, until we got home and heard the news on the radio. At the time, we did not think the Japanese Americans would be considered a danger, since most of us were born in America of Japanese Americans. My parents were Isseis (first generation), and those of us born here were Nisei (second generation). It wasn't long until a curfew was imposed, and Japanese Americans could only be outside their homes from 6:00 a.m. to 6:00 p.m.

In 1943, President Roosevelt and Congress declared that all Japanese Americans would be "evacuated" to various locations. They were called internment camps, and a General Dewitt was in charge of seeing that Japanese Americans were assigned to the various camp locations throughout the country.

When I was eighteen, my family and I were sent to internment camps in Poston, Arizona, where 20,000 Japanese Americans were relocated. The camps were named I, II, and III. We were in camp I, which had 10,000 people. Later in the war, the WRA (War Relocation Authority) took charge of the camps. I guess they thought "relocation" sounded better than internment camps.

Many of the older men thought Japan would win the war, and I am sure some hoped they did. It is interesting to note that the German and Italian second-generation Americans, as we were, did not have to relocate to internment camps when Germany and Italy declared war on the United States.

Our camp was located on a large Indian reservation in Arizona, which was surrounded by barbed-wire fence about five feet high. The conditions were hot and crowded, and all ten of us lived in a small two-room barrack made of wood with tar paper roofs and sides. When the camps and barracks were built, it was done so fast that the wood was still green and had not cured. This resulted in gaps between the boards, which let in dust and sand when there were high winds. Snakes were also a problem, and once a rattlesnake got into our barrack, and my father killed it.
We ate in army barrack-type mess halls, and the food was terrible. When it was time to take a shower or use the bathroom, we had to use communal showers and toilets.

There were a few military guards inside the camp and armed MPs outside of it. To my knowledge, there was no mistreatment of us by any of the guards. It was like a small community and town with people having different jobs, including janitors, laborers, farmers, nurses, and doctors. We also had our own schools and teachers, and people were paid according to their position of responsibility. As teenage boys, we swam in the canals, which were used for farming by the

Indians; however, we didn't mingle with the Indians. Sometimes, we would sneak under the fence and go down to the Colorado River to swim and fish. The guards would see us but never stopped or bothered us.

When I was nineteen, I volunteered to go to Nebraska with my dad and four other kids to work on the sugar beet farms. While sugar was scarce and rationed on the home front, it was harvested to send to our troops overseas. The government asked for volunteers because most of the white and Mexican workers were being drafted or worked in essential civilian jobs. If you said you wanted to go to work or school somewhere in the Midwest or East, you were usually permitted to go. I went to Chicago because I wanted to go to art school but, instead, worked in a display company making posters for banks and conventions located in large hotels.

When I was twenty-two, I decided to join the army, since my brother was drafted while in the internment camp. After basic training in Camp Hood, Texas, I was sent to Southampton, England, on to France, and eventually I ended up in Italy.

I was first assigned to a medical unit as a stretcher bearer to carry the wounded to ambulances. As medics, we didn't have guns, but when we were doing our job, the Germans would shoot at us. I finally went to my captain and told him, "If I am going to be shot at, I might as well have a gun." I was reassigned and issued a Browning Automatic Rifle (BAR) with the 442nd Regiment Combat Team.

One time, we were trying to capture a small Italian village that the Germans occupied. I was digging a foxhole, and my sergeant told me to dig it deep enough for two. Later that day, we came under heavy fire, and a German Tiger tank's 88mm shell exploded near our foxhole, killing my sergeant. I was severely wounded, with shrapnel in both legs. If I had been in my sergeant's position in the foxhole, I would have been the one killed. War taught me that you had to have the attitude to kill or be killed.

After being hit with shrapnel, I was sent to a hospital in Naples, Italy, and after a few weeks they sent me to a military hospital in Utah. I had asked to go to a hospital in Chicago where my family was living, but it wasn't to be. That's the "army way." They do what they want to do. I spent two years in various hospitals recovering from my wounds.

My unit became the most highly decorated unit for its size in military history. Our unit had 21 Medal of Honor recipients, and I am proud to have served my country.

Marshall Samms

Army Air Corps: First Lieutenant, 15th Air Force
Hometown: Indianapolis, Indiana
Career: Partner and founder of a CPA firm

Samms (right) receiving the Distinguished
Flying Cross on September 4, 1944

I was a navigator on a B-24 Liberator bomber with the 720th Squadron, 450th Bomb Group. We flew most of our missions over Eastern Europe, and we were also involved in the bombing of Munich, Germany.

On June 24, 1944, we took off from Manduria, our base in southern Italy, to bomb oil refineries in Ploesti, Romania. When flying missions over Ploesti we always encountered scores of German and Romanian fighter planes, and we knew we were going to experience a very rough time. We considered it to be the hottest target on the face of the earth. The Germans depended on these oil fields for much of their fuel supplies, and it was the remaining refinery operating at capacity. I was the navigator of our plane, which was called the "Shoo Shoo Baby."

About ten minutes before our target area, the squadrons experienced heavy attacks by at least 50 German fighter planes. The attack lasted for about twenty minutes. On this mission, 29 of our bombers returned, four were shot down, and two others were missing.

We flew across Albania, Yugoslavia, and Bulgaria, reaching our bombing altitude as we approached the Danube River, south of Bucharest. Several of our planes had dropped out of formation, due to engine trouble, and headed back to the base. Our plane's number four engine was smoking, but we continued on the bombing run. At this time, we saw no enemy or American fighter planes anywhere around us. However, it wasn't long before we came under German fighter attack again. Luckily, we had not been hit seriously by the first pass of fighters.

All of a sudden, a bright flash burst a few inches from my head. I looked up and saw a hole about eight inches in diameter in the side of our fuselage. Far worse was that flak had knocked out our number three and four engines on the right wing.

I quickly called to the others, and we began putting on our parachutes for evacuation. I felt the plane start diving out of control. We bailed out. I thought I was going to die, especially when my chute did not open on the first try. After my chute finally opened, far below I could see the green and brown of the Romanian countryside. The sky was a beautiful blue, and I felt gently suspended in air, as if I would never reach the ground.

I landed in a gully or streambed. My hands were cold and numb as I struggled to get rid of my chute and hide it. A group of peasants armed with clubs passed by and eventually saw me. There was a German soldier with them, but they would not let him near me. At first they seemed friendly, and I thought they might help me. I was led down a road still thinking I was safe. The old farmer and German soldier led me to a German major. I knew then that I would become a POW. My combat days were over.

The German major interrogated me, but I refused to answer his questions. Up until this time, I had not really been scared. I was taken to a large airport where the Germans had set up their headquarters. I was met by a young, blond German officer. I will never forget his cold, steel-blue eyes.

Later, I was taken to the city of Bucharest and placed in a garrison for German and Romanian troops. A few hours later, more American prisoners were brought in. I could not believe it; one of them was my bombardier. He knew nothing about the rest of our crew. The officers were placed in an old schoolhouse. Throughout most of our imprisonment, we experienced many air raids by British and American bombers. The ground would explode and shake violently. During these bombings, I was just as afraid as when our plane was hit. I decided it was better to be in a plane dodging flak than on the ground being bombed.

We were finally liberated by the Russian army. For a few days, the bombing attacks had stopped, but it wasn't long until German bombers and fighters strafed our shelters, which were trenches covered with boards and dirt. The Germans had poisoned the water, so we had none for drinking, washing, or cooking.

On August 28, we saw some of our B-17s circling the city. On the thirty-first, we were finally evacuated and boarded our B-17s. We were going home! When we landed in Italy, we finally got "deloused" of our filth and lice. I later learned that one of my friends in pilot training was shot down and killed.

This was my 37th and final mission with the "Shoo Shoo Baby."

Benito Mussolini

"The truth is evident to all who are unblinded by dogmatism that men nowadays are tired of liberty."

Mussolini (left) seated with Adolf Hitler

Mussolini, Il Duce (the leader), and his Fascist Party, came to power in Italy in 1922. Prior to World War II, Mussolini invaded Ethiopia in 1936, and in the same year he provided Italian troops to Franco during the Spanish Civil War. While he enjoyed popularity for a while, his support never reached the level of Hitler's in Germany. As the war progressed, and his military faced defeats, Hitler looked upon Mussolini as an embarrassment. In April 1945, Mussolini was captured and shot. His body was publicly hung for all to see.

Joe Talbott

Air Corps: Staff Sergeant, 15th Air Force
Hometown: Indianapolis, Indiana
Career: Insurance company district manager

Talbott (left) with the Eugene Barter crew

I was assigned with the 15th Air Force and was stationed in San Giovanni, Italy. I served aboard a B-24 airplane as the nose gunner and flew in 35 bombing missions over Germany, Italy, and the Czech Republic.

At the altitude we were flying, it would get close to fifty degrees below zero, so we had to wear electric flying suits that plugged in to give us heat. When we went on our bombing missions, our four bomber squadrons were escorted by P-51 Mustangs and P-38 Lightning fighter planes. The mission of these fighter planes was to defend against and attack any German fighter planes that attacked us on our bombing raids. We always wanted the Tuskegee fighter pilots to escort us because they were the best.

On one of our missions, we took two bad hits to the right wing and landing gear by German antiaircraft guns. When we returned to our base, the pilot was forced to do a crash landing on the nose wheel; we all got out of the plane safely. However, the plane coming in behind us had a bomb stuck on board, and when it landed the bomb exploded, killing all of the crew. We had to dive in a ditch along the side of the runway because the ammunition from the plane's turret guns was going off. Our plane was far enough away, or we would have been killed too. Throughout our missions we all knew our job, worked together, and depended upon one another.

I believe that the Great Depression affected and helped those of us in the military. During the Depression we had to learn to do certain things to live, and we had to do without. This experience contributed to our feeling of patriotism, sense of duty, and commitment.

14

Utah, Omaha, Gold, Juno, Sword

The Great Crusade

"You are about to embark upon the great crusade toward which we have striven these many months. The eyes of the world are upon you. I have confidence in your courage, devotion to duty and skill in battle."
—General Dwight Eisenhower

And so, the German soldiers waited. Peering out across the English channel, they waited and wondered where the massive Allied invasion would occur. From General Erwin Rommel, architect of the Atlantic Wall, to the lowest-ranking German soldier, no one knew exactly where the much-anticipated invasion along the four-thousand-mile coastline would take place.

The Allied soldiers waited. On army bases and airstrips, in crowed ships and landing craft, they waited. For thousands of young men, the long hours of training were over, and now they waited for the word to move out, so they could put Operation Overlord into motion.

General Eisenhower waited. The commander of the Allied Expeditionary Force waited for word on when there would be a break in the weather, so that his boys could ship out and take the war to the beaches of Normandy, France, and then to Hitler's Germany. On June 4, 1944, terrible weather was hanging over southern England and the English Channel, and Ike needed a break in the weather to be able to put his troops on the beachhead. That evening, Group Captain J. M. Stagg, of the Meteorological Committee, briefed Eisenhower and his staff that a break was going to occur in the storm. This is what Ike had been waiting for, and at 9:30 p.m., he set forth the operation, but would reconvene his staff early the next morning for one last meeting to ensure they would proceed.

At 4:15 a.m. on June 5, with a terrible rainstorm raging, Eisenhower met for one last session with his American and British advisors. Stagg delivered an updated weather report and was more confident that there would be a break in the storm. Eisenhower sought the opinions of his high-ranking staff, but in the end, it was Ike's decision to be made. With thousands of young men bobbing up and down in landing craft and ships; with bomber crews waiting at airstrips, and with airborne troops waiting with their loaded packs; Ike said, "Okay, let's go."

With those words, the date June 6, 1944, became another date that would live in infamy as 175,000 American, British, and Canadian troops became engaged in the battle that was the beginning of the end for Adolf Hitler's Third Reich. The beach areas code-named Utah, Omaha, Gold, Juno, and Sword became cemented in American history because of the heroic actions of teenagers and young men in their twenties—mere boys.

During the early-morning hours of D-Day, the naval and air armadas blanketed the English Channel and the skies above. More than 5,300 ships and landing craft carried the men, equipment, and vehicles necessary for the invasion and operations that would continue inland, and 11,000 aircraft conducted bombing runs and participated in dropping airborne paratroopers behind German lines. Thirteen thousand American and 7,000 British paratroopers dropped from the dark skies to conduct vital missions that captured bridges and secured river crossings and beach exits.

As the invasion troops began to unload and move ashore into their sectors, they encountered various obstacles, mines, machine-gun and artillery fire, and the chaos and confusion that go with such a complex military operation. In the midst of the fierce German resistance, which was pinning the landing force down on the beachhead, something else began to emerge—leadership! From the officers, to sergeants, and down to the enlisted men, natural leaders began to surface and seize the initiative. Across the different sectors, men grasped the mantel of leadership with their "follow me" attitude, which ultimately helped win the day for the Allies.

As this historic day started to fade, the boys of the Great Crusade had gained a foothold on the Third Reich and would not let go. Operation Overlord had succeeded, and a new phase of the war in Europe was about to begin. But one cannot forget that 4,900 brave young men gave the ultimate sacrifice on June 6, 1944.

For the people of Europe, the invasion had finally arrived, and now they waited to be free from the grip of Nazism.

Dr. Raymond Beights, Sr.

Army Air Corps: First Lieutenant, 8th Air Force
Hometown: Kendallville, Indiana
Career: High school music teacher and medical doctor

In the fall of 1941, I began my teaching career in Porter County, Indiana. On December 7, 1941, my father and I were at a Christmas tree farm when we heard the news on the radio that Pearl Harbor had been bombed by the Japanese. He looked at me and said, "Son you could get involved in this."

I thought about the possibility of being drafted, so a visit to the Navy Pier in Chicago, Illinois, was arranged. Since I had a strong background in music, it was my hope to qualify to join the navy band. However, I was informed that an enlistment must first occur, before I could be considered for the band.

After traveling to Lafayette, Indiana, I enlisted in the Army Air Corps, since I was unable to get into the navy. I was still teaching, so the Air Corps placed me on a waiting list until the end of the school year. Due to my enlisted status, the superintendent would not hire me for the following school year. While I waited for an official notice from the Air Corps, I worked in a refrigeration plant making parts for Liberty ships.

Finally, in October 1942, at age twenty-five, my orders from the Air Corps arrived. My father took me down to the train station, and I left Kendallville, Indiana, on a troop train headed to San Antonio, Texas. I took the tests to determine my eligibility to become a pilot, bombardier, or a navigator. After-hours, when we were not testing or training, I enjoyed playing the piano with a group of other musicians as we entertained local civic groups.

After all of the testing was completed, I was selected for pilots' training. I traveled to an air base in Corsicana, Texas, where I received classes in aircraft identification, weather, and flight technology. After successfully completing all of these courses, I received my pilot wings! I had achieved my goal of flying planes, and this led me to becoming a bomber pilot and getting my commission as a second lieutenant. The level of training intensified at Greenville and Ellington fields in Texas, where I learned how to fly multiple-engine aircraft. Once this training was completed, I reported to Tarrant Field in Fort Worth, Texas, where I trained with the B-24 bomber. First, I received a ten-day furlough, and I traveled to Philadelphia, Pennsylvania, and married my fiancée.

After my furlough was over, I returned to Tarrant Field and was introduced to the B-24 Liberator, becoming one of the first pilot groups to fly this huge new aircraft. When my crew was assigned, we trained together for a month in Arizona. We traveled to West Palm Beach, Florida where our orders to fly overseas awaited our arrival.

While en route, I remembered a promise I made to my mother that a "visit" over our house would happen if at all possible. Violating almost every rule in the book, my promise became a reality. As we approached my hometown of Kendallville, my mom heard us coming well before we arrived. As we approached my home, I could see my mother waving a white towel in our backyard. I "buzzed" Kendallville in our big bomber, flying at about 500 feet above the ground. Being a mother, she contacted the local newspaper and, with a great deal of pride, announced that the person who flew over was her son. I realized what I did was a dangerous and poor decision, but, fortunately, our escapade was never discovered.

From West Palm Beach, we headed overseas with stops in Trinidad, Brazil, and Dakar, in Africa. It was a long and boring trip, and at one point, we received a weather alert warning us of an impending storm front. Feeling confident of having mastered our plane, we decided to ignore the forecast. Engaging the autopilot, we fell asleep listening to the BBC radio network. Sure enough, the storm found us. Almost instantly, flashing red warning lights lit up our instrument panel like a Christmas tree, causing us to think we had come under attack. Needless to say, we never fell asleep again.

Our navigator guided us to southwest England and then to our assigned air field at Halesworth Air Base, where we were part of the 459th Bomb Group. Our crew kept busy with practice missions as we prepared for the invasion of Normandy, France. Sadly, during the last practice mission, two of our planes crashed, killing all of the crew members. If there had been any doubt as to the seriousness of what we were doing, the tragedies we witnessed made us realize the dangers involved.

The following day was June 6, 1944, D-Day. We flew as part of the largest bombing group ever assembled, dropping bombs on German fortifications on the cliffs and beaches of Normandy. After heading back to our base for more fuel and bombs, we returned to action. Realizing I was a part of history brought about feelings of soberness and quiet resolve.

My 10th mission nearly cost me my life. Flying directly through heavy antiaircraft flak, I was hit in my head with shrapnel and was knocked unconscious. Fortunately, I was wearing my metal helmet, or I would have been killed. The hole in my helmet was seven inches in width. Our plane began to drift out of formation, but my copilot was able to get the plane back on course. As our radioman was administering me first aid, I regained partial consciousness. I told my copilot I wanted to land the plane. Because of my condition, he could have overruled me and taken charge; however, he let me land the plane. Once we landed, the crew set off the flares signaling there was wounded aboard.

I was immediately sent to a field hospital, but they were unable to determine the seriousness of my injury, so I was sent me to a hospital in Diss, England. After being released from the hospital, I returned to my crew. Due to my head injury, I was not allowed to fly again, so I trained copilots and checked out crews for qualification.

Three years after the bombing of Pearl Harbor, our bomb group returned to the States in December 1944. A Christmastime arrival reunited me with my wife and newborn son. In retrospect, I was never afraid to fly a mission. A strong faith helped remind me that God had been with me always and saved my life. At the age of ninety-four, the indentation on my skull, where a piece of flak (shrapnel) had lodged, can still be seen. A small piece of that shrapnel has been kept as a reminder of what could have been. With the grace of God, and the fact that I was wearing my steel helmet when hit, I am alive today.

Gene Cogan

Army: Private First Class, 29th Infantry Division
Hometown: Avilla, Indiana
Career: Teacher, coach, and principal

USO artist Jo Stein drew twenty-one year old Cogan, while in Billings General Hospital, Fort Benjamin Harrison, Indiana, October 7, 1944

In May 1943, I was sent overseas to Scotland. Once we arrived, our company, part of the 29th Infantry Division, took the train to England. None of us was aware that we were going to be trained to become a part of the largest land invasion in military history. For the next year, we were involved in numerous mock battles off the coast of England in which we practiced storming the beaches in every kind of imaginable landing craft.

On the evening of June 4, 1944, two days before the actual D-Day invasion at Normandy, our captain called us all to the deck of our transport ship. He told us what we were going to do and asked that everyone write a letter to his family and tell them what we were doing. He said, "For some of you, it will be the last letter you write."

We landed on Omaha Beach in the second wave; ninety minutes after our first troops had landed. Our LCIs (Landing Craft Infantry) lowered the gate planks, and we jumped into the water and headed toward the beach. As a scout, I was the first off of our craft. All I remember is the tremendous noise and chaos, German machine guns firing at us, and the explosive booms of our ships' big guns shelling the Germans. As I saw all of the tanks, artillery, and other equipment being unloaded, I thought, the American people at home had really come through for us. It was an amazing sight to see. Unfortunately, many men, tanks, and equipment never got to the beach. There were soldiers who drowned in the water after leaving their landing craft, and tank crews that drowned because their tanks sank.

When I finally got to the shore, I lay on the beach next to another soldier. I said to him, "This is the kind of thing that could get you killed." When he didn't respond, I looked more closely and saw that he had been shot through the head. I knew then that war was real! I have no memory of how I moved across the beach and got off the beachhead to move inland.

After the landing, we were involved in some heavy fighting with the Germans. Once an artillery shell exploded near me, and a piece of shrapnel went through my backpack and lodged in my neck. If it had been an inch lower, I would probably have been killed. I never thought I would be shot, but a few days later, I was shot twice in the same day. The first was by a German sniper, who shot me across my upper back.

A short time later, I was standing by a hedgerow, and out of the corner of my eye, I saw a German with his rifle aimed at me. We were only about fifteen feet apart, when he shot first. He shot me in my hip, and my thighbone shattered and came through my skin. It was the most terrible pain I have ever experienced.

For over twelve hours, I lay wounded and bleeding with other GIs around me who were dead. I prayed for God to keep me alive and help me get home. That night, it was very cold, and I crawled to a backpack and took a raincoat and put it over me. I passed out, and when I woke up the next morning, I could see what looked like a hazy fog with people standing above me. It was my sergeant and some other soldiers who had come back to collect the dog tags from the dead GIs. He couldn't believe I was still alive, because he was told the medics had already evacuated all of the wounded. They missed me.

I was flown to a hospital in Liverpool, England, and later was placed on a ship to be sent home. On the ship, I met Ernie Pyle, the famous war correspondent, who is from Dana, Indiana. He was later killed when he went to the Pacific.

People have asked me if I was ever scared during battle. I remember soldiers saying, "If anyone told you they were not afraid in combat, they were a liar." I must be a liar because I don't remember being scared. I felt I was well trained; I had a job to do, and we all had a common goal. A good soldier has to believe in himself, his buddies, and the cause for which they are fighting.

In combat, every day is a lifetime. One of my best friends was killed in the war. He and those who fought for the freedom of others and never came home are the real heroes. I feel the military should award only two medals. The Purple Heart for those who are wounded in battle, and the

Medal of Honor, for all who are killed in combat. Many years after the war, I had nightmares where I would relive seeing others killed and me being shot.

My hope for the present and future generations of young people is that, if called upon, they would serve our country with a sense of pride and patriotism as did the hundreds of thousands of us during World War II.

A place in Normandie

By Gene Cogan

I stood among the crosses—
of my buddies from Company "B,"
their crosses glistened in the Normandie sun
what a beautiful sight to see.

For just a moment my buddies were standing—
each by his battle cross, in battle dress,
silently they pass in review—
I saluted them as they returned to rest.

Three score years have passed—
since we landed in Normandie,
many times I have wondered—
why did they, and not me.

I have no answer to the question—
but a little bit of me
rests with my buddies—
at a place in Normandie.

(Printed with permission of author Gene Cogan.)

Paul Hedges

Army Air Corps: Captain, 8th Air Force
Hometown: West Valley, New York
Career: Car dealership manager

A B-24 Liberator with the 389th Bomb Group

I was originally assigned as a bombardier instructor, but later I volunteered to be a replacement head bombardier on B-24s because I knew this would get me into combat.

In England, I was assigned with the 565th Bomb Squadron, 389th Bomb Group at Hethel Air Field, which is west of Norwich. On June 6, 1944, my bomber group was part of the D-Day Invasion at Normandy, France. We received a 2:00 a.m. briefing, and then we took off at 4:00 a.m. to form our bombing squadrons and groups in the air. This was my sixth mission, and I was the lead bombardier for our squadron. There were over 1,000 bombers involved in the assault on the coastline of Normandy.

On the flight across the English Channel, I will never forget looking down and seeing our ships and amphibious landing craft sailing toward the beaches. I could even see the ships firing their guns at the German positions along the beachhead. There were so many ships it looked like you could walk on top of them and cross the channel.

Our mission was to drop bombs on the Germans operating in the area of Caen. The timing of our mission was so precise that we dropped our bombs on our targets at 6:25 a.m., and our troops hit the beaches at 6:30 a.m. We usually dropped the bombs from an altitude between 18,000 to 25,000 feet, but at Normandy, we were flying at only 8,000 feet. When we were two to three miles from our target, we dropped our bombs.

Later, in an attack on Hamburg, Germany, we were taking heavy fire from German antiaircraft guns, when one of our waist gunners was seriously wounded. My command pilot told me to go back and help him. When I got to him, I found him in shock with a hole in his thigh the size of a softball. When we landed, he was dead.

On nearly every mission, our planes would were damaged by antiaircraft guns or strafed by German fighter planes. On one occasion, we lost one of our engines, and we had to fly back to base with only three engines. During our bombing missions we would lose about 25 percent of our planes. I can still remember looking from my plane and seeing my friend's plane explode after being hit by flak.

On one mission, 45 bombers took off, but only 16 were airworthy the next day. To keep a bomber flying, it took ten people on the ground for every plane flying. I had great respect for our ground maintenance crews, mechanics, and technicians. Without them, we couldn't fly.

Before I left for the war, my mother gave me a small New Testament Bible. I carried it with me everywhere including our 30 successful bombing missions. After our required 30 missions, I was glad to be alive. I never looked for an easy way out of anything. I had a job to do, and I did it with a sense of duty and pride.

E. Carver McGriff

Army: Private First Class, 90th Infantry Division
Hometown: Indianapolis, Indiana
Career: Pastor

I was nineteen-years-old when we landed on the beaches of Normandy on D-Day, June 6, 1944. The beach was nearly sixty miles in length. The Americans were responsible for Utah and Omaha beaches, while the British landed on Juno, Sword, and Gold beaches. It was an experience I will never forget, as we came under heavy German artillery and machine-gun fire.

I had a naïve, untested faith, at that age. We were to stand our ground no matter what. I was scared, as were thousands of American soldiers that day. I remember seeing the dead soldiers around me. We had a job to do, and we did the best we could. I did not consider myself a hero. To me, those who died were. On my first day in combat, I saw one of my buddies shot in his arm and leg by a German sniper. It could just as easily have been me. Two of our men then killed the sniper. That sniper was the first person I saw killed, and I realized why we were there. I knew I was in a war and could die. Later, I thought, the German sniper was just doing his job as we had ours to do.

My first day in combat was pretty much a matter of following the person in front of me. That night we moved into a field, and I saw a dead soldier. No one seemed to pay any attention. Death was the reality of war. Today, I think back to that moment, remembering that dead soldier. Like most of the rest of us, he had loved ones and friends waiting at home. He, like me, was not long out of high school, a kid with hopes and dreams. Now, he was dead, shrouded in darkness, lying uncared for along a nameless road in a country far away from home. No one should die that way. These are the photographs still in my mind that dispel any idea of the romance of war.

There are no words to adequately describe the terror of war when you are under heavy machine-gun or artillery fire. You visualize each incoming round, thinking it might hit you. We would flatten ourselves to the ground and experience the ultimate feelings of fear, isolation, and helplessness. If a man panics and jumps up to run, his odds of survival are minimal. Pieces of slashing hot steel rip through the air, tearing everything in its path. The ground vibrates, soon accompanied by cries of shock and pain, and the calls of "Medic, medic!"

During a battle, I was wounded, and a Mexican soldier carried me to safety or most likely I would have been killed. I never knew his name. Prior to that time, many of us had a prejudice toward the Mexican soldiers, and we did not want to associate with them. Eventually, I was captured and became a German prisoner of war. After a two-day fierce gun battle, we were rescued a month later by the 8th Division.

Years after the war, I came to understand the significance of the D-Day landing. As a teenager, I was involved in the largest land invasion by American troops in history. There was a tremendous loss of life for us and the Germans. The hard-fought victories after landing on the Normandy beaches proved to be the turning point in the war for the Allies. Our troops were then able to go through France on their way to Berlin.

Another thing that I think is important for people to understand is that only 17 percent of the soldiers were actually involved in combat, and most of them were under twenty years old. The other 83 percent were providing direct or backup support for those of us fighting. These included medics, doctors, nurses, various supply divisions, mechanics, engineers, chaplains, and cooks. The war was truly a team effort.

My experience in the war helped me to grow spiritually, and I realized the importance of the values and work ethic that I learned when I was young. I was proud to have served my country.

Field Marshal Erwin Rommel

"Don't fight a battle, if you don't gain anything in winning."

Rommel was one of the most celebrated and fearless German generals. He was commander of the 7th Panzer Division when the Germans invaded France in the spring of 1940. As a brilliant military leader and military tactician, the "Desert Fox" led his Afrika Korps to victories in North Africa. He was given the mission of building the German defenses along the French coastline in preparation for the Allied invasion. Later in the war, he was implicated in a plot to kill Hitler. Hitler had him arrested, but rather than having to face trial as a traitor, he was allowed to poison himself.

William Schubert

Army Air Corps: Sergeant, 53rd Troop Carrier Wing
Hometown: Indianapolis, Indiana
Career: Architect

General Eisenhower speaking with 101st Airborne paratroopers on the eve of the Normandy invasion

I was stationed outside of London, England, with the 53rd Troop Carrier Wing. In preparing for D-Day, the section I worked in studied aerial photographs of the territory behind the German lines. By studying the photographs, we were able to provide the troops with reconnaissance information that helped determine safe drop zones for our paratroopers and landing zones for our gliders. These landing zones and flying routes were displayed on large maps in our war room. The gliders carried the necessary supplies and equipment, including jeeps, for the paratroopers to fight the enemy once they landed in France.

During the airborne mission of D-Day, many of our paratroopers landed in trees and were shot by the Germans. One of the paratroopers I knew landed in a tree and was shot by a German soldier. The German soldier thought he had killed the man, and he left him there. My friend was in fact shot, but he was hit in the leg and didn't die. However, the wound was serious enough that his leg had to be amputated.

"One of my lasting memories was when I saw the supreme Allied commander, General Eisenhower, speak to the paratroopers at Greenham Air Force Base in England. This was the same day they departed for the D-Day invasion of Normandy."

General of the Army Dwight David Eisenhower

"I hate war as only a soldier who has lived it, only as one who has seen its brutality, futility and stupidity."

Eisenhower was the supreme commander of Allied Forces in the European Theater. "Ike," as he came to be called, was the only American general without battlefield experience. He was a superb leader in managing the American and British generals as they worked together to formulate a strategy for defeating Nazi Germany. Eisenhower led the planning and preparation for the D-Day invasion at Normandy, France, on June 6, 1944, and it was he who made the final decision to send thousands of Allied troops to the beaches of Normandy. After the war, in 1952, he was elected as the 34th president of the United States.

Orrin Tovson

Navy: Lieutenant, USS *Corry*
Hometown: Decorah, Iowa
Career: Actuary

USS *Corry* sinking after hitting a mine off of Utah Beach on June 6, 1944

In 1942, I was attending Luther College in Iowa. I had a special graduation date in March 1943, since I had been accepted into the navy's V7th Training Program. Thirteen of us were sent to Columbia University in New York City to begin our midshipman training.

During the summer of 1943, I boarded the USS *Nevada* battleship and sailed to Belfast, Ireland. The *Nevada* had been one of our ships at Pearl Harbor, during the Japanese attack. We changed to a smaller ship, which took us to Glasgow, Scotland. When we arrived, we took a train to Duncan's Head, Scotland, where we boarded the USS *Corry*. The *Corry* was a destroyer and operated with the British Home Fleet, based in Scapa Flow, in the Orkney Islands, Scotland.

In October, we headed to Bodo, Norway, as part of the escort for the aircraft carrier USS *Ranger*, which was the first aircraft carrier the navy had built from the keel up. As destroyers, our job was to protect the *Ranger* from any German U-boats. We used echo ranging (sonar) to detect and locate the U-boats. This mission was known as Operation Leader. Planes flew from the *Ranger* and bombed German shipping vessels at the far northern naval base. Several German ships were sunk or damaged during this attack.

We had the mission of escorting the USS *Nitro* to Plymouth, England. This aircraft carrier was transporting ammunition for the D-Day invasion. We were told to stay our distance from the *Nitro* to prevent a collision, since several destroyers were part of the escort group. We remained in Plymouth and prepared for D-Day. As an assistant communications officer, I was assigned various duties. One of the duties was to go ashore and retrieve secret messages.

We were chosen to be the lead destroyer for the entire Normandy invasion. On D-Day, June 6, 1944, we were part of the largest naval armada ever assembled in the history of the world. Our ship was to drop anchor and commence firing off of Utah Beach. Off of the coast of Normandy, we endured heavy German artillery shelling from the beaches and cliffs for several hours. One of our planes was to provide us with a smoke screen, but it was shot down by enemy fire. Destroyers did a zigzagging pattern to try to avoid the enemy shelling.

We moved straight ahead, since the area had been swept for mines. The firing from the beach was so close the captain maneuvered the ship, and we were hit midship by a mine. The explosion was horrendous, and the ship began sinking immediately. This occurred at approximately 6:32 a.m., two minutes after our troops landed on the beaches.

Men were trapped in the forward firing section of the ship, and the captain asked someone to go and help them. I volunteered, but when I got to the area, live rounds of ammunition and shells were all over the floor. We were finally able to get most of the men off the ship and into life boats. Many of the men were severely burned, and some would later die from their injuries. I admire our captain because he remained on ship until every injured crewman was safely off the ship.

After jumping into the water, I could not get my life vest to inflate, so I got back on the sinking ship and used a hose to inflate my vest. When I ended up back in the water, my life vest still was not working well, so I had to float on two ammunition containers. Other men also were using ammunition containers for flotation devices. If any shells had exploded nearby we would have been killed. One of my buddies died while floating in the water, when an enemy shell exploded nearby. Many of the worst casualties were the men who were burned in the steam room during the explosion. Some men died from exposure to the frigid water temperature, which was about fifty-four degrees.

After being in the cold water for some two hours, with enemy shells still exploding around us, the captain's whale boat from the DD 462 *Fitch* and PT boats rescued us from the water. The continuous enemy artillery fire and the water mines had prevented anyone from getting to us sooner.

There was a crewman who remained on board the sinking ship and climbed the stern to get the American flag. At his own peril, he swam and scrambled to hoist the flag on the main mast. He was able to get off the ship safely, after this act of courage. There were 260 men on board; 24 were killed, and many others were seriously wounded.

On the same day, many of us survivors were sent back to England on the USS *Barnett*. After six months, we returned to the States, and I had to go through gunnery and communications school again, even though I had previously done this. Our next assignment was to the USS *Soley*, one of the navy's largest destroyers. The navy had begun to make the destroyers larger, because they needed to be able to carry more fuel going to the Pacific.

Once we received our orders, our ship left from Norfolk and headed to the Panama Canal. It was during this time we learned the atomic bombs had been dropped. We knew the war would soon be over. We sailed to Hawaii and then to the Japanese island of Kusaie. Here, we accepted the surrender from the Japanese garrison commander. There had been no food supply ship on the island since 1943. The island was used for raising food for the defeated Japanese soldiers and sailors. On one occasion, I visited a hospital on the island with a Japanese officer. When we entered, the Japanese soldiers who were very sick had to get up and stand at attention. In the United States, we never would have done that.

As an Allied Occupation Force on the island, we were received warmly by the Japanese civilians. They were happy to see us rather than the Japanese army, who often brutalized and killed their own civilians. From Kusaie, we departed for Enewitok and then to the Japanese naval base at Yokosuka. Later, I took a train to Yokohama, Japan, and as I traveled, all I could see was the total devastation from the bombing. In one large field, there was but one chimney standing.

I returned to the States on the USS *Soley*, docking at the Brooklyn Naval Yard in early March 1946. I never knew how many thousands of miles I traveled on ships, during and after the war.

15

Through the Hedgerows and on to Berlin!

The Breakthrough

"I love the infantry because they are the underdogs. They are the mud-rain-frost-and-wind boys. They have no comforts, and they even learn to live without the necessities. And in the end they are the guys that wars can't be won without."
—Ernie Pyle, war correspondent

The "Atlantic Wall," full of its concrete bunkers, mines, Belgian gates, hedgehogs, and German soldiers, was not the great deterrent that Hitler had planned. The Allied troops, full of dogged determination, were not thrown back into the English Channel, but, instead, they pushed forward yard by yard, and gradually moved beyond the bloody beaches and into the French countryside. Every man's role was vitally important as the Allies began to fan out in all directions with their new missions to penetrate and clear out German resistance.

To achieve the breakthrough from the Normandy region, through the hedgerows, across France and into Germany, a combined effort from every soldier, regardless of his job. The hard-fought drive across Europe would eventually take the Allies across the Rhine River and result in control of Germany.. In the end, the infantrymen bore the brunt of the responsibility for driving the German army back to their Fuhrer.

As the Allied troops took the fight into the French countryside, they faced stiff resistance within the maze of French hedgerows and villages that dotted the landscape. For many American boys and their Allied companions, the French towns of St.-Lo, Avranches, Mortain, Brest, St.-Malo, and Le Mans soon became their final destination. As the battles and retreating Germans moved eastward, the liberation of the "City of Lights" came into view—Paris! On August 25, 1944, the French 2nd Armored Division and U.S. 4th Division secured and liberated Paris from German control.

While Parisians celebrated and rejoiced, the troops continued their drive across France. The fast-advancing Allied machine was assisted by what became known as the Red Ball Express. This 700 mile long supply line was full of trucks carrying the necessary fuel and supplies for the spearhead across Europe. This one-way express highway was a key reason for the rapid advance across France.

As the battles wound down in France, difficult and hard-fought battles awaited the Allied troops as they made their way into Belgium, Luxembourg, and the Netherlands. As the American

First and Third Armies entered new regions, they encountered natural and man-made terrain features that played pivotal roles in upcoming battles.

Along the Belgium-German border, south of the German town of Aachen, lay the dense and dark Hurtgen Forest. These features, along with the wet and muddy terrain, made the daily grind of battle equally difficult for the American and German troops who fought in the Battle of the Hurtgen Forest. Initially, the Germans sat in their defensive positions and let the fight come to them. As the Americans gained ground, the Germans counterattacked, and at times soldiers engaged in brutal hand-to-hand combat as they fought over small patches of terrain.

In the spring of 1945, with the Germans in retreat, the grand prize of being the "first across the Rhine" went to a small group of American soldiers with the First Army. The Germans fired on the American troops as they ran across the Ludendorff Bridge at Remagen. These brave men captured the last standing bridge across the Rhine.

These young boys—men—landed on a continent that was controlled by the Nazis. They fought, and died or survived battles that took place in foreign cities and villages whose names they could not pronounce. Each man carried with him the desire to return home as quickly as possible, but before returning, they delivered freedom back to its rightful owners—the European people.

Robert Borton

Army: Private First Class, 26th Infantry Division
Hometown: Richmond, Indiana
Career: Regional manager, Link Belt Company, Bearing Division

Camp Rucker, Alabama, 1943

I was nineteen and had completed my first semester at Purdue University, when I was drafted and sent to Fort Rucker, Alabama, for my basic training. The invasion at Normandy, France, had already occurred, and the army was experiencing a lot of casualties, and replacement troops were desperately needed.

After a brief assignment at Fort Dix, New Jersey, we boarded the Queen Mary and headed to Europe. We were to be replacements troops for units that had been depleted by combat deaths, wounded, AWOL (Absent Without Leave), or those with combat fatigue.

In the fall of 1944, we landed in Glasgow, Scotland, and traveled to the southern coast of England; from there, we boarded troopships that took us to the beaches of Normandy. This was about four months after D-Day, so most of the obstacles had been removed, and there was not any German resistance. I looked up the steep cliffs and saw the large German pillboxes that had housed the heavy defensive guns that our troops had to endure when landing on D-Day. I thought to myself, "Thank God I didn't have to experience what they did."

We climbed the steep cliffs, past the shattered pillboxes, and moved through the thick hedgerows that divided miles of flat French pastureland. We did not know what to expect, as we loaded onto boxcars and traveled to our destination, which was a "repo depot" (replacement depot). Over 1,000 troops waited processing to become part of a combat unit.

I was assigned to a weapon's platoon with Company A, 101st Infantry Regiment, where I was a mortar man and carried a forty-two-pound mortar on my back. I was unable to carry a rifle, so I carried a Colt .45 By that time in the war, the Allies already occupied Paris, and the Germans were retreating toward Germany. Our job was to keep them retreating.

My first combat experience was the worst one. We were assigned to take a small French village called Guebling. We spent the night about three to four miles away from the town. Early the next morning, my unit of 200 men was moving across an open field toward the village. All of a sudden, we were hit with heavy German 88mm artillery fire, and we had no cover. Some of us ran about three hundred yards to a shallow creek embankment to take cover. After the heavy shelling had stopped, my group realized there were only 30 of the original 200 left. The rest were lying in the field behind us either dead or wounded.

It did not appear any help was on the way. I was only twenty, and I thought, "What do I do?" We crawled to an area at the base of a forty-five-degree, ten-foot-high creek bank. We stayed at the base of the hill, because we did not know what was beyond the top. Finally, one of our guys crawled to the top of the hill to take a look. When he got to the top, a German machine-gun bullet ripped through his face. He crawled down the hill with his chin hanging from his face. Even in his condition, he was still able to use his bayonet to draw the German machine-gun location in the dirt. He survived, and I saw him after the war.

We could not move anywhere, so we started digging foxholes in the embankment for protection. While we were digging, the German machine-gunners had moved to a grove of trees, which placed them slightly to the right and behind us. They began firing nonstop, and this loosened the dirt of the embankment above our foxholes. Lying in the foxhole, I was covered with about six inches of dirt. I thought to myself, "I will be shot if I stand up, or be buried alive, if I don't." Using my helmet as a shovel, I began throwing the dirt out of my foxhole. Somehow, word got back to our headquarters from one of our staff about our location, and it wasn't long until our artillery wiped out the German machine guns. We remained in our foxholes the rest of the night, but still no one came to help us.

Our headquarters had assumed none of us made it out alive, or we had been captured. My parents received a telegram from the War Department saying I was MIA (Missing in Action) in France on November 16, 1944. My parents did not believe this and contacted the Red Cross to find out my status. However, my name was in the newspaper as MIA, and a memorial service was held for me. I had written a postcard to my parents on November 24, but they did not receive the telegram until December 4. My postcard arrived a few days after December 4. I can only imagine what they experienced thinking I was dead and then knowing I might be alive.

Shortly after November 24, we received new orders to head up to the front lines near Metz, France. We did not know it, but soon we were to become involved in the Battle of the Bulge in the Ardennes Forest in December 1944. This would be the Germans' last major offensive thrust toward the Allies. Our unit headed north a few miles southeast of Bastogne, Belgium, and for the next two weeks we engaged in heavy, and what seemed like nonstop, fighting.

During the war, I was never really aware of my exact location. However, on New Year's Eve, December 31, 1944, I was on guard duty near Wiltz, Luxembourg, from 2200 to 0200 hours. I was positioned on top of a tree-lined ridge on a beautiful moonlit night. The temperature was ten to fifteen degrees below zero, and my feet were so frozen they felt like heavy fireplugs. A few minutes before midnight, I was standing behind a tree when I heard a screaming noise. It was a half-crazed German soldier charging toward me from only five or six feet away. I had to decide within seconds if he was drunk, freezing from weather, or was about to stick his bayonet in me. Fortunately, he wanted to surrender.

I took him down the hill to our company command post, where the executive officer quizzed me about my prisoner and my condition. I told him I thought my feet were frozen. He had me take off my socks and boots, examined my feet, placed them near a stove and massaged my ankles, heels, and toes with "eye salve." What really caused me pain was when he said the company was shorthanded, and I had to go back to the lines. I finished this cold and beautiful night without further incident.

For the next several months, my unit moved north into Germany and across the Rhine River. While standing by a tree in Fulda, Germany, I had another brush with death when a German sniper fired and just missed hitting my head.

We traveled southeast through Germany liberating small towns, where many Jews were living. When we arrived, they came outside cheering wildly and kissing our boots. If the Germans had remained in control, the Jews would have been sent to the gas chambers in Passau and Linz.

One of the things I remember about combat is you don't take the time to try to become close buddies with someone, because you don't know how long they will be around.

James Enzor

Army: Private First Class, 103rd Infantry Division
Hometown: Indianapolis, Indiana
Career: Senior vice president, property and casualty insurance

Enzor with his parents and sister Ruth

In the summer of 1943, after one and a half semesters at Indiana University, I entered the army and was sent to South Carolina for basic training. With two weeks remaining in my basic training, I applied for, and was accepted into, a new program to train new air force pilots. After my air force basic training and several pilot training schools, I was chosen to become a pilot. However, during my Primary Flying School, I flew out of a regulated area and was discharged from the program. It was back to the infantry for me.

When I returned to the infantry, I was assigned to the 409th Infantry Division with an intelligence and reconnaissance platoon. When we learned we were going to be shipped overseas, we were given two-week furloughs. However, my platoon leader felt we needed more training and told us that anyone who left on furlough would be reassigned. It was a tough decision, but I chose to visit my family before I was shipped out. My platoon leader kept his promise, and when I returned, all my belongings had been sent to another company.

We shipped out from Camp Shanks, outside of New York City, and after a long ten-day trip across the Pacific, we landed in Marseilles, France. After landing on the beaches, we walked thirty-five miles northwest into the hills, ending up at the Vosges Mountains. My combat experience began.

Our unit was assigned to take the high Vosges Mountains in France. The French Army Command had advised the American Command not to try to attack through the high mountains. They said it had never been successfully accomplished in the history of France. Our unit made history and did it! We were replacing the 3rd Division, which had been involved in heavy fighting. As our battalion advanced, we experienced an almost impenetrable forest of large fir trees and narrow dirt roads.

The orders came down for us to attack the Germans who were located in a small French village on the other side of the mountain. With the help of C and D Companies, we circled the town and caught the Germans by surprise. From the hillsides, we fired our machine guns and mortars on them. We were able to kill and wound a large number of Germans who were standing in line to get their food. They counterattacked, firing into the hills and killing all of our officers and several of our machine-gun and mortar men. Finally, we were able to take control and captured over 200 German troops and officers.

Later, we moved on to Alsace, France, where the Germans attacked us in great force. We had set up a defensive line and roadblock at the end of town. The Germans came down the hill with a massive force, but we stopped them. I manned one of our machine guns at the time. As a result of the firefight, four of our men were killed and four more were wounded.

The next day, we had orders to capture a walled town called Dambach La Ville. The wall surrounding the town had been built by the Romans centuries ago. It was about ten to twelve feet high and six feet thick. After our heavy artillery blasted the town for several hours, we were able to take it without much resistance. We captured a regimental headquarters with several hundred German troops and a Gestapo officer.

That night, we had discovered that the Germans had cut our communication lines to our headquarters. I was assigned to go with a wire team to reconnect the wires. The woods made it so dark you could barely see your hand in front of your face. We were so close to the Germans we could hear them talking. A line was reconnected, and we returned to the village. If it weren't so dark, I think that we would have been shot or captured.

After a day of rest, we headed out again and passed a small village, where we saw some German tanks. We were told we didn't need our antitank weapons because the Germans had no armor on our side of the Rhine River. As we neared our objective, Selestat, France, we entered a grape farm where the vines were three to four feet high. We had to move down the rows with very little room to maneuver, and the Germans hit us with heavy machine-gun fire. After we experienced heavy casualties, we finally were able to take out their machine guns and enter the town. We occupied three houses and captured nearly 30 more German soldiers.

Our job was to secure the town from any advancing Germans. We knocked out a German command car and turned it over on a small bridge to serve as a roadblock. I was on sentry duty at predawn, and all of a sudden, I saw a large group of German infantry headed toward us. I yelled at my buddies, who were resting and sleeping, to get up. We set up a heavy machine gun and a BAR (Browning Automatic Rifle) and fired down the street. While we were able to stop the advance of the German infantry, we soon heard tanks coming behind us. We thought they were our tanks, but we soon found out that they were German Tiger tanks. As soon as the lead tank realized we had no antitank weapons, they fired two 88mm rounds at our house.

The ceiling and walls crumbled around us. When I woke up, I had shrapnel wounds in my leg. Shortly after, a German soldier stuck his pistol in my face and told me to surrender. When he realized I couldn't move, he and two other soldiers dug me out of the debris rather than shooting me. I was carried outside on a door used as a stretcher. I was put with other American prisoners, and we were taken as POWs and moved to various German prison camps and hospital units. The first camp was the infamous Buchenwald concentration camp where many Jews had been exterminated. The smell was terrible, and we were placed in crowded barracks. Fortunately, we were only there for one day before being moved to Stalag XII-A and Stalag IV-B POW camps.

My leg wound developed gangrene, and they thought they would have to amputate my leg. A French doctor, with no medical supplies, took care of me and was able to save my leg. While we were in the hospital POW wards, the Germans treated us fairly well and saw that most of us got medical attention.

Another thing I will never forget was when a German intelligence officer interviewed me after I was captured. He knew more about my unit than I did. After I told him my name, rank, and serial number, he smiled and said, "For you the war is over." And it was! Months later I was shipped back to the States, where I recuperated in an army hospital. I finally returned to Fort Benjamin Harrison in Indianapolis, Indiana, and spent some time in the fort hospital. After recuperating, I took the bus to my home in Indianapolis.

During that one week in November 1944, I experienced days of heavy fighting and saw numerous American and German soldiers killed. Some of those Germans I probably killed. I survived the war, but there were many times I thought I never would.

Bernard Heeke

Army: Tech Sergeant, 78th Infantry Division
Hometown: Siberia, Indiana
Career: Junior high and high school teacher

Berlin, Germany, 1946

As a nineteen-year-old kid, I had never been away from home until I joined the army. After six months of basic training, I was made a temporary first sergeant and was in charge of 200 men, mostly seventeen to nineteen years of age. I learned to be a leader fast, since I felt responsible for them. The skills I learned helped me later in life.

After arriving in Liverpool, England, we moved on to France and then to Belgium, where the Germans were trying to break through our American lines during the Battle of the Bulge. For transport to our location, we had to get in railway boxcars. There were about 30 men to a car, and it was cramped, smelly, and cold. Horse manure was on the floor. We finally arrived at our destination in Verviers, Belgium. I got my rifle from a pile on the ground. It was a beat-up M-1, and I hoped it worked. The first night I had to stand guard duty. This was a scary experience because it was dark, and you couldn't tell if there were enemy soldiers or trees out there.

In March 1945, we crossed the Roer River, headed to the town of Euskirchen. It was rainy, when we came under heavy enemy fire from the German 88mm field artillery guns. We were pinned down, and, for cover, we lay in our tank track ruts, which were full of mud. I saw our sergeant hit by mortar fire.

We then moved to the Rhine Valley. Several of us rode on the back of our tanks. Fortunately, we jumped off our tank before it got hit by a German shell. We would probably have been killed. Our orders were to cross the Remagen Bridge over the Rhine River. We crossed the bridge and made a steep climb up into the hills. The Germans were shelling the bridge to keep our troops from crossing. A German plane dropped bombs on one of our platoons, killing most of the men. I was so close, the blast bounced me off the ground.

As we moved forward to Rottgen, we came under fire, and another of our sergeants was shot. I then became the squad leader. I gave orders to one of my men to use his automatic rifle and shoot the approaching Germans. His response was, "I can't kill anyone." After some intensive fighting, the Germans finally surrendered. We looked for our men who had been captured the night before, but we could not find them. A few days later, some of my unit and I were sent to a rest center in Belgium for three days. It was hard to go back to the front lines and face enemy fire again.

In April 1945, our unit moved to a small town called Alzen. We came under small-arms and mortar fire, and we ran for cover. A mortar round exploded near me, and I got shrapnel in both legs. The pain was severe. I was sent to an army field hospital, and I remember seeing the doctors and medical staff in their bloody aprons. The doctors operated on one leg but forgot to do the other one, and I had to remind them.

Before we were sent home, we had classes in which we were taught to be civilians again. We had been "trained to kill," and now we were being "untrained" so we would know how to act when we got back home.

In June 1946, after being in combat for over a year, I was sent back to America. I will never forget approaching New York City and seeing the Statue of Liberty welcoming us home.

Kathryn "Katy" Huehl

Red Cross Services
Hometown: Indianapolis, Indiana
Career: Teacher and professional volunteer

Huehl passing out newspapers to the troops

After my graduation from high school and Indiana University, I became a high school history teacher at Lawrenceburg High School, in Indiana. I also served as a USO volunteer in Indianapolis, where I played the piano and danced with the soldiers. My brother was a B-17 bomber pilot in the war, and I too wanted to help in some way. Since I had done some volunteer work with the Red Cross, I finally decided to make application to be a Red Cross Service worker. After my acceptance, in 1943, I was sent to Washington, D.C., for management training. Eleanor Roosevelt spoke at our graduation, and she was a very inspirational and gracious person who contributed to the war effort in so many ways.

In December 1943, I received orders to report to New York City. It was Christmas, and while I was walking through the city, I heard Bing Crosby singing, "I'll Be Home for Christmas" over the street speakers. It brought tears to my eyes, and it still does. On December 28, we boarded an English troop ship, the HMS *Samaria*, headed for Liverpool, England, as part of a large convoy of troop ships, battleships, and destroyers. The conditions on the ship were so filthy that we called it the "HMS *Malaria*." About 1,000 Australian soldiers and 24 of us Red Cross gals were on board.

Upon arriving in England in January 1944, we took a bus to London, which was under "blackout" at the time. We stayed in an American Red Cross club, and we could hear the

German bombs exploding around the city. The English lady who served in the club told us not to worry. She said, "We have the best neighborhood air warden in the area. He will never stop digging until he finds your body." A little humor in tough times can help. I was never really scared, even though many of the bombs landed around our area. I thought if I were going to die, so be it; otherwise, I had coffee and doughnuts to make. I feel the Lord had his hand on my head throughout the war.

I was trained to drive a truck called a Clubmobile. We were a mobile unit staffed by Red Cross workers, and we drove the trucks to designated locations. Our job was to make coffee and doughnuts, and hand out hometown newspapers to the soldiers who were back from the front. The soldiers often referred to us as "Donut Dollies", a name we never liked, because we knew how hard we worked. Wearing our paratrooper boots and playing records, we would even dance with the GIs in the mud. I remember so many of them were frightened, homesick, and bewildered. Most of the soldiers were only eighteen or nineteen years old. We knew many of them would never return home to their families. It was our privilege to be there and provide encouragement, comfort, and friendship.

I was in Dorchester and Bristol, England, for several months. On the evening of June 5, 1944, I heard hundreds of planes flying overhead all night. I went outside to look, and the sky was covered with Allied bombers heading for France. The next day, the Normandy invasion began.

We crossed the English Channel in July 1944. Our Landing Ship Tank (LST) 157 landed at Utah Beach, and we drove our Clubmobile onto the beach where the invasion had occurred only a month before. Our first night in France, we slept in a barn. There were holes in the roof, and we could hear and see the artillery fire. From then on, we slept wherever we could find a place, which included a convent, open fields, schoolhouses, a bombed-out chateau, a barracks in Verdun, France, and the stables of the Rothschild Estate outside of Paris, after the city was liberated by the Allies.

I was assigned to General Omar Bradley's First Army and followed him through France, Holland, Belgium, and Luxembourg and across the Rhine River into Germany. We were honored to be with the 1110th Combat Engineer Group as they built one of the first pontoon bridges across the Rhine. Our Red Cross unit was the first group of women to cross the Rhine during the war.

At times, we were only about a mile behind the front lines. I never worked harder in my life, but it was the most worthwhile service I have ever done. We provided coffee, doughnuts, encouragement, and smiles to about 500 soldiers each day. Everywhere we went, the GIs were wonderful. They treated us with respect, like we were their wives, sisters, girlfriends, or the gal next door. Of course, we would get whistles now and then.

After the war ended in Europe, I was assigned to Munich, Germany, and became a supervisor. While I was there, we always knew when General Patton was coming to town because the GIs would have to sweep the sidewalks and streets prior to his arrival. Everything had to be in "spit-and-polish order." I experienced a memorable event on February 12, 1945. A birthday party was held for General Bradley, and I was invited. Whenever I saw the general, the first thing he would ask me was, "How are my boys?" He was a very gracious and kind man. I have the birthday program, which he autographed for me—something I will always treasure.

In September 1945, I boarded the *Grisholm* in Marseilles, France, and returned to New York City. The passengers on the ship were war brides, children, and Red Cross workers. There were no soldiers aboard. My brother had been killed when his plane was shot down over Germany earlier that year, and I knew I was needed at home with my family.

Approaching New York Harbor, I saw the Statue of Liberty, and I cried. It was the end of the two most challenging years that I shall never forget.

General of the Army Omar Bradley

"We know more about war than we know about peace, more about killing than we do about living."

Bradley was one of the Eisenhower's key generals in the European Theater. He was responsible for coordinating the logistics for the invasion of Normandy. As the Allies advanced across Europe, he would command the First Army and later the Twelfth Army. Bradley was extremely popular with the soldiers due to his polite and courteous manner, which earned him the affectionate title, "the GI's general." After the war, he earned his fifth star and became the Army chief of staff and chairman of the Joint Chiefs of Staff.

Jack Leslie

Army: 79th Infantry Division
Hometown: Indianapolis, Indiana
Career: Founder of Leslie Brothers Company Inc.

I was thirty when I was drafted into the army. Our company landed on Omaha Beach after D-Day, and by this time the fighting was over on the beaches, so we did not come under fire. As we moved through France, I had no idea where we were going. We would determine our destination by the rumors we heard.

In the summer of 1944, I remember resting in an apple orchard when we started to receive sporadic fire as the Germans were retreating. We would find them in small groups of ten to twelve, mostly young boys with an older sergeant. Many would surrender, and we would take them as POWs. They gave us little resistance.

Although the Germans were in retreat, their heavy artillery still shelled us. Being under artillery fire was a frightening experience because you never knew where the shells would land. When we moved to different places, we would see dead American and German soldiers in the fields and villages. It is something you never forget.

If we could find a previously dug German foxhole, we got in it. Their foxholes were always deeper and bigger than ours because they had larger shovels. In October 1944, our unit came under heavy artillery fire. A buddy and I scrambled into a German foxhole to protect ourselves from the incoming artillery fire. It wasn't long until I heard a big explosion near our foxhole. We were buried in dirt. When I looked over at my buddy, he was dead. I held him for a while before I realized I had been seriously injured. When I looked at my leg, it was barely attached to my hip. If I had not had a belt to tie around my leg as a tourniquet, I would probably have bled to death.

One of soldiers who uncovered me from the dirt and pulled me out of the foxhole was from Indiana. I told them to bring my leg, since I thought it was no longer attached to my body. I was sent to a field hospital behind the lines. The doctor told me to hold tightly to the stretcher because I would feel severe pain when he pulled my mangled leg from its distorted position; he was right. The pain was almost unbearable because there was no good painkiller or anesthesia to give me. I later learned that my buddy died from a concussion because of the shell that exploded in front of us. He didn't have a mark on him, and I was cut up with shrapnel. I thought, "Why was he killed, and I wasn't?" We were right next to each other in the foxhole.

I was flown to a military hospital in Naples, Italy, where I had extensive surgery. The American surgeons were outstanding and saved my leg. One of the doctors, who was from Indianapolis, observed every one of my surgeries. When I saw him after the war, at an event in Indianapolis, he immediately recognized me. He told me he couldn't believe I was walking, due to the severity of my injury. I never had to use a cane or walker. From the time I was injured and sent back home, I had been in combat for only eleven months.

Albert E. "Gene" Liston

Army: First Army Headquarters
Hometown: Robinson, Illinois
Career: Controller and general manager; real estate broker

Liston with wife Betty on wedding day August 4, 1945

As a supply sergeant, my job was to see that soldiers and officers on the front lines had the necessary supplies they needed. This included water, food, ammunition, fuel, pontoons for building bridges, and other items. Our supply lines remained about a mile behind our front lines.

We landed on Normandy D-Day Plus Three and followed the First Army through France and Belgium and into Germany. The weather conditions were often rainy and muddy when we were in France. Our foxholes would often be filled with water, making them unusable. I remember how difficult it was advancing through the thick hedgerows throughout France. These provided the Germans with cover and slowed our advance. Along with the extreme weather conditions, it made it difficult to keep our front lines supplied. General Patton was a "pain" because he was always demanding more fuel and supplies for his Third Army. However, without his courage and leadership, the Allies might not have won the Battle of the Bulge. In the Ardennes Forest, we encountered deep snows and freezing weather. The conditions were horrible.

We were in a small French village right before the Battle of the Bulge. The Germans were advancing toward us. Our sergeant told fifteen of us to be prepared to defend the village. This was ridiculous to think that fifteen of us, with only rifles, could stop the Germans from entering the village. A German tank was advancing toward us but got bogged down in the snow. If the tank had gotten through, we probably would have been killed. As they continued to move closer, we moved out and ended up in an open, snowy field where we spent the night. The Germans could easily have killed all of us, but they did not fire upon us. One of the scariest things I remember was when the Germans would fire their V-2 rockets at us. You could hear them coming, and they sounded like a large washing machine.

Two times I was given the general's jeep. The first time, I was ordered to find the pontoons we needed to cross the Rhine River, after the Germans had destroyed the Remagen Bridge. Another time, I was told to go find our tents. It seemed strange to be driving the general's jeep with his star on the front. Traveling on ice, I slid and hit another truck, but I was finally able to get the tents back to camp.

After Germany had surrendered, we were sent on leave for 30 days. We found out that the First Army was going to be sent to the Pacific, and we were going to invade mainland Japan. Luckily, President Truman had ordered the dropping of the atomic bombs, and the war soon ended. As controversial as Truman's decision was, it saved millions of lives on both sides. Since I was married, I had enough points necessary for discharge.

I have been asked if I was ever scared. I guess I was too young and didn't have the sense to be scared. Looking back, I should have been. My faith carried me through, and I had confidence that we would win the war. I was very proud to have served my country during the war.

Many years after the war, my wife and I returned to Normandy. While sitting on a wall, I gazed over the beaches and the thousands of white Allied Crosses at Normandy. I cried, as I thought, 'There, but for the grace of God, go I.''

Ernie Lorch

Army: Tech Sergeant, Allied Forces Headquarters
Hometown: Louisville, Kentucky
Career: Manufactures agent

Hermann Goering and other German leaders
stand trial for war crimes at Nuremberg, Germany

In 1923, I was born in Nuremburg, Germany. On November 10, 1938, which is known as Krystalnacht, my father was taken away by the Nazis and killed. At the time, I was fifteen-years-old and was away at school in Berlin. My father's body was returned later in a sealed casket. We believe he was beaten to death. In the spring of 1939, my mother and I immigrated to New York City to escape the Nazi persecution. In December 1942, at nineteen, I was drafted into the U.S. Army, and my basic training in infantry was at Fort McClellan, Alabama.

Directly after basic training, our company was shipped out to North Africa, and we landed at Oran, Morocco. We spent some time in replacement centers waiting for an assignment. One day, I hitchhiked on a truck, planning on going to Tunis but ended up in Bizerte, Tunisia. I was sitting having coffee when a major sat down beside me and began talking with me. He found out that I spoke German and asked me to meet him the next day to talk about becoming a part of a newly formed special intelligence unit. This sounded intriguing to me, and I told him my buddy also spoke German, so the major said to bring him along.

At that time in the war, the Americans had no organized intelligence units, so 13 of us German-speaking American soldiers, most of us still teenagers, were assigned to a British intelligence unit that trained us. The British were very good at this and had been at the game for a very long time. They taught us how to interrogate German prisoners. Although we did not realize it at the time, we were probably some of the first American soldiers to be trained in intelligence work.

We interrogated German pilots and navy personnel who had been shot down over Gibraltar, as well as others captured by the Allies. We asked questions about troop movements, battle plans, supply lines, armament, personnel, numbers in units, and other information we thought would be helpful. Most prisoners voluntarily gave up information when told that they had three choices. They could be sent to POW camps in the United States, where they would receive good treatment, or we could turn them over to the French Foreign Legion or the Russians. Most opted to tell us what they knew to avoid the likely torture and possible death from the French and Russians. Another technique we used was placing small, hidden microphones in their tents, so we could hear what they were saying to each other, after their initial interrogation. We never used any physical or verbal abuse during interrogations.

On July 4, 1944, we landed in Naples, Italy, and spent free time along the Amalfi coast. One month after the D-Day invasion, we landed in Marseille, France. The Allies were fighting their way north when, one day, a captured German general was brought to our unit. I sat in the backseat with him while riding around Marseilles. I showed him the massive war supplies and weapons we had amassed preparing for our northern movement through France on the way to Berlin. I said to him, "General, after seeing all of this, how do you possibly think you can win the war?" He soon talked, which proved to be very helpful.

In October, our unit moved to Northern France, and we located on the Meuse Loop, in a city named Revin. We were near the Ardennes Forest, and one cold morning in December we heard the rumbling of tanks and artillery. It was General Patton's Third Army advancing on the Germans during the Battle of the Bulge, which was the last major German offensive. We were evacuated from the area to Rheims, France, where we stayed until the battle was over. It was a hard, icy, extremely cold and snowy winter. There were heavy casualties and difficult and intensive fighting.

In the spring of 1945, five of us from our unit were assigned to go to Spa, Belgium, where we set up in a large chateau. The chateau had been the command headquarters for Generals Eisenhower and Montgomery, during the Battle of the Bulge. It wasn't long after we occupied the chateau, when six members of the Nazi high command were brought to us as prisoners. I could not believe it when I found out that some of them were Hermann Goering; Franz von Papen, former chancellor of Germany; Field Marshal Gerd von Rundstedt, one of the highest-ranking German generals; and Albert Speer, Hitler's architect. They were administered questionnaires, and my job was to translate them. During their stay at the chateau, I was able to have informal conversations with most of them, since they were free to walk the grounds. At the time, I did not think of this historic interaction, but it was a heady adventure for a twenty-two-year-old soldier.

On May 7, 1945, the Germans had surrendered to the Allied Forces, and plans were being made to conduct the War Crimes Tribunals in Nuremberg, Germany. By this time, we were located in Luxembourg, where we held most of the Nazi High Command in a prison camp. In September, I was given the assignment to transport 24 of the most notorious German war criminals to the trial at Nuremberg. We transported them in a truck followed by a jeep and two armed guards, and I was in the lead command vehicle. The prisoners were delivered without incident to the sergeant of the guard at the jail in Nuremberg. He provided me with a document confirming "24 live bodies."

For the next three months, we were stationed in Oberursel near Frankfurt. During this time, I found my grandmother in an Allied refugee camp. She had survived incarceration in the concentration camp of Theresienstadt—a very emotional reunion indeed.

In December 1945, I returned to the United States. After three years, the war was over for me, and I was discharged at Fort Dix, New Jersey. Later on, I reflected on how ironic my experience was. I had come full circle from my birth in Nuremberg, having been kicked out of Germany as a Jew, and then as an American soldier delivering these Nazi war criminals to the tribunal at the "Palace of Justice" in Nuremberg, Germany. There was "justice" after all.

Prime Minister Charles de Gaulle

"Nothing great will ever be achieved without great men, and men are great only if they are determined to be so."

He was the grand figurehead of free France during World War II and became the minister for national defense and war. After France's fall to Germany, he made a famous radio broadcast calling on the French people to resist the German army with all their hearts and souls. A group of French citizens and soldiers formed the French Resistance, inflicting damage on the Germans by providing valuable intelligence information to the Allies.

Gerald Mansbach

Army: Sergeant, 8th Armored Division
Hometown: Fort Wayne, Indiana
Career: Stockbroker

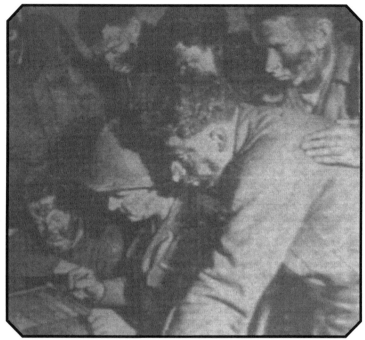

Mansbach (top right) and soldiers are briefed before their next mission. The photo appeared in the *Stars and Stripes* newspaper. (Courtesy Gerald Mansbach)

I left Indiana University and was drafted in January 1943. My basic training was in Fort Benning, Georgia, where I was assigned to the 88th Calvary Reconnaissance Squadron, 8th Armored Division. From there, I went to Camp Polk, Louisiana, for combat training. Eventually, I went to Fort Dix, New Jersey and boarded a Liberty ship. We crossed the Atlantic in January 1944, as part of a convoy that consisted of 55 different types of ships. Somewhere in the Atlantic, our ship had engine trouble, and we fell behind the convoy. This was not a good situation, because it left us vulnerable to German U-boat attacks. Fortunately, we got our engine repaired and made it safely to Liverpool, England. Training exercises were conducted in preparation to cross the English Channel on June 12, 1944, D-Day Plus Six. Most of us were eighteen- or nineteen-year-old kids at the time.

When we landed at Normandy, our tanks and other mechanized armor and vehicles had a very difficult time getting through the thick hedgerows. As a recon unit, we were a lead tank looking for the enemy. This makes you a higher-risk target for enemy fire. When we arrived in the St.-Lo area, we were under fire continuously. By this time, I had been promoted to vehicle commander of a Sherman tank. When you got a promotion, you didn't necessarily want the stripes or bars that went with it, because the Germans targeted our NCOs (Non-Commissioned Officers) and officers. In fact, we joked if you were still alive, you might get a promotion.

In December 1944, during the Battle of the Bulge, we joined with the 4th Armored Division and went to Bastogne. At Bastogne, members of the 101st Airborne had suffered heavy casualties, and it was our job to help break through the German units surrounding them and evacuate the injured.

After the Battle of the Bulge, the Germans were in retreat. Their losses were so great that I remember seeing thirteen- to fifteen-year-old boys they had conscripted to fight. Our next significant combat occurred in Berg, Germany. While my tank was on a recon mission, an enemy antitank gun hit the tank's tracks and immobilized us. A second hit took out our tank, killing all four of my men who were inside the tank. At the time, I was in the turret with our .50 caliber machine gun, trying to hold off a large group of German infantry heading toward us. The second explosion knocked me out of the tank and rendered me unconscious. My clothes were shredded; however, other than a severe head injury, I was not seriously hurt in any other way. My dog tags were blown off, so no one could identify me.

I developed what was called "military amnesia," which is a means to block bad memories due to a traumatic experience. I spent months in ten different hospitals undergoing various psychiatric treatments. I was given a fairly new drug called sodium pentothal, also known as "truth serum." It was amazing how I could recall some basic information two hours after the treatment; information such as my name, where I was born, and where I lived.

My parents had not received letters from me for months. They had no idea where I was, because I could not remember who I was, and the army had not yet determined my identity. However, once I received the sodium pentothal drug, the army was able to notify them of my location and condition. I was still not able to remember the tragedy that happened to my crew and me. At times, I still question myself as to why I did not tell my crew to get out of the tank after the first hit. That is a regret that will always be with me. Sometimes, I still have dreams.

I still try to forget many things about the war that were unpleasant. There is nothing good or glamorous about war.

Richard Mote

Army: Sergeant, 82nd Airborne
Hometown: Indianapolis, Indiana
Career: Middle school social studies teacher

Rheims, France, 1945

On D-Day, June 6, 1944, we were on a transport ship heading for an unknown destination. Our ship had about 5,000 men aboard ready for combat. The conditions were crowded and smelly.

On June 8, 1944, D-Day Plus Two, we landed on Utah Beach. The sight is one I will never forget. There were thousands of Allied ships and troop carriers still in the channel unloading troops onto the Normandy beaches. Before we got to shore, I saw one of our troop carriers hit a mine. It exploded, most likely killing everyone on board. We could still hear the shelling from the fighting that was taking place near Omaha Beach, which was several miles east of us. Omaha was the bloodiest battle of the five beachhead landings at Normandy.

Three days after our landing, we experienced our first enemy fire. On the next day, we were still receiving enemy fire. In the evening, a German fighter plane flew over our camp. Our machine gunners fired at it, but unfortunately hit and shot down one of the British Spitfire fighters pursuing the German fighter. We later heard that the pilot had bailed out and was okay.

As we continued to move inland, the Germans were firing at us. Getting through the thick hedgerows was hell because of the cover it provided for the Germans. When I explored our area one day, I saw four dead American GIs. They had been killed by mortar fire. One was shot right between the eyes. Another horrible sight I saw was one of our Piper Cub scout planes that had been shot down. The pilot was sitting upright burned to a crisp. We were going through the small French town of Chef du Pont, and as we moved out of the town, we saw dead bodies of our paratroopers lying in the mud and water.

While I saw much death and destruction, one of the most terrible sights I saw was when we entered a German slave labor camp that had been liberated by the Russians. German villagers were made to stack the dead bodies of those who had died in the camp due to starvation or by other means. There were stacks of human skeletons, and those who were still alive were "living skeletons." That experience will haunt me forever.

On D-Day Plus Thirty-Seven, we were told we were going back to England for preparation to return to the United States. I was in combat for 34 days. In our battery, we lost one man due to enemy fire, and five others were wounded. During our time in France, we had accomplished all of our objectives, but so many American soldiers had paid the ultimate sacrifice by dying on foreign soil.

Harry Phariss

Army: Private First Class, 13th Airborne Division
Hometown: Shawnee, Oklahoma
Career: Postal Service

Florence Phariss

Home Front
Hometown: Paris, France
Career: French professor

Harry and Florence Pharris the day after their wedding in France

I volunteered for the army and was assigned to the 13th Army Airborne Division, 515th Parachute Infantry Regiment. After the war had ended, and I returned to the States, I was reassigned to the 82 Airborne Division.

At Fort McArthur in California, I was an MP (military police). For my airborne training, I was sent to Fort Benning, Georgia, where I earned my wings. If you were a paratrooper, you volunteered to be one, and you had to go through rigorous training. We were prepared to jump and fight anytime, anywhere, under any circumstances. As paratroopers, we were sent as advance and as diversionary troops. We were not usually backed up by tanks or heavy artillery.

We landed on the Normandy beaches, six months after the D-Day invasion. I will never forget the devastation of the terrain and the destruction. There were huge craters where our ships had fired their shells. We moved through Ste.-Mere-Eglise after the German army had retreated into Germany and across the Rhine River. We had been making practice jumps in France out of our C-47 planes, preparing for the troop drop around the Rhine, but Patton's Third Army beat us to the Rhine River and pushed the Germans back.

The best thing that happened to me during the war was I met my future wife in France. We were married in Auxerre, France, and she became a 'World War II war bride.'

When I returned to the United States, I marched in the V-J Day victory parade in New York City, where we were greeted by thousands of people. How fortunate we are to live in a free country. This would not have been possible had we not won the war.

Mrs. Phariss

My family and I lived in Paris, France. My father was in the military, and my mother worked in the city. Before the war began in September 1939, my parents sent my brother and me to the small village of Boissy-le-Cutte, France, about fifty miles south of Paris, to live with a lady for the summer. My mother thought it would be safer. When the Germans passed through Boissy-le-Cutte, we hid in a cellar.

On June 6, 1944, D-Day, I was only fifteen-years-old and remember seeing and hearing the Allied planes fly over our school; the sky was full of them. The Germans had placed their antiaircraft guns on top of our schools, and we knew something big was taking place. Once the Allies took Normandy and started moving through France, we would see the German soldiers retreating through our village. Many of them were old men and young boys. They were a ragtag group.

We were still in Boissy-le-Cutte, when the American troops liberated us. We came out of our houses and lined the streets greeting the Allied soldiers with cheers, wine, and champagne. I remember seeing General Patton's jeep, which had his general's flag with stars.

My mother, siblings, and I walked several miles to find a train we could take back to Paris. With several others, we finally got on a flatbed railcar, and as the train went along, we could see the devastation and destruction of the countryside. As we neared Paris, we learned that the Allies had stopped at the edge of France and allowed the French to liberate themselves.

Harry and I met in Paris while he was on leave. When a friend and I came out of the subway tunnel, Harry and his friend started walking beside us after they had decided which girl each one was going to approach. Harry and I walked about a mile before he even said anything to me. He finally asked me for a date. We were married in Paris, but I did not get to come to America until after the war, in 1947.

What impressed me were the spirit, perseverance, and integrity of the American soldiers and people.

General of the Army George Marshall

"Military power wins battles, but spiritual power wins wars."

Marshall was the army chief of staff before and during the war and was an expert at planning and organizing the army, which reached eight million men before the war started. While he desired to command the invasion at Normandy, President Roosevelt considered him too valuable as the Joint Chiefs of Staff. After the war, Marshall served as the secretary of state and secretary of defense, and he created a plan to help rebuild the economies and infrastructures of Europe. This became known as "The Marshall Plan."

Paul Richert

Army: Tech Sergeant, 78th Infantry Division
Hometown: York, Nebraska
Career: Auctioneer

I left for WWII from Camp Kilmer, New Jersey, on train 13 and on track 13. I boarded the ship to go overseas on Friday the 13th, and it took us 13 days to cross the ocean. I landed in England at port 13 and went into combat on December 13. I was in Germany for 13 months before being sent back to America, which again took 13 days to cross. Believe it or not, I was discharged from the army on January 13, 1946. Thirteen was my "*lucky number!*"

I experienced my first day of combat in December 1944, in the Battle of the Bulge. The battle lasted for 125 days and was fought in the heavily wooded forests of Ardennes, Belgium. It was the coldest winter in Germany in the last thirty years, and the weather conditions were terrible. The snow was up to a foot deep, and because of the extremely cold temperatures, many GIs got frostbite on their fingers and toes and had them amputated. If your feet got frozen and infected, it was called "trench foot." When we weren't fighting, we were told to keep our extra pair of socks in our helmet to keep them warm and dry. We lived like animals, and some of our guys even froze to death in their foxholes.

I saw General Patton several times in his jeep going up to the front lines to survey the situation and direct his tank division. It amazed me that he never got shot because he led from the front and exposed himself to enemy fire.

We rode in trucks when we could get them. One time we were near the front lines, and our driver got lost. To turn around, he started backing up, and the driver behind us did the same. When the truck behind us backed up, it hit a land mine, killing all of the soldiers on board. It could have been our truck that hit the mine.

When a unit moved into an area it would place "hasty" mines on top of the ground in case it was attacked. If the unit had to quickly move out, it could easily see the mines, disarm them, and load them. One day we came across an area covered with "hasty" mines, and we had to get out of our trucks and disarm them, so we could move through the area. The driver got out to help us. I was only about forty feet away when he picked up a mine and threw it in the back of the truck. The truck exploded, and the sound was deafening. The driver had forgotten to put the pin back in the mine to disarm it. When I hit the ground, I thought I was dead. After the rest of us got up off the ground, all we could find of the driver was his heel in his boot. It was a terrible sight.

When we were on the Siegfried Line in Germany, our lieutenant told us we had to capture a German machine-gun bunker, or a "pillbox." I felt we were going to get killed trying to take it. All of a sudden, a British tank came over the hill, and the driver asked if we needed help. He had a flamethrower, so he shot flames into the bunker, and the Germans came running out and surrendered. He not only saved our lives, but he saved the German soldiers' lives because he could have blasted that pillbox.

One time, I went out to a clearing to sight my rifle, when I heard a bullet zing past my ear, just missing my head. I took off running and zigzagged, hoping the German sniper wasn't a very good shot. That was the third time I had come close to death. I had another close call when we were in a small German village. We took cover in a building because German artillery was shelling us. One wall of our building was completely blown off, but somehow we all survived.

On one patrol I came across a German officer and six of his soldiers. All of them jumped out of a wooded area and surrendered. I raised my submachine gun and in German I told them to put their hands up and drop their weapons. The officer spoke to me in German and asked how I could speak German so well. I told him I was from a German community in Nebraska, and my grandfather was from Germany. He then said to me, "Isn't war hell?" I still have his German Luger pistol, with his name on it, when he surrendered it to me along with his officer's dagger.

On Christmas Eve 1944, during the Battle of the Bulge, the Allied and German guns were silent, as there was usually no fighting at night. That night, I witnessed a remarkable and emotional sight that I will never forget, and I still think about it each Christmas Eve. An American soldier, who had been a singer with the Fred Waring singers, stepped out onto the open battlefield and began singing "Silent Night." The forest was completely silent, and it was an eerie sight. A German sniper could have easily shot him.

On March 7, 1945, the men with the 9th Armored Division were the first to cross the Rhine River. They crossed the Rhine on the Ludendorff Bridge, which was the only bridge still standing on the Rhine. It was a critical bridge for us to capture. As they were about to cross over, the Germans were trying to blow it up, so the Allies could not cross, but their attempts with explosives failed. While our troops were moving across the bridge, they were being shot at by the Germans.

Early the next morning a battalion from our division was the first infantry unit from an infantry division to cross the bridge. When I was crossing, the Germans were firing down on us with everything they had. As we were crossing the bridge, the Germans were shelling us with their big 88mm guns, and a jeep behind me got hit. I watched the man burn alive—another close call with death.

The Germans wanted desperately to destroy the bridge, so we could not keep sending our troops across. They even sent floating mines down the river to try to explode the bridge. Ten days after we had taken the bridge, I had to make another trip back across to get ammunition for us. I had just crossed the bridge, when I heard a terrible noise. The bridge had just collapsed into the Rhine, killing 28 American soldiers. Another brush with death.

As we continued to move eastward, we liberated a German concentration camp and captured some German soldiers and Nazi SS (secret police) officers from the camp. They were taken to our POW camp, but the next day we learned that the German soldiers had killed the SS officers during the night because they also hated the SS for their brutality and what they had done to German civilians and Allied prisoners.

When we finally pushed the German army back and arrived in Berlin, we saw that most of the civilians were starving. The food from our camps was being thrown away. Some old German ladies came up to us and asked if they could have some leftover food. I asked our captain if we could give them food. He said, "Okay. They didn't start this war." Later on, an order came down from headquarters that said Allied troops were to give German civilians all of our leftover food.

This was just one example of the many humanitarian things the Allies did throughout the war. I know that we saved many German lives by keeping them from starving to death.

After all of my combat experience, I came home without a scratch. I know the good Lord had been watching over me, and I had lots of prayers from my family members at home.

Virgil Stamm

Army: Private First Class, Third Army
Hometown: Anderson, Indiana
Career: Tool and die maker

American convoy moving through
the war torn town of St.-Lo, France

When I was drafted on July 13, 1943, I was eighteen-years-old. My basic training was at Fort Belvoir, Virginia, and after basic training I went to the New York Trade School in New York City to be trained as an electrician. From there, I was sent to Indio, California, where I became a part of the 133rd Combat Engineers. As combat engineers, we were trained in bridge construction and demolitions. We could build a bridge overnight.

After boarding a troopship to Belfast, Ireland, we then headed to Oxford, England. From there, we crossed the English Channel and landed at Normandy on July 13, 1944, exactly one year to the day after I was drafted. For several weeks we moved up and down the twenty-mile beachhead awaiting our orders. We dug a lot of foxholes.

On July 25, 1944, the Allies made their breakthrough at St.-Lo, France. During the breakthrough, my company was assigned to check out the town in nearby Lessay, France. The night before we were to leave, intelligence informed us that Lessay was the most "booby-trapped" city in all of France. I was assigned as the head scout when we headed out the next morning. Upon arriving, we saw that the entire town had been leveled by Allied bombs. The Germans had "booby-trapped" the town with hundreds of land mines before they left. One of the colonels from another company ran over a mine with his Jeep and was killed. A medic in our unit went to help another guy injured by a mine, and he stepped on a mine and lost his foot. The thing I remember about Lessay is the terrible stench of the bloated dead Germans, who had been dead for weeks prior to our arrival. I couldn't eat for three days.

During our engagements around St.-Lo, we experienced a real morale booster. We saw hundreds of our B-17 bombers, only about five hundred feet above the ground, dropping their bombs on the Nazis who were entrenched on one side of the road while we were on the other side. It was a sight you can't imagine. The Nazis were completely demoralized, and those who lived, retreated. During this time, the Allied infantry troops were moving farther into France.

I was assigned to the 121st Calvary, which was part of General Patton's Third Army. He boasted that we would be in Paris in 21 days. None of us believed this was possible because of the distance we had to cover. On the drive to Paris, we liberated several French villages and towns. Again, the Air Corps came through for us. We could see our P-57s flying low, strafing villages, killing Germans and causing others to retreat. Driving along the roads, we saw hundreds of former POWs clustered in small groups in the trees. Many of them looked like walking skeletons. We could not stop to help them, because we were an armored division and had to keep moving.

When we arrived in the villages, the French people treated us like heroes. Church bells would ring; they cheered, waving French and American flags, and brought us wine and food. The villagers sang World War I American songs. They did not know the World War II American songs, because they had been under Nazi rule and occupation for four years. I remember a unique sight, as we traveled through these small villages. Nearly every village had a small town square. All the girls and women who had fraternized with the Nazis were taken to the square, and their heads were shaved to humiliate them.

Patton was right. It was only about three weeks, when we arrived near Paris. We were instructed to remain outside of Paris and let the First French Army occupy the city. After about three days near Paris, we headed to Nancy, France, in early December 1944. I was transferred to the 4th Armored Division.

Orders were given to hook up with another company, and along the way our captain got us lost. While trying to turn around to go back the other way, one of our bulldozers got stuck. We were all lined up in our trucks and other vehicles when, all of a sudden, we were hit with heavy mortar fire by a Nazi armored outfit. I saw a corporal in the vehicle in front of me get shot in the spine by a German sniper. We jumped out of our trucks, not realizing most of us were jumping out on the side that the Nazis were firing at us. We ran to get into the ditches to take cover. The Nazis were hidden behind the trees, and we could not see them, but they could sure see us. While still under fire, we were finally able to escape. Within an hour, we lost 52 of our men, who were either taken prisoner or killed. In combat, sometimes you feel all alone, even though you know that hundreds of other guys are fighting around you.

By late December, with the Battle of the Bulge still going on around us, we arrived in a small Belgian town that had not been bombed or damaged. On a beautiful, extremely cold, snowy Christmas Eve 1944, we were treated to a full-fledged Christmas dinner. It was the only hot meal I can remember during the war. While we were there, the Allies wired a bridge with explosives to serve as an escape route, if they had to return. My squad of ten was told to stay behind and watch the bridge. If our troops came back over the bridge, we were to blow it to keep the Nazis from crossing over.

In January 1945, the Third Army was making preparations to attack the Nazis' last stronghold, the Siegfried Line. This was the Nazis' "last stand," before Allied troops moved on to Berlin. The line was divided by the Saur River, with the Allies on one side and the Nazis on the other side, heavily armed with machine-gun pillboxes, artillery, and mortars. We were in the Luxembourg area of the Siegfried Line. My unit's job was to transport infantry troops and supplies across the river. We used wooden boats with oars to cross the river. Four engineers to a boat did the paddling, carrying 12 to 14 soldiers in each boat. Twelve boats left on the first crossing. The current of the river was so strong we were swept downriver from our original location. The Nazis were constantly firing at us from high ground. We could see the bullets and explosions hitting the water nearby. Amazingly, we lost none of our soldiers or boats.

After dropping off our infantry, we rowed back to our side to get more troops. We were "sitting ducks" all of the time we were in our boats. When we took the members of the 5th Infantry across for the second crossing, our boat was the only one in the water. I felt a sensation like I was being hit with a fly swatter. I did not want to look at my stomach, because guys had told me that when you're shot, you don't feel anything at first. Luckily, the bullet just grazed me and landed in the bottom of the boat. I picked up the bullet and have it framed in my home.

When we got the squad across the river, the Nazis pinned us down with heavy fire. Two of our soldiers lay seriously wounded on the river bank. My buddies and I got out of our boat to help them. The guy I was trying to help asked me to remove his boots. I later learned that when a soldier was wounded or dying, one of the first things he would ask is to have his boots removed. I was standing at the time, and my three buddies were on the ground. Suddenly, four mortar shells exploded around us. A piece of shrapnel went through my left leg and came out the other side. My clothes were ripped to pieces, but, miraculously, I had not been hit in any other part of my body. All four of us were wounded from the blast, but we were able to get back in the boat and cross the river, while being constantly fired upon. I learned later that my platoon sergeant and several officers and infantrymen had been killed on that day.

When we got ashore, I was sent to a field hospital, and my leg wound was treated. The next morning, I was back on duty and returned to our base camp. The 5th Infantry had penetrated the Siegfried Line. A week later, we crossed over a bridge, moving our heavy armor into Germany. After crossing the bridge, a building was obstructing our ability to make the turn with our tanks and armored vehicles. Since I was trained in demolitions, I was asked to blow off the corner of the building. I loaded so much TNT in that building that it blew down the entire building and those around it. Our equipment had no trouble getting around the corner.

I was now assigned to the 11th Armored Division, and we were moving toward Austria. Along the way, we came upon a large German roadblock made out of stone. The roadblock was attached to a villager's house. I was asked to blow the roadblock. When I got to the roadblock, the German guy who lived in the house came out yelling at me. He thought I was going to blow up his house. I blew away the roadblock without even touching his house. I think he was a pretty grateful German civilian.

On the way to Linz, Austria, in May 1945, the war was almost over. Along the way, we encountered thousands of Nazi soldiers walking the opposite way along the sides of the roads with their hands above their heads. They were surrendering to the Americans, because they did not want to be captured by the Russians. They feared what the Russians would do to them. When we arrived in Linz, American and German soldiers mingled together with no hostilities.

I was sent to Regensburg, Germany, for a few months, as part of the Allied Occupation Forces. I returned to the States in November 1945, at Camp Kilmer in New Jersey. I was not the only one who served from my family. One of my brothers served on Iwo Jima, and the other one was a navy airplane mechanic.

16

THE ARDENNES

Battle of the Bulge

*"To me, it is a never-ending marvel
what our soldiers can do."*
—General George S. Patton, Jr.

It was 5:30 a.m. on December 16, 1944, and history would soon be made. For the German soldier, a new energy filled the air, a new confidence had emerged, as once again it was like the early days when they were on the offensive taking the war to different countries and different enemies. This enthusiasm was prevalent along the German front, from Monschau, Germany, in the north, to Echternach, Luxembourg, in the south. The hour had arrived for the youth of Hitler to once again show the fanaticism they had given to their leader, and turn it upon their enemy and drive him from the border of the Fatherland. As the German soldiers looked westward, their enemy was unaware of the attack that was about to occur.

"I have made a momentous decision. I am taking the offensive. Here—out of the Ardennes!" With these words, Hitler started to show signs of his old self, confident and giving out orders to his top generals, which he had not displayed in some time. At a top-level meeting in the fall of 1944, Hitler instructed his generals to devise a more detailed operation that would secretly bring a massive amount of troops, supplies, and equipment closer to the Western Front for an all-out assault on the American front line. As Hitler began to lay out his mission, he knew it could only be successful if secrecy was maintained. If they kept the American intelligence arena from discovering the massive buildup, the element of surprise would be achieved!

To help ensure a successful attack, Hitler would not initiate the offensive until bad weather conditions prevailed. This would help neutralize American air power, and keep the front-line troops from being resupplied. An overwhelming concentration of German infantry and tanks would break through the porous American lines and advance at a rapid rate toward the Meuse River. Once the Meuse was crossed, the forces would drive to Antwerp and capture its port, where the majority of the Allied supplies were located.

Hitler also believed Eisenhower and his staff would not respond to the attack quickly and would have to consult Roosevelt and Churchill on the next steps. Finally, Hitler could not fathom that his troops would not be able to overrun the American soldiers, who he believed were unmotivated, too green, and would run in the face of the advancing onslaught. Hitler believed history would soon be made.

Along the winding eighty-eight-mile front, foxholes were dug into the frozen, snow-covered ground, as American soldiers peered eastward. They did not realize they were about to become part of the largest land battle ever fought by the United States Army. On the American front line were inexperienced and battle-weary units filled with green replacements. The German soldiers, on the other hand, had been rejuvenated by the fact that they were no longer in a defensive posture, but were now on the march to the west.

At 5:30 a.m., German troops moved out and quickly advanced into the thick and dark, pine-tree-filled Ardennes. It was here, at the lowest level of the German and American armies, that the outcome would be determined. The Germans quickly routed many of the American front-line troops. Rattled by the overwhelming assault, many panicked and ran. However, the majority of the greatly outnumbered American soldiers, held their ground. From company commanders, to sergeants, and down to privates, there were heroic acts of defending small areas of terrain to keep the Germans from advancing. These small scale engagements, with companies and platoons fighting to the last man, were reminiscent of the fighting at the Alamo.

Generals Eisenhower and Bradley received reports of the German counterattack, but Bradley did not believe this was the main counterattack. Eisenhower however, realized the seriousness of the situation. He deployed the 82nd Airborne (All American) and the 101st Airborne (Screaming Eagles) into the fray. The 82nd was sent to the northern flank, and the 101st deployed to Bastogne, Belgium, and moved directly to the perimeter in a hold-at-all-cost mission.

On December 19, the town of Bastogne, and the troops defending this important crossroads town, had become surrounded by the German army. Per Hitler's directive, the town of Bastogne must be taken. The thirty-kilometer perimeter that protected Bastogne consisted of the 101st, the 10th Armored Division, combat engineers, and antitank units. On this day, while being battered by German artillery, the Bastogne defenders fought off a fifteen-division assault. As the days passed, the situation grew bleaker for the defenders of Bastogne. Casualties were mounting and the heavy cloud cover prevented the C-47 transport planes from delivering much-needed supplies. With the noose tightening around the defenders of Bastogne, the Germans were confident of victory.

As the defenders of Bastogne were making their valiant stand, another daring event was developing south of Bastogne. At 11:00 a.m. on December 19, Eisenhower met with his commanders to develop a plan to help Bastogne. During the meeting, Ike told General Patton that he wanted him to take his Third Army, which was on the southern boundary of the Bulge, turn it ninety degrees to the north, and conduct a counterattack to Bastogne. When Ike asked Patton how soon he could start, Patton responded, "As soon as you're through with me." Eisenhower asked Patton to be more specific. With confidence, Patton told Ike, "The morning of December twenty-first, with three divisions."

Believing this was too quick, as Patton's forces were driving east at the moment, Eisenhower told Patton, "Don't be fatuous, George. If you try to go that early, you won't have all three divisions ready, and you'll go piecemeal. You will start on the twenty-second, and I want your blow to be a strong one." The dialogue between the two generals electrified those at the meeting.

The thought of being able to turn the Third Army northward in such icy conditions and counterattack brought a new energy to the leaders. In fact, Patton and his staff had already drafted three plans for just such an operation, and prior to leaving his headquarters, each plan was given a single-word code. When Ike's meeting adjourned, Patton called his headquarters and delivered the code word. The men of the 4th Armored, 26th Infantry and 80th Infantry Divisions were on the move.

On December 22, a German officer, and a four-person delegation carried a white flag toward the American lines. With him was a letter from his commander addressed to the commander of the American forces at Bastogne. Contained in the handwritten message was the opportunity for an honorable American surrender. If the American commander rejected the proposal, then the American troops in Bastogne and its vicinity would be annihilated.

The message was delivered to the acting commander of the 101st Airborne, Brigadier General Anthony McAuliffe. Upon reading the message, McAuliffe responded with, "Nuts!" With no thought of surrender, McAuliffe conferred with his staff on what to say. They suggested that his initial reaction to the proposed surrender was fitting. Colonel Joseph Harper happily delivered McAuliffe's response back to the German officer. As Harper escorted him back to the perimeter, he could see the German was not sure of its meaning. Harper replied, "If you don't understand what 'Nuts' means, in plain English it is the same as 'Go to hell.'"

On December 26, after an amazing dash and counterattack to the north, through difficult terrain and harsh winter conditions, Patton's Third Army had made its way to the perimeter surrounding Bastogne. A vehicle from the 4th Armored Division was the first to enter into the 101st lines, and was soon followed by others. Bastogne would never fall into German hands. The heroic defense at Bastogne, and the counterattack of Patton's boys made history.

After the standoff at Bastogne, there was still a month's worth of fighting left to come. And while Bastogne had grabbed the headlines and the attention of the home front, there were plenty of other inspiring acts of bravery occurring at St.-Vith, Krinkelt, Noville, Café Schumann, Trois Ponts, Stavelot … The GIs in these areas possessed the same grit and will to win as those at Bastogne, and they too played major roles in turning back the German assault in the Ardennes.

While the Germans advanced deep into the Ardennes, the tide started to swing in favor of the Americans, and the German leaders in the field began to realize they would not reach Antwerp.

What Hitler and his leaders had not anticipated was the deadly weapon that had been deployed in the Ardennes—the American GI. His will to fight, his tenacity, and his adaptability during battle surpassed what the Germans believed he was capable of doing.

In all, 600,000 GIs were engaged in the fighting while 400,000 were in support roles. During this battle, almost 20,000 brave young men would perish. Another 40,000 were wounded, and 20,000 were taken as POWs. For the Germans, they sent close to 500,000 soldiers into the battle, and nearly 100,000 were killed, wounded, or captured.

Hitler's soldiers did not make history at the Battle of the Bulge. Instead, it was made by the American GI.

Andy Anderson

Army: Corporal, Third Army
Hometown: Indianapolis, Indiana
Career: Craftsman for AT&T

Anderson (center) in a German village

After graduating from high school in 1942, I was drafted at age eighteen, and in January 1943, I was sent to Camp Ellis, Illinois for basic training. After basic, I was sent to Camp Siebert, Alabama, where I learned I was to become part of a top-secret experiment. I ended up in Bushnell, Florida, for special training with the 94th Medical Gas Treatment Battalion.

While at Bushnell, some of us were assigned to the Canadian Army for thirty-one days. During this time, we learned about and saw the effects of mustard gas, which the Germans had used during World War I. The Allies were concerned it might be used again. We were also trained on how to disengage chemical weapons. Our group was sent to some wooded locations and fields, where we noticed stray dogs and cattle. The Canadian Air Force planes would fly overhead and drop mustard gas canisters. When they hit the ground, they exploded, releasing the gas, which caused a purple haze. You could see the effects dripping from the trees. The animals died almost immediately.

We wore special uniforms and gas masks to supposedly protect us. One of our guys did not get his mask on correctly and died. After we returned to our base and were ordered to remove our clothes and take a shower, we noticed that we all had burns on our skin. Seventy years later, the burns are still visible on my skin, especially if I am exposed to the sun. I found out years after the war that some of the guys involved in this experiment had health complications and had died prematurely. Many of their deaths have been attributed to exposure from this mustard gas experiment.

In May 1944, we left for England on the USS *Uruguay*. I remember looking at the Statue of Liberty as our ship pulled away. I thought to myself, "What is a nineteen-year-old kid going to do about that mess going on overseas?" I just wanted us to get there, take out Hitler, and return home. I still have the memory of "Lady Liberty" holding her torch of freedom high above her head, as we pulled away.

After our unit docked at Liverpool, England, we transferred to Pontypridd, Wales. In August, some thirty days after the D-Day invasion, we landed at Omaha Beach. Once inland, we set up our medical unit. To our surprise, a lot of our medical supplies, equipment, and food had been sunk on ships. In the meantime, the Germans had made a counterattack on the Americans who were in the area. After a few days, we continued on northward through France. I knew a lot of soldiers had been killed during and after the invasion and knew many more of us would die. I went to confession and asked one of our chaplains to baptize me again. I was glad he did this.

One day, we pulled into a field between thick hedgerows and unloaded our gear. That night, I was assigned as corporal of the guard. It was my first night in France and in enemy territory. Another guard and I didn't have a weapon. All we had were tent pegs. Can you imagine guard duty with only a tent peg? That was a very long night.

Since we had not experienced any mustard gas threats, our unit was assigned to perform medic duties and assist the doctors at the field hospitals. The first patient we received had been liberated from a German hospital. He was in a full-body cast and was so thin he could almost turn over in his cast. We sent him back to England for further medical attention.

Later, we moved through the Avranches Pass, where General Patton's Third Army had penetrated and was heading full blast toward Paris. During this time, our patients were German soldiers who had been wounded. Something I will never forget is when I saw one of our surgeons remove a German's gangrened leg with a meat saw. This is just one of the many terrible experiences I witnessed while working in the combat field hospitals. We were trained to do everything the medics could do.

One day, on an improvised airfield, there were about 100 of our big C-47 transport planes, which had landed to unload supplies and transport our wounded back to England. Within an hour, they were all gone. What an amazing sight!

During the Battle of the Bulge, which took place in France and Belgium, our medical unit was in Bastogne. We treated the casualties in tents, and there were so many casualties. Our C-47 air evacuation units were unable to land, and we could not take out our sick and wounded. We worked a lot of twenty-four-hour days attending to large numbers of wounded soldiers. We were so darned busy; I didn't have time to take a shit.

The first time I gave a guy a shot, I closed my eyes because I thought I was going to hurt him. We did not have food or water for about seven days, because the Germans made their counteroffensive, and we were surrounded. The weather conditions were terrible, with extreme cold and deep snow. Several of our new replacement soldiers were just eighteen-year-old kids with no experience. The Germans moved so quickly, and these kids were no match for the Germans. They were just in shock when they came to our medical tents.

When we, the Americans, were able to turn back the Germans, we were able to air-vac our sick and wounded back to England. During the Bulge, we treated about 1,200 a day. What we witnessed was terrible. Some of my former 94th buddies and I figured we had helped care for over 100,000 wounded GIs and Germans throughout the war. This figured out to be about 10,000 per month, including prisoners of war.

I treated all kinds of injuries, including burns. One guy was wrapped in a complete head bandage, which had two small holes for his nose and a small hole for his lips. His eyes were even covered. I can remember one guy who was severely wounded asking me for a razor blade or knife, so he could end his life. He said, "I lost my buddy, who had a wife and kids. There is nothing for me to live for."

Being able to help our wounded GIs was such an honor and privilege. When a wounded soldier was brought in for treatment, the first question many of them asked was, "How long will it be before I can get back to my unit?" These were brave men; most of them were only eighteen- to nineteen-years-old. One guy left a note for me under his pillow thanking me for helping him. He said he needed to get back to his outfit; he was gone the next morning.

There were only two times during the war that I remember sleeping under a roof. One time, we stayed in a German castle in the Bavarian Alps. The scenery was beautiful and seemed so far removed from the killing and pain of the war. A woman who was staying in the castle would repeatedly return to us and ask for food. When we became suspicious, some of us went upstairs and found a wounded German general for whom she had been caring. The general was actually glad to see American medics and doctors. We attended to his injuries, put him in an ambulance, and sent him to a place where he would receive more help. Overall, our doctors and medics did a tremendous job of caring for our men as well as the Germans. We tried to honor the Geneva Convention.

Since I traveled with the Third Army, I saw General Patton about four times. I never spoke to him, because I was afraid of him, as were many officers and his own soldiers. He was a great general and commanded respect from his troops. He showed no fear in combat. When we were in Gotha, Germany, I saw General Patton and General Bradley arrive in their Jeeps. The generals always had air cover. Being part of General Patton's Third Army meant we were always on the move. He was often called "Blood and Guts Patton," our blood and his guts. Patton was a great general and leader, but he could also be a "son of a bitch."

We remained in Gotha three to four days. One day, our chaplain took a group of us to Weimer to see the notorious German extermination camp at Buchenwald. This was the camp where the Nazi commander's wife made lamp shades out of human skin. When we entered the camp, we saw hundreds of dead bodies stacked like cords of wood on top of one another. Most were dead, but those still alive were so thin and weak they could not eat regular food. If we could find a vein, we fed them intravenously. The survivors, and those who were dead, looked like human skeletons. You could see their bones though their skin.

We went into the barracks and saw prisoners living among dead bodies, and fecal material was all over the floor. The odor was terrible. Bony hands reached out for food. Bodies were stacked against walls and in closets. After I saw the extermination ovens and the conditions in the camp, I began to question humanity. We could smell the stench of burning flesh from miles away. How could people in the nearby towns say they did not know this was happening? This is an experience I will never forget as long as I live. I took several pictures of these atrocities, and I still have them today, over sixty years later.

When we passed through French villages, we would often see some women with their heads shaved and walking naked in the streets. We learned that after the Germans had left the town, other townspeople punished these women for collaborating with the Germans.

We did not have time do anything but provide medical help for the wounded. We did whatever we were asked to do and whatever needed to be done. One time, I was asked to accompany the 11th Armored Division across the Rhine River. Stockpiles of mustard gas had been found, and we had to dispose of it. My training was put to use.

We were headed to Regensburg, Germany, when the war ended. Then, it was on to Paris, where some of the guys got a three-day pass and saw all of the sights. I did not get to go to Paris or Berlin. Our unit was assigned to watch for German SS members who were trying to escape. The SS would put on any uniform, other than their own, to try to avoid capture. A German SS soldier could be identified by a special tattoo stenciled below his left armpit. Many tried to burn off their tattoo, but it was obvious when they did. The SS would rather be captured by the Americans than captured by the Russians, because the Russians would brutally torture or kill them.

In July 1945, we returned by ship to Boston. I'll never forget the sight as we approached Boston. We were greeted by cheers and people waving flags; bands were playing, and there were fireworks. Walking down the gangplank made me feel thankful and proud to be an American. We even kissed the ground when we got off of the ship.

Throughout the war, I had witnessed and experienced many terrible things. I know the Lord was with me through all of this and helped to keep me going from day to day.

Phyllis Funk

Army: First Lieutenant, Third Army
Hometown: Corydon, Indiana
Career: Nurse

Funk serving in France

After graduating from nursing school at twenty-one, I enlisted in the army in October 1943. I was sworn in at Fort Harrison in Indianapolis, Indiana, and was sent to White Sulpher Springs, West Virginia.

The facility had been a luxury resort but was converted into a hospital. My first nursing experience was treating our injured soldiers who returned from the battle on Anzio Beach in Italy. As nurses, we treated all kinds of combat-related injuries and worked eight-hour days. While at White Sulpher Springs, I met General Eisenhower, who came to our ward to visit the wounded soldiers. He took time to shake the nurses' hands. Japanese Americans from Washington, D.C., were also interned here, at this time.

While awaiting orders to go overseas, I was married in the chapel in White Sulpher Springs. My husband returned to Fort Harrison, where he served as the provost marshal. It was fairly unusual for a military husband to remain stateside, while the wife was scheduled to go overseas.

In December 1943, we shipped out on the *Queen Mary* with troops and medical staff. We zigzagged across the Atlantic to avoid German submarines and landed in Scotland five days later. On the way there I saw the beautiful White Cliffs of Dover. From Scotland, I took the train to Stone, England, and we nurses stayed in private homes for three months. We would hike two to three miles to headquarters outside of Stone and hike two to three miles back later in the day. Our headquarters was a large country estate called Meaford Hall.

We landed on Omaha Beach on June 24, D-Day Plus Eighteen. In the rough seas, I remember climbing down the side of our transportation ship on rope ladders, just as the troops had to do. We loaded into boats called "Ducks" and waded ashore with the troops and our equipment. The Germans were firing at us from locations above the beach, and our ships were firing over our heads at the Germans. I guess I didn't have time to be too scared, because I knew we had an important job to do.

As part of the 35th Medical Evacuation Hospital, we had 40 nurses, 39 doctors and 217 enlisted men, who served as ward attendants. We were able to set up and break down our entire field hospital within three to four hours. My area of trauma care was to treat our soldiers who had serious head, chest, and abdominal injuries. We treated 39 patients in each of twelve wards. Twelve operating tables were in use twenty-four hours a day. Our evac hospital had 400 beds and was the first or second Allied hospital in France. The first week we provided medical care for 1,200 wounded soldiers. Our goal was to treat them and get them onto hospital ships within three days.

In late June 1944, we began our travels throughout France, and went to Carentan, Rennes, Le Mans, Insigny-sur-Mer, Ste.-Mere-Eglise, St.-Lo, Fountainebleau, Metz, and Nancy. At Nancy, we cared for nearly 4,900 injured troops in sixty-seven days.

During my nineteen months in France, Luxembourg, and Germany, we treated over 27,000 soldiers in 18 different locations. The wounded were brought to us by Red Cross trucks, jeeps, or any way they could get them to us. Once, I was assigned to care for a German POW, but the doctor I was with would not operate on the German because the doctor was Jewish. He told me what to do, and I did it. We treated several German POWs. I knew it was the right thing to do, but I didn't like to do it, because our boys needed care. I do think most of the injured German POWs were grateful to us for helping them.

While in St.-Lo, I particularly remember the "smell of death" all around us. Gangrene was another smell you don't forget. I know it was everywhere we were, and I do not know why I recall St.-Lo so vividly. It was at St.-Lo where we saw hundreds of our bombers fly over, bombing the Germans with 2,000 pound bombs. The ground would shake beneath our feet.

There were times when we were going through the Normandy hedgerows, and we came under German artillery and small-arms fire. One night, I left my tent and got in a foxhole with a GI, because we were under fire. When I returned to my tent, I saw bullets had ripped through it. At times, we were very close to the front lines, usually one to three miles back. Many times we could see and hear the artillery fire throughout the day and night.

I was transferred to the Third Army's 4th and 6th Armored Divisions, which were under the command of General Patton. Wherever Patton went, we followed him. At times, I saw General Patton return from the front lines, and he would visit with the soldiers in the hospital tents. He would give them a medal, if he thought they deserved one. He despised those soldiers whom he thought had "SIWs" (self-inflicted wounds), in order to get out of combat.

In late December 1944, it was extremely cold, and we were lying in the snow near the Ardennes Forest. It wasn't long until an officer came by and told us to move our field hospital back immediately. At the time, we did not know the Germans were advancing with their attack, which came to be known as the Battle of the Bulge. This was a brutal battle, and many of our soldiers were killed or severely wounded. On Christmas Day, 1944, we were sent to Metz, France. It was a miserable Christmas, and the weather was twenty-five degrees below zero with a heavy ground cover of snow.

While in the Ardennes, as we did in many locations, we had our hospital set up on one side of the road and our morgue on the other side. We treated most of the wounded in Luxembourg. One day I lost five young boys within an hour. I told my supervisor I wanted to go home, and she told me to get back to work. On another occasion, I was treating a severely injured GI. I gave him a stimulant to try to revive him. When he responded to the stimulant, he got angry with me and said, "Why did you do that? I saw a peaceful and beautiful place where the streets were lined with gold." He asked me to let him die peacefully. I feel he must have had a "glimpse of heaven."

One time, three of my nurse friends and I were on leave and decided to hitchhike to Paris, something we did not have permission to do. A French farmer picked us up and took us into Paris. Later on, a group of navy pilots saw us and asked if we wanted to ride along. They took us around Paris to see the sights. We all got lost and did not know how to get back to our units. The navy guys did not want to take us back, because they knew we were in trouble. Finally, we saw an American officer, and he had us returned in a command car. Needless, to say, when our colonel found out that we had been AWOL, he gave us the "what for!" using some "choice words."

Another time, I was on a troop train leaving the French Riviera when our train was wrecked because the Germans had sabotaged the railroad tracks. I was not hurt, and the other nurses and I provided emergency care for those who were injured. I heard that over 12 soldiers died in the crash.

One of my scariest memories is crossing the pontoon bridge over the Rhine River at night. I thought anytime we could go over the edge into the water. I have the greatest respect for our combat engineers and the work they did.

During my time overseas, I was involved in 227 days of combat nursing, often working nonstop twelve-hour days. My fellow nurses and I received five "Battle Stars," three of which we earned during the Battle of the Bulge.

We learned about the German surrender when we were in Erlanger, Germany. We were treating soldiers in a vacated school building and later moved out to the field. Since we slept on the ground, we had mice run through our hair and make nests in our bed rolls.

In the fall of 1945, I was sent to Camp Lucky Strike in France and shipped back home in October 1945, landing where I started, in Camp Kilmer, New Jersey. I called my husband, and he came to get me. As I look back, I think my nurse friends and I were young and dumb, but we were also brave. During my time in the war, I learned to live one day at a time doing whatever I had to do.

Irv Heath

Army: First Lieutenant, 4th Armored Division
Hometown: West Somerville, Massachusetts
Career: Insurance agency owner

General George Patton with his pearl handled pistol
(courtesy Andy Anderson)

I graduated from DePauw University in Greencastle, Indiana, in June 1941. After graduating I was hired by Brewer and Company in my hometown of Worcester, Massachusetts. When Pearl Harbor was attacked on December 7, 1941, I was in Baltimore, Maryland. The next day I called my boss and told him that I was coming home because my draft number was high on the list. Since I was not married, I figured I would be in the army very soon.

Right after Christmas, I joined the army and was sent to Fort Knox, Kentucky, for my basic training in the armored forces—tanks. Since I was a college graduate, I attended and graduated OCS (Officer's Candidate School) at Fort Knox as a tank officer. I was assigned to the 35th Tank Battalion, 4th Armored Division.

We were in England for six months before D-Day, and one day near the end of May 1944, the officers of the division went to a large theater on a U.S. base to hear General George S. Patton. It's something I'll never forget.

General Patton walked out onto the stage wearing his helmet, riding britches, and his two pearl-handled pistols. There was a shadow from his helmet, so I never saw his eyes. He stood there welcoming us to the "main event." He told us he had been involved in the sideshows in North Africa and Sicily, but now it was time for the main event. He said, "You have hunted deer or bears or wildcats, but they didn't shoot at you! Now, you will be hunting Germans, and those sons of bitches will kill you, if you don't kill him first." He went on and on talking in a very high-pitched voice. When he paused for a moment, you could hear a pin drop! He had blood running down the aisles! We hardly breathed for one and a half hours!

We landed on Utah Beach at Normandy D-Day Plus Thirty-Six. The beach was still a mess with burned-out vehicles and equipment. After the breakthrough in Normandy, we headed toward Germany. As we left Normandy, the French people stood along the roads giving us cider since they did not have much wine because the Germans had taken everything. One day, riding in the turret of my tank through a little French town, a Frenchman handed me a bottle. I took a big swig. I swallowed a mouthful, and it took my breath away. I could not breathe! It felt like I was on fire from my throat to my toes! What I swallowed was not hard cider or wine. It was Calvados, French liquor. My gunner realized what had happened and said, "Lieutenant, you are supposed to sip liquor."

In December 1944, we were in Alsace Lorraine, France, heading east when we received General Patton's order to change our direction. His orders were to head north over one hundred miles to Bastogne. We knew nothing about the big German offensive that had started. All we knew was the 101st Airborne Division had been trucked into Bastogne and ordered to hold it. They were completely surrounded by the Germans! The 4th Armored Division was to break through and relieve the 101st Airborne! A foot of snow was on the ground, and it snowed on and off every day, and the temperature was close to zero each morning.

By December 24, we were just two miles south of Bastogne, but we were not fighting yet. The weather was rotten, and the air force could not fly supplies into Bastogne. On the morning of December 26th, everything changed. The clouds were gone, the sun came up, and the sky was blue. The sun almost blinded us reflecting off the snow-covered ground. Overhead, we heard the roar of over one hundred cargo planes flying low to drop supplies to the 101st Airborne. Each item dropped had a different-colored parachute, red, orange, blue, green, which represented items such as food, ammunition, or medicine. The 4th Armored Division broke through into Bastogne before noon on December 26, 1944.

On December 27, my tank battalion was on the west side of Bastogne. My company had just taken a ridge, and we were waiting for the armored infantry to catch up. It was quiet and my tank driver got out of the tank to take a smoke. Suddenly, German artillery came in on us, and my driver was hit. I waited for the artillery to let up, and then got out to help him. He was dead. Just then more artillery came in, and I was hit in the leg. My leg was operated on in a big field hospital tent several miles west of Bastogne. I was put on a hospital plane and flown to England.

I returned to the 4th Armored Division on May 15, 1945, after the war in Europe had ended. We were in Pisek, Czechoslovakia, to link up with the Russian Army. There was a bridge in which we controlled one side and the Russians the other. The policy was that all German soldiers that fought the Russians had to be turned over to the Russians. When German soldiers were transported across the bridge, the Russians watched to see if the Nazi SS patch was on any of the collars, or if it had been torn off. If a German was suspected of being SS, the Russians would slit the soldier's shirt under the left arm. This is where an SS officer had his blood type tattooed on him. If an SS officer was found, he was shot on the spot and thrown over the bridge. We could never have gotten by with this, but the Russians did.

General Patton was a taskmaster. He was tough and demanding, but he knew what he was doing. On many occasions Patton passed us in his special field jeep heading to the front lines but never returned. It was all psychology on his part. The troops would always say, "Patton is up front, so it must not be that bad. We better get there." During battle, he would be at the front lines encouraging and directing his tanks and troops. When he told you to do something, you had better do it with no excuses. His charisma inspired us, and he was a respected leader who led from the front.

Time after time General Patton would use the 4th Armored as his lead division for the Third Army. We never let him down. General Patton said, "The accomplishments of this division have never been equaled. And by that statement I do not mean this war; I mean in the history of warfare. There has never been such a superb fighting organization as the 4th Armored Division." We were proud to be "George's Boys."

President Harry S. Truman saved my life in August 1945. The 4th Armored Division had already been assigned to an army base in California, and I would have been involved in the invasion of Japan. The death toll on both sides would have been in the millions, and the Japanese Islands would have been a wasteland. Japan started the war for the United States, and President Truman did the right thing to use the atomic bombs to end the war. If Germany had discovered how to make the atomic bomb before the United States, it would be a different world today.

World War II was a time when everybody was involved. It's hard to explain. It was almost two wars—one in Europe and one in the Pacific. No automobiles were made for four years. Many items were rationed, and many items you just could not get. Citizens got used to it and did not complain. Everyone just made the best of it and said, "Wait until the war is over." We have to tell the next generation how important it was to win World War II.

Lieutenant General George S. Patton, Jr.

"An Army is a team. It lives, sleeps, eats, and fights as a team. This individual heroic stuff is pure horseshit."

Patton was a tough, hard-charging leader whose flamboyant style inspired his troops to perform to the highest standard. Patton's lead from the front style earned him the respect of his soldiers, who nicknamed him "Blood and Guts." He commanded II Corps during Operation Torch in North Africa, and then led the Seventh Army in the invasion of Sicily. After the Allies secured the beachhead at Normandy, Patton's Third Army led the breakout of Normandy and raced across France. In December 1944, during the Battle of the Bulge, his forces raced northward to relieve a surrounded Bastogne and helped to repel the German offensive.

Merrill Huntzinger

Army: Staff Sergeant, 2nd Infantry Division
Hometown: Matthews, Indiana
Career: Print and broadcast sales

I was only twenty, when I was first introduced to combat. On June 21, 1944, D Plus Fifteen, we landed on Omaha Beach. Our infantry group assembled in an orchard above the beach, and three of us loaded into a jeep trailer. Our squad leader, Sergeant Ivy, sat in the jeep in front of us. I asked him where we were going, and he said, "We're going to hell, and if we are lucky, we will soon end up in heaven." It wasn't long before we smelled the terrible stench of dead farm animals and the dead German soldiers. As we pulled to the side of the road, our trailer ran over a land mine and the three of us were thrown from the jeep; fortunately, none of us was seriously hurt.

I was assigned to a machine-gun squad, and shortly after arriving, I was involved in heavy hedgerow fighting against the Germans as our unit pushed them back. During the night, we took turns pulling guard duty. It's a lonely, scary assignment because you're all alone, and you feel that the enemy has you in his sight, and you could be shot at any time.

On my eighth day in the hedgerows, Sergeant Ivy and Sergeant Cunningham met up with a jeep driver who was delivering rations and ammunition for our squads. When the sergeants were returning across an open field with our food and supplies, along with the jeep driver and a guy in a clean uniform, they got caught in a heavy mortar barrage and were pinned down about sixty yards from our foxholes. The jeep driver and the other guy got up and ran for it and jumped into my foxhole. They made it safely, but Ivy and Cunningham were both hit and still out in the field.

Ivy started yelling for help and said that Cunningham had been hit pretty badly. I asked the two guys in my foxhole if one of them would go with me, but they let me know there was no way they were going back out in the field. One of them said it would be suicide. I got my first aid kit and took off running out to Ivy and Cunningham with mortar shells hitting around me. I hit the dirt and started crawling to them when I felt something burning in my leg. I had been hit by shrapnel.

I kept crawling toward them, and when I finally reached Sergeant Ivy, I bandaged his wound above the knee. Sergeant Cunningham's chest was ripped open and full of shrapnel. He was barely conscious, and when the shelling stopped, Ivy and I dragged him back to the foxhole. Cunningham was dead by the time we got to the foxhole. Later, I was awarded a Bronze Star for Valor, and I thought, "Why?" Sergeant Cunningham was dead. The "other guy" turned out to be the chaplain, and he's the one who put me in for the award.

Our next combat activity happened when we were fighting our way through a residential area of Brest, France. We came under heavy German machine-gun fire and scrambled to an abandoned house. Once we were entrenched in the house, I began to lay down heavy machine-gun fire. The fighting in Brest was pure hell.

My unit was later engaged in the Battle of the Bulge in the Ardennes Forest. We were attacking a dam and were told to report to a small Belgian town, since the powerful German armored forces were headed toward Krinkelt, Belgium. We did a forced ten-mile march in heavy snow to reach the small town. Upon arrival, we took cover in a house. There was heavy fire from German infantry and Mark V Tiger tanks. Eight of us were captured by the Germans for about twelve hours. Later, some of our troops routed the Germans, and we were free.

Seeking cover, we came to another abandoned house and moved up to the attic. We took positions looking out windows, so we were able to shoot the Germans below us in the street. We were 'picking them off until a German Mark V tank spotted us and fired on our location and hit us twice. Before he could fire another round at us, one of our antitank crews fired and took out the tank. We would have been killed if the tank had not been destroyed. Later on, some of the guys from other companies came through, and we went with them until one of our half-tracks came by picking up dead GIs and let us go with them.

After getting a bad case of trench foot, due to the cold and snow, I was sent to French and English hospitals and finally sent home. In less than two years, I had witnessed and taken part in so much killing and saw many dead and wounded GIs and Germans. It was an experience

I will never forget. To me, the worst thing about combat was worrying about being killed without anyone in my family realizing the misery I was going through.

John Kerr

Army: Tech Sergeant, 78th Infantry Division
Hometown: Greencastle, Indiana
Career: Elementary teacher and principal

Kerr (back left) with men from his unit

I served in northern France, and was assigned to an Intelligence and Reconnaissance (I&R) section/platoon. Our job was to help gather and report intelligence to our troops in the field. We provided vital information for General Patton's Third Army as they prepared for the Battle of the Bulge.

During the Battle of the Bulge, our troops had to take out German machine-gun nests, and many were engaged in hand-to-hand combat, especially the 106th Infantry Division. We lost two entire regiments of men. They were either killed, wounded, or captured. We were reminded that "If you can see the enemy, they can see you."

One of my lasting memories about the Battle of the Bulge was the cold, harsh weather and the total darkness at night due to the heavy forest area. Soldiers walked through snow with the tanks, and due to long exposure to the freezing conditions, many developed severe frostbite, known as trench foot. It was true "hell on earth!"

Wayne Mocas

Army: 83rd Infantry Division
Hometown: Indianapolis, Indiana
Career: Laboratory Technician

American soldiers in the Ardennes during the Battle of the Bulge

As a nineteen-year-old young man, I was involved in heavy combat fighting in the Ardennes forest in northern France. It was called the Battle of the Bulge. The forest was so thick you couldn't drive a truck through it, and at night, it was pitch black and very cold.

I will never forget the day I killed a German soldier at close range; I didn't want to do that. Another time there were three German soldiers crossing a river, and my sergeant shot one, and the others surrendered. A German medic came up to try to help the two soldiers, who were wounded. My sergeant ordered me to shoot him, but I refused since he was a medic.

Two other lasting memories were when I saw one of my buddies killed and the other wounded. That day I grew up real fast. I also remember going into an old building after we shot a German sniper. I went down to the basement and found three German soldiers. They were only fifteen or sixteen years old and were scared. They surrendered, and I turned them over to the MPs, who sent them to an American POW camp.

I received my Purple Heart because I had severe frostbite on both feet and was sent to an army hospital for eight months. One of my buddies was captured and sent to a German POW camp. He had frostbite so bad that they had to cut off both of his feet.

17

SUPREMACY IN THE SKY

The Air Corps

"Offense is the essence of air power."
—General Henry "Hap" Arnold

Their names ranged from the sweet, *Betty Jane*, *Mary*, and *Paulette*, to those that sent a message, *Special Delivery*, *Hitler's Headaches*, and *Slightly Dangerous*. Some became famous, *Memphis Belle* and *Enola Gay*. The names painted on the noses of the aircraft had special meaning to the flight and ground crews, as did the planes upon which the crews worked and flew.

The aircraft themselves gained their own place in World War II lore, as they ventured into the blue enemy skies. Crews debated and shared their opinions as to which aircraft were superior. The bombers who delivered their payloads were called Mitchell, Liberator, Flying Fortress, and Superfortress. American planes maneuvered through the skies and fought wing to wing engaging the Axis. Our pilots flew the Lightning, Mustang, Corsair, Hellcat (all fighters), Avenger (torpedo bomber), and Dauntless (dive bomber).

Air battles and raids were etched into history as defining moments that helped turn and sustain supremacy in the sky. Still reeling from the attack on Pearl Harbor, and with America's morale low, President Roosevelt ordered a high-risk bombing raid. The name Tokyo was on the briefing board. On April 12, 1942, the aircraft carrier USS *Hornet* carried sixteen B-25 Mitchell bombers to the liftoff point in the Pacific. In bad weather, Colonel Jimmy Doolittle and his "Doolittle's Raiders" vaulted off the *Hornet's* deck and journeyed to the capital city and officially delivered the war to Japan. While the raid itself did little damage, the psychological impact was great, as Japan's citizens and leaders now realized they were not out of harm's way.

As ground forces gained control of small islands throughout the Pacific, airstrips were rapidly constructed, so they could be used for intensive bombing operations against Japan's homeland. In June 1944, 60 Superfortresses conducted a bombing raid on Yawata to destroy a steel and iron facility. This was the first raid against Japan since Doolittle's raid. Throughout 1944, daylight missions were conducted against aircraft production facilities. In 1945, the missions switched from daylight to nighttime attacks, and on March 10–11, for more than three hours, 300 Superfortresses pounded Tokyo with deadly incendiaries. Other cities would soon encounter the same devastating raids.

In the European Theater, Ploesti, Schweinfurt, and Berlin are synonymous with significant bombing raids. On August 1, 1943, 176 Liberators attacked the high-value oil complex at Ploesti, Romania, in a daring raid that severely damaged the refineries. Fifty-four bombers were lost in the raid, along with 500 airmen. Within a few weeks, the target was Schweinfurt, a ball bearing plant deep within the Reich. The Flying Fortresses encountered several waves of German fighters as they made their way to their targets. Sixty planes and 600 airmen did not return to their airfields. In March 1944, while being escorted and protected by Mustangs, American bombers delivered their first payload to Hitler's Berlin. Air battles and bombings continued above the Reich into spring 1945, with the last major bombing being the blanketing of Dresden.

Based out of Italy was the famed black fighter squadron known as the Tuskegee Airmen. Bombing crews were delighted to see the "Red Tails" as their escorts on the long bombing raids.
During their escort missions, it was reported that not one bomber was lost due to enemy fighter planes.

The names of individuals play a significant role in honoring the heroics of all who served in the Air Corps and air forces of World War II. Some names have become legendary, such as Paul Tibbets, who piloted the Enola Gay; Pappy Boyington of the "Black Sheep Squadron"; Jimmy Doolittle, leader of the first raid on Tokyo; Benjamin O. Davis, Jr., commander of the Tuskegee Airmen; and the top ace fighter pilot, Richard Bong. By knowing these names, we realize there are thousands who we are not familiar with, men who helped ensure victory in the skies above. They were mechanics, crew members, and pilots who did their jobs without glory.

Arthur Carter, Sr.

Army Air Corps: Sergeant, 477th Bombardment Group
Hometown: Indianapolis, Indiana
Career: Federal auditor

When I was drafted at age nineteen, I was recruited to become a pilot. The War Department thought that blacks weren't smart enough to be pilots. Finally, the War Department decided to recruit blacks to form an all-black fighter and bomber squadron. I was sent to the Alabama Tuskegee Institute for my training and started as a member of the 320th College Training Detachment. Part of our job was to train the cadets to become pilots. Later, I was trained as a mechanic to work on the engines of the B-17 and B-29 bombers.

We became known as the American Black Air Corps. We had over 450 fighter pilots (nearly 1,000 trained overall) in Italy and Europe, and our fighter squadrons were considered some of the best and most highly decorated in the war. One of our P-51 Mustang fighter squadron escort units never had an American bomber shot down during its escort missions.

One of the things I remember most is that we were segregated from the white people on the base. These were the doctors, nurses, support staff, and officers. We had to stay in our own area. I was even angry and bitter after the war because of this. I also earned a college degree and still could not find a good job due to the racial prejudice that still existed. However, I am a patriot and proud that I served my country and am proud to be an American.

My most special memory is meeting the famous black inventor, scientist, and educator, George Washington Carver. I was able to go through his laboratory to see his inventions and projects.

Walter Copper

Army Air Corps: First Lieutenant, 2519th Unit
Hometown: Newark, Ohio
Career: Director of market development, IG Technologies

Copper at Curtis Field in Brady, Texas, 1943

When I was a young boy, I built model airplanes, and I always wanted to be a pilot. I was originally trained to become a fighter or bomber pilot, navigator, or bombardier. My training was extensive, as we studied at the University of Alabama for engineering science and received flight training at various bases across the country

At this early time in the war, the United States did not yet have enough fighter planes or bombers. Since there were very few military-trained flight instructors, we were trained by civilians. I learned to fly my first plane after about eight hours of instruction. We then had to learn how to fly twin-engine planes in our advanced training. After our advanced training, we were sent to Fort Worth, Texas, to learn how to fly the B-24 Liberator bomber. The first B-24s saw action in the Pacific, where they flew combat missions, dropping bombs on Japanese shipping ports.

After our training, 250 of us were commissioned as second lieutenants, and I was twenty years old at the time I received my pilot's wings. I was hoping to be sent overseas to be a bomber pilot. When the orders came down, 175 of my classmates were sent overseas for combat missions, but my name was not on the list, and I was concerned why it wasn't. A couple of days later, I was informed that I would become one of the first pilot instructors for our B-24 bombers. This did not ease my disappointment because I had wanted to go to Europe with my buddies; however, I later realized what I was doing was very important.

Today, there is only one B-24 Liberator bomber remaining, and it is used to fly in air shows across the country. It has been flown in air shows for the past twenty-one years. As an aircraft commander instructor, I was one of the first to fly this same plane during training.

At the beginning of World War II, we had 319,000 aviation cadets assigned for pilot training, but only 193,000 graduated as pilots. I was fortunate to have trained many of them. Another interesting fact that many people do not know is that when World War II started in 1939, the United States had only 175,000 military personnel. By the time the war ended in 1945, we had over 16,000,000 men and women who served in some military capacity at home and abroad.

Fred DeBruzzi

Air Corps: Captain, 8th and 11th Air Force
Hometown: Chicago, Illinois
Career: Aeronautical engineer

P-38 Lightning

I was a student at the University of Florida when my friend and I heard that the Army Air Corps needed pilots. The pilot training requirements were changed so an applicant needed only two years of college rather than four. We went through our preflight and pilot schools together and finally earned our fighter pilot wings after two years of intensive training. He was later shot down and killed during the Korean War.

As part of a fighter squadron, my friend and I were sent to the Allied Army Air Force base in Andover, England, as part of the 8th Air Force. Upon our arrival, the Allies had control of the skies. The German fighter pilots and planes were outstanding, but we had more planes, fuel, and pilots. My first combat action was serving as fighter escort for our B-17 bombers flying missions over Germany.

We flew in formations of four planes, and I served as wingman for our element leader. My job was to protect his back when we broke off to engage enemy fighters. I learned from flying bomber escort missions that the bomber pilots and their crews were some of the bravest people I knew. They experienced high casualty rates because they had to contend with heavy antiaircraft fire, enemy fighter planes, and the possibility of running out of fuel. Another high risk factor was they had to fly 35 missions. Some of the men even flew more.

After we completed our escort runs, we were ordered, "with no official approval," to engage in what were called "hit-the-deck" runs. This involved making attacks on railroad tracks, trains, convoys, oil refineries, ammunition supplies, and other suspected enemy targets. During these attacks, we flew as low as fifty feet above the ground at a speed of over 200 miles per hour. We were told to return to base with our ammunition trays empty. I'm not proud to say that I know innocent civilian farmers and families were killed in some of our attacks.

My first "kill" was when we attacked a German airfield and one of their fighter pilots was taking off. I hit him with my .50 caliber machine guns. His plane exploded, and I had to fly through the flaming debris. It was tough returning to our base after a mission and finding out some of our buddies would not be coming home. Some were shot down, and others ran out of fuel on the way back and crashed. I never kept track of my total number of combat missions (sorties). I know there were too many for me to remember.

After four months in Europe, we were sent to the Japanese-controlled Aleutian Islands in the Pacific Theater as part of the 11th Air Force. During my time there, some of us had the distinct privilege and honor to work with the American aviation hero and pioneer Charles Lindberg. Lindberg was the first person to fly solo over the Atlantic in a single-engine plane. At the time, he was an employee of the Lockheed Aircraft Company, which produced our newest and most effective fighter plane, the P-38. He taught us the aerodynamics involved in flying the faster and more heavily gunned plane and how best to conserve fuel. I am convinced many American pilots' lives were saved because of what they learned, minimizing their chance of running out of fuel.

The P-38 was the best plane I flew. It had such great maneuverability in an aerial dogfight and was armed with four .50 caliber machine guns and a 20mm cannon in the nose of the plane. On one of our sorties, the air controller radioed to tell me a Japanese Zero was flying above me, and I was to take him out. The cloud cover was so heavy I couldn't see him. It was freezing cold in the cockpit, and my engines almost stalled on me. I finally saw him and was able to dive and shoot him down; again flying through the explosion was a scary experience. This was my second recorded kill.

While flying in the Pacific Theater, we also had to shoot down Japanese hot air balloons they loaded with bombs. By using the easterly jet streams, the intent was to get the balloons to land in the Pacific Northwest of the United States and explode upon landing. I remember shooting down six of them. It was like shooting fish in a barrel. If any of the explosive balloons would have landed, it could have caused a panic. This is why the government kept our mission secret.

After serving about twelve months in the Pacific, I eventually returned home to the States. A proud moment in my military career was earning my silver fighter pilot wings. It is a highlight of my life besides serving with many outstanding men who shared a common purpose—win the war and go home. We won the war, but, sadly, many never returned home. At the beginning of the war, I did not think there was any way for us to win, since we were so desperately unprepared. I am so proud of my country and what we accomplished at home and abroad.

E. Stuart Felton

Army Air Corps: First Lieutenant, 13th Air Force
Hometown: Cincinnati, Ohio
Career: Investment banker and financial analyst

Felton (L) with his brother Lawrence

I was nineteen when some of my college friends and I enlisted one day after the bombing of Pearl Harbor, December 7, 1941. My pilot training courses took place at Santa Ana and Visalia, California, and I did my bomber navigator training at Mather Field in Sacramento. A close friend and I chose to fly combat missions.

Our training was completed in 1942, and our first assignment was on a B-18. We flew several missions searching for the Japanese naval fleet, while trying to locate World War I American pilot hero Eddie Rickenbacker. His plane was lost en route to an island in the Pacific. We did not find him, but he did survive his plane's crash-landing in the Pacific.

In 1942, I was sent to Espiritu Santo in the New Hebrides to obtain jungle gear, where I joined an experienced B-17 crew on Guadalcanal in the Solomon Islands. We were part of the 13th Air Force but became known as the "Cactus Air Force." My first completed mission was to the island of Bouganville. From January 1943, my crew and I flew our bombing missions "island hopping" across the Pacific.

After rotating among three different bomb squadrons, I eventually became a part of the 72nd Bomber Squadron, 5th Bomb Group. I became the squadron lead navigator. As the navigator, I had to do what is called "celestial navigation," which is memorizing sets of constellations and stars in order to establish a flight pattern. I completed 62 missions throughout the Southwest, the West, and the Central Pacific. Some of the bombing runs were made at Suva, New Guinea; the Northern Solomons; the southern Philippines; the Fiji Islands; and Truk. On the mission to Truk, on June 7, 1944, I was assigned to fly as a trainer pilot for a new crew's first combat mission. I protested, because I wanted to fly with my own crew, but my protest was rejected. Had I gone with my own crew I would have been killed, as my plane, the *Faunce*, did not make it back.

Any bombing mission was dangerous because of enemy fighters, antiaircraft flak, and running out of fuel. On one mission, I was flying with hundreds of other planes, trying to locate the Japanese naval fleet when we flew into a full-blown typhoon. I wasn't sure we were going to survive.

Another mission involved an emergency landing on Guadalcanal. While returning to our airfield, a Japanese light cruiser hit us and knocked out three of our four engines. Our pilot had to do a belly landing, since we had no wheels and no engines remaining. How he landed our plane safely is a miracle. At the time, I was not scared, because it happened so quickly. I was just glad to be alive. Someone once said, "There are no atheists in foxholes or on airplanes."

During our 62 missions, the last 40 were staged from the Admiralty Islands. We flew some of the longest over-water bombing missions ever flown without an electronic guidance system. Flying long distance missions increased the danger. On one of our missions, our plane was only one of three to return safely out of seventy other planes. In some cases, planes did not have enough fuel and had to return to base. In other situations, our planes ran out of fuel and crashed into the ocean. The fatality rate of our squadron during the war was 60 to 65 percent. The 13th Air Force became the principal destructive force attacking Japan's powerful and distant bases.

Bougainville was a major air and naval base for the Japanese, who were using this location to try and retake Guadalcanal. Our navy decided to bombard the area, leaving us just enough room so our planes could land and refuel, since we were headed to bomb the Japanese headquarters at Truk. When the navy captured the landing strip, the Japanese controlled the mountain ridge facing the landing strip. The Japanese used their heavy antiaircraft guns and shelled our planes while refueling. The shelling was constant and went throughout the night. The sound reminded me of freight trains. Eventually, the Japanese began their retreat, and Bougainville was no longer of logistical significance.

On June 4, 1945, I returned to the States. Our captain flew under the Golden Gate Bridge, which was prohibited and was a dangerous thing to do.

Bill Goodman, Jr.

Army Air Corps: Captain, 5th Air Force
Hometown: Chicago Heights, Illinois
Career: District sales manager for Inland Steel

Goodman's crew in Tonopah, Nevada, April 1944

I served in the Pacific for nineteen months with the 408th Squadron, 22nd Bomb Group. I was a pilot of a B-24 Liberator bomber, and I flew in 38 combat missions.

Many times during our combat missions, several planes were shot down or crashed. The reality of losing our buddies hit us when we returned from the next day's missions. As we departed from our plane, we would see the footlockers of the dead airmen gathered up and ready to be sent home.

The commander of our squadron was Colonel "Robbie" Robinson. He had bright red hair, so his nickname was "Red." On one mission, our plane was second in line to take off, and the colonel was in the lead plane. While we were waiting to take off, we watched his plane move down the runway. When he tried to lift off, his plane could not get enough elevation. The plane crashed into some trucks at the end of the runway and burst into flames, killing all ten crew members. All they found of Colonel Robinson was some of his red hair in the wreckage. In our colonel's memory, we named our bombing squadron the "Red Raiders."

On another mission our plane was hit by antiaircraft fire, and two of our engines were knocked out. My copilot and I were ready to ditch the plane into the China Sea, and the crew was ready to bail out, but, fortunately, we landed the plane safely.

Another time, we were taking off, and our landing wheels collapsed. We slid one thousand feet down the runaway, and the nose wheel of the plane came right through the cockpit where my copilot and I were sitting. We couldn't believe we all walked away without the bombs exploding.

Mark Griffin

Army Air Corps: First Lieutenant, 8th Air Force
Hometown: Indianapolis, Indiana
Career: Retired Air Force; chief architect of Indiana for the
Department of Housing and Urban Development

B-24 Liberators drop bombs on the Ploesti oil refinery in Romania

After my high school graduation, two friends and I joined the Army Air Corps. I was eighteen when I enlisted. During my pilot training I learned to fly some of the Army Air Corps' best planes, the B-17, B-24, B-25, and the P-51 Mustang. One of the buddies who enlisted with me was killed on his first bombing mission, and the other one was killed in a plane crash after the war.

I was stationed in England as a member of the 66th Bomb Squadron, 44th Bomb Group, where I was a pilot of a B-24 Liberator. My crew flew 35 combat missions, and we were a part of the bombers who dropped the first bombs on Berlin, Germany, and on the Germans' oil fields in Ploesti, Romania. Most bombing missions were designed for mass destruction of the targets— Nazi factories and oil fields. Bombing runs would last about twenty to thirty minutes, but an entire mission could last eight hours from takeoff to target and the return to our base.

The German fighter pilots were very good, and we were often under attack since, early in the war, we did not have fighter support. Later on, we had the P-51 Mustang American fighter pilots, who provided us excellent air cover and shot down many German Messerschmitt fighters. German antiaircraft guns were constantly bombarding us on our missions. Contrary to what you see in the movies, when the big shells explode in the air, the flak is not black smoke clouds. They are bright red fireballs.

Most of the time, we flew in close formation in groups of three bombers. This allowed more visibility and firepower for our turret gunners. Besides being hit by fighter planes and antiaircraft flak, one of our main concerns was having enough fuel to return to our base. Some bombers were lost because they ran out of fuel; however, most bombers lost were shot down. On one of our missions, our number three engine was blown off by an antiaircraft shell. I knew we were going to have to make an emergency landing, which was always dangerous. Fortunately, we were able to do a "belly landing" on an emergency airstrip in Dover, England.

My most memorable mission was a bombing run we made over Royan, France. The Germans were entrenched in concrete bunkers shelling our ships off the French coast. The Germans' big guns had to be taken out, so the entire 8th and 15th Air Corps was dispatched to bomb them. It was amazing to see about a 1,000 bombers involved in one attack. We destroyed the German fortification in two days.

All of the bombers carried four 2,000 bombs, which were our most powerful bombs at the time. Our bombardier dropped three of the bombs on the targets, but the fourth bomb got struck in the bomb bay area. I told my engineer to kick it out with his feet. He was finally able to dislodge it. The terrible part was we were beyond our target, and the bomb exploded on a French farmhouse. If we had not been able to get rid of the bomb, there was danger of being hit by enemy fire or landing and the bomb exploding. If that had happened, the force of the explosion would have killed many pilots and crews.

In World War II, we had a common cause and a defined purpose. We were in it to win, and we did! I was proud to have served my country, and I hope that the present and future generations realize that America is the best country in the world. We are not perfect, but we are the best of the rest!

Ken Hamilton

Army Air Corps: First Lieutenant, 340th Fighter Squadron
Hometown: Tipton, Indiana
Career: Business owner-Exhibits and Displays

Hamilton (L), Tex Williams (C), and Crew Chief
at Itami Air Strip in Osaka, Japan, January 1946

I joined the Army Air Corps at age twenty. My four brothers also served during World War II. Two of them served in the South Pacific, and the other two were in Europe. Five brothers serving at the same time was fairly unusual. Luckily, all of us came home safely from the war.

I had a lot of training before I earned my wings to become a pilot. It started with basic training in Miami, Florida, and after that I was sent to Indiana Central College in Indianapolis, Indiana, for training in mathematics, weather, and aircraft identification. I was sent to San Antonio, Texas, where I was selected for pilot training. For my advanced training, I was stationed at Moore Field in Mission, Texas, where I received my wings.

On a training flight in Idaho, we were about to land when one of the wheels locked up. When the plane hit the landing strip, it flipped over. During the accident I was knocked unconscious for a period of time. Somehow, while the plane was flipping over, I remembered to turn off all of the control switches. This probably kept the plane from catching fire or exploding.

From Hamilton Field in San Francisco, California, we were transported to the South Pacific to serve as part of the 340th Fighter Squadron, based in Biac, New Guinea. The plane we had trained to fly was the P-47 Thunderbolt, but one morning, we were given new flight manuals and told to read them. We were going fly the P-51 Mustang. While I had no previous training with the Mustang, it was a great plane to fly. We transferred from Biac to Ie Shima, a small island off the northwest coast of Okinawa, and this became our permanent base of operations. Ie Shima is where war correspondent Ernie Pyle was shot and killed by a Japanese sniper.

The first plane I flew was named the *Big Mac II*, but later I changed the name to *Bonnie*, my wife's name. It was our job to fly escort missions for our B-29 bombers, which were dropping bombs on strategic locations on Okinawa. By this time, the Japanese air force was pretty much decimated, and they offered us little resistance. We also flew escort for our PBY Navy rescue planes, which picked up our downed pilots in the Pacific. These pilots performed some amazing rescue missions.

Our flight group flew many missions as fighter escorts or performed dive-bombing runs. On one of our dive-bombing runs over southern Japan, I was flying at about eight thousand feet, and my engine totally stalled. I did all of the functions we were taught, but the engine would not start. I had to make a decision. Was I going to remain on natural cruise or parachute out of my plane? By a miracle, my engine restarted, and I was able to return to base. On that day, God was my copilot. Another pilot in our squadron experienced the same engine problem. However, he was not able to restart his plane and had to parachute out over the ocean. Parachuting out of a P-51 Mustang is hard and dangerous, if you do not get yourself into the right position. Evidently, when he was bailing out, the rear stabilizer of the plane caught him. His body was not found for over a week.

When we did dive-bombing runs, we carried one 500 pound bomb under the belly of our plane. When we got to our target, we broke formation and formed a "string." We lined up behind each other single file, made our dives and pulled up. Often, there was flak from the Japanese antiaircraft guns. Fortunately, no one in my flight group was ever hit. On one of our missions, I was the flight leader. A flight consisted of four fighter planes flying in a formation. We were flying low to the ground, and when I saw we were approaching some high tension electrical wires I radioed for my team to pull up. Upon our return, we noticed one of our pilots was missing. Below us, we saw his crashed Mustang. He must have hit the wires.

On another mission, we saw four Japanese Zeroes flying below us, and we pursued them as they tried to break away. I was so close to one of the Zeroes I could see the pilot's face. He looked about sixteen years old. One of our guys shot down one of the planes. If you shot down an enemy plane, and it was confirmed by another pilot, when you returned to your base you would do a "rollover" indicating you had made a "kill."

I witnessed a part of history. After the atomic bombs were dropped, P-38s and a B-25 were selected to fly from Ie Shima to Tokyo. Their job was to escort the Japanese bomber carrying the surrender party to Ie Shima. I had hoped our P-51s would be assigned as part of the escort, but we were not. I watched as our planes returned, and I saw the Japanese delegation board one of our C-54s for the flight to the USS *Missouri* to sign the surrender documents.

Our fighter squadron, the "Sky Devils," was sent to Japan during the occupation. We flew surveillance missions out of Osaka over various airfields in Japan to ensure there was no military activity.

I was asked if I thought we would win the war. There was never any doubt in my mind that we would win.

James Lee Hutchinson

Army Air Corps: Tech Sergeant, 8th Air Force
Hometown: Bedford, Indiana
Career: Elementary teacher, principal, and assistant superintendent

A drawing made by Hutchinson while sitting in his plane

I grew up in the hills of southern Indiana in the poverty of the Great Depression, as did many of the teenage boys who served in World War II. Drafted out of high school, I was too young to vote but not too young for combat. Teenagers on aircrews were part of the sixteen million young men who fought and died for their country.

It was June 12, 1943, my eighteenth birthday, when I received my draft notice. I was a high school junior who needed only six credits to graduate. My induction into the army took place in Louisville, Kentucky, on August 4. I was then sent to Fort Benjamin Harrison in Indianapolis to be processed for the infantry, but I volunteered for the Army Air Corps.

My basic training was in Amarillo, Texas, as a member of the Army Air Cadet Program. I was a volunteer for the Volunteer Flight Trainees (VFT), and as an air cadet, I was ready for training as a pilot, bombardier, or navigator. We were mostly a group of high school kids. I bought a sterling silver air cadet ring that became my "lucky ring" throughout the war. I still wear it today.

I eventually "washed out" as an air cadet and was assigned to radio school. My next destination was Sioux Falls, South Dakota, where I received my radio training. After radio school, I was sent to gunnery school in Yuma, Arizona. I was proud to have earned my coveted silver (pewter) gunner's wings and my corporal's stripes.

In August 1944, I was sent to Sioux City, Iowa, for aircrew training and was assigned to a B-17 Flying Fortress bomber crew as a radio operator and gunner. Our crew was now in the combat training phase. The crew represented a cross section of the country, as not one of the ten crew members was from the same state.

On November 4, 1944, we left from New York Harbor aboard the HMS *Queen Mary* headed for the 8th Air Corps base in Eye, England. Shortly after I arrived, I learned that my best boyhood buddy had been killed during combat in France.

Our crew was one of three replacement crews assigned to the 490th Bomb Group. We trained in flying close formations for three days and were considered ready for combat. The tour of duty for bomb crews at the time had been raised to 35 missions, and we thought, "Let's get on with it!" Little did we realize, of those 30 boys, 13 would die, and 3 would be wounded.

Two days after our assignment to our crew, we were alerted to fly our first mission, and it was almost our last. I remember that cold, snowy December morning when we rode out to our bomber. I was "shaking like a leaf," but not just from the cold.

Our target was Berlin, the German capital, which was one of the most heavily defended areas in Germany. The 8th was told to expect 300 or more antiaircraft guns and lots of German Luftwaffe fighters. We had a large protection from our P-51 and P-47 fighters, which did an excellent job. Our targets were technical buildings and labs as well as railroad yards and fuel supply areas. We were flying in last place in the low squadron of the bomber formation, which was called "Tail-end Charlie or "Coffin Corner," since it was a place you did not want to be, because it was easier to get picked off by German fighter planes.

Somewhere over enemy territory, our number three engine developed a fuel problem, and we began losing power and air speed, and lagging behind the formation. A lone bomber is in a dangerous situation flying over enemy territory. It is "easy money" for enemy planes. To see your group moving away from you is a sickening feeling. We were too late to abort, and our only chance was getting our engine running or if one of our fighters escorted us back to friendly territory. Since there were no escort fighters in sight, we were lucky that our engine regained power, and we were able to catch up with our group and take our place in formation.

When we reached the Initial Point (IP), it was my job to send radio information back to our base. The formation was to complete a fifteen-mile bomb run to the targets. Our gunners manned their .50 caliber machine guns preparing for the hell they knew was coming. It was our crew's first flight into a sky filled with antiaircraft fire. The black smoke from the bursting 88mm shells spewed thousands of pieces of jagged metal flak into the sky. The plane shook from close explosions, and flak pinged off of our plane. The shells exploded, just like a shotgun shell shoots buckshot at a rabbit, but this time we were the "rabbit"! This was a very frightening experience.

Thirty-six B-17 Flying Fortresses followed their squadron leader, and each dropped ten 500 pound bombs on target and then headed back to our base in England. Dozens of German fighters began pursuing us but were intercepted by escort fighters. Our heavy bombers were escorted by more than 800 P-51 Mustang and P-47 Thunderbolt fighters.

We witnessed an unbelievable series of air combat, called "dogfights." Our fighter pilots were superior and outnumbered the enemy. The German fighter pilots took heavy losses, which never could be replaced. The next morning, after returning to base, the *Stars and Stripes* newspaper said our 8th Air Force bombers had hit a vital munitions plant in Berlin, and our fighters had shot down 80 German fighters. Only one of our 490th Bomb Group's planes went down on that raid. It had been damaged by flak, fell behind the formation, and was shot down by a group of Luftwaffe FW-190 fighters.

The entire crew was listed as MIA (missing in action). They had met the terrible fate that we had escaped earlier in the mission. Violent deaths and injuries were facts of life for the men and teenagers on the heavy bombers. There were times when I wondered if I would ever see my twentieth birthday. My "lucky air cadet ring" may have helped, but I know it was my mother's prayers and God's help that got me through the war.

As bomber crews, we often flew on oxygen at 25,000 feet, nearly five miles high. The temperature would reach forty degrees below zero, and our oxygen masks could freeze up. We had to wear special electric suits, gloves, and socks under all of our heavy clothing to keep from freezing. Our 8th Air Force bomber formations were never turned back from a mission by enemy ground fire or fighters while flying over deadly skies. Some 26,000 men (mostly boys) of the 8th Air Force—bomber crews, pilots, and ground support units—were killed in the World War II aerial crusade to destroy Hitler's Third Reich.

World War II was a battle of survival for the United States. It is my hope that present and future generations will know the sacrifices these men and women made to preserve our freedom and the freedom of others.

During the war, I flew 20 combat missions, fourteen of which were as lead crew. Before I returned to the States in the summer of 1945, I calculated that I had spent over 300 hours in a B-17 Flying Fortress.

Harry Leavell

Army Air Corps: Sergeant, 1170th College Training Detachment
Hometown: Richmond, Indiana
Career: Firefighter

Harry Leavell (second row, far left) at Tuskegee Institute

As a boy, I wanted to be a pilot, so I saved some money when I was in high school and took some flying lessons. I volunteered to go into the service because I wanted to be a fighter pilot. I was sent to basic training in Biloxi, Mississippi. When we took the train to Biloxi, the other black soldiers and I had to stay in a designated train car away from the whites. One of the white guys told me if I didn't, they would start beating on me. On one of my furloughs home, I took my wife to a movie in Richmond, Indiana. I tried to buy tickets, but they would not sell them to me; however, they sold them to a group of white boys in front of us. I was so embarrassed and angry. I thought, here I am in uniform, serving my country, and I can't get into our local movie theater. I was mad as hell.

In January 1943, I left my job as a janitor at the Perfect Circle factory in Richmond to accept an appointment to aviation cadet training at the Tuskegee Institute in Tuskegee, Alabama. This is where blacks were trained to be fighter or bomber pilots, navigators, bombardiers, gunners, or were assigned to various ground support duties. First, we had to take college classes in advanced math, engineering, and other subjects since we didn't have a college education.

Lieutenant Colonel Benjamin O. Davis, Jr., was a 1936 graduate of West Point, and he became the commanding officer of our squadron. While at West Point, he had to live in a room by himself; he ate alone and was not allowed to take part in social activities with the white cadets. He was appointed as the first black general in the armed forces. He taught us discipline and pride in what we were doing, and he demanded that we had the best training. This training included mental toughness and preparation, pilot and crew training, and extensive physical training.

With B. O. Davis, it was all about *duty*, *honor*, and *country*, and he made sure we all understood that. Even though he experienced segregation and racial prejudice, he was not a bitter man. However, there were white soldiers and officers who were nice to us. He instilled a sense of patriotism in all of us even though we experienced segregation and racist attitudes. Those of us who were privileged to serve under B. O. Davis are better men today.

During pilot training, the cadet pilots were taught to do acrobatic moves in open two-seat planes, so they could learn how to maneuver their planes in aerial combat. One time, a pilot instructor was in the back seat flying the plane. Somehow he didn't have his seat belt fastened. When the plane did an upside down spin, the instructor pilot fell out. The cadet pilot thought the instructor was still flying the plane, and it crashed, killing the cadet pilot; two lives were lost in this training exercise. A lot of pilots were killed during training.

I went through all of the basic and advanced pilot training at Tuskegee before I washed out and couldn't become a pilot. I was assigned to the army with the 1869th Aviation Engineering Battalion at Harmon Field on Guam, where I became a construction and supply supervisor. Our unit helped build roads, runways, warehouses, and Quonset huts. We also installed culvert pipes for waterlines and ran heavy equipment. The work was hot and dirty, but it had to be done, and we did it well. One time we were digging up the road to lay our cement culverts, and the bulldozers unearthed dead Japanese soldiers.

I will never forget some incidents. One of our planes was trying to evacuate children from a village and take them to America. As it took off it exploded, killing everyone. Another time, one of our fighter pilots was firing-up his plane, and the engine got too hot, causing the plane to explode, killing the pilot. Once while overseas, two of our guys went AWOL and left camp. They went into a native village to steal food. They got caught and were killed. One had his head cut off, and the other one was shot in the head. There were tragedies like this, but we also did good things like taking food to the villagers.

We thought we were going to be sent to Japan for the land invasion, but the atomic bombs were dropped. We could see the flash from Guam, over 1,600 miles away.

One of my classmates and friends who I trained with was James Harvey III. In 1949, after the war, he and a team of Tuskegee Airmen participated in the first "Top Gun" competition, which was held at the Las Vegas Air Force Base in Nevada. The United States Air Force fighter plane competition featured the best combat pilots in the navy, air force, and Marines. This team won the entire competition.

Quentin Smith

Army Air Corps: First Lieutenant, Tuskegee Airman
Hometown: Gary, Indiana
Career: High school Latin teacher

A Tuskegee Airman featured on a war bond poster

I was first assigned as a civilian primary pilot instructor for black cadets in the Army Air Corps. I was not allowed to train white cadets, since I was black. I volunteered to become a Tuskegee Airman because I wanted to fly fighter planes. When I got to the Tuskegee Institute in Tuskegee, Alabama, I was required to take my instructor training again, even though I was already a primary pilot trainer.

As black instructors, we were not allowed to teach the advanced pilot training. At this time in the war, to become a pilot, blacks had to have a college education, while whites only had to have a high school education. This rule was in place to discourage blacks from becoming pilots because our military didn't want blacks to fight. Later in the war, when our Air Corps was losing so many planes in combat, the requirements to become a fighter or bomber pilot were changed. Blacks could become pilots without a college education, but they first had to go through rigorous academic training in what were called college training detachments. Since I already had a college education, I earned my pilot wings and was assigned to become a B-25 bomber pilot. I wanted to be sent overseas to fight.

We could not go overseas as bomber pilots, because there were not enough trained black navigators, bombardiers, engineers, and waist gunners. Since we were not allowed to fight with whites, we had to have an all black crew. After our training in Tuskegee, we were sent for more training to Fort Knox, Kentucky, but the runways were too short for our big bombers to land. In one instance, one of our planes crashed upon landing, and the entire ten-man crew was killed. The military kept this quiet, and we were sent to Freeman Field, near Seymour, Indiana, where the runways were designed for landing bombers.

At Freeman Field, I was part of 546 Tuskegee Airmen on the base. Most of us wanted to exercise our privilege and use the officer's club facilities. When we tried to use them, the colonel, who was the commanding officer, denied us use. He said that we could only use the facilities before 5:00 p.m. The problem was we didn't finish our training until after 5:00 p.m. This was an excuse to keep us from using the dining room, bar, and tennis, swimming, and other recreational facilities available to only the white officers. The colonel told us we had to sign a paper saying we would agree not to use the officers club after 5:00 p.m.

I was one of 101 black officers who refused to sign the paper. We were ordered to be placed under arrest for failure to follow the orders of our commanding officer. The military police handcuffed us and took us to a confinement area. Later, we were returned to Fort Knox and were confined under guard in a segregated two-block area. We heard that we were going to be court-martialed and sent to Fort Leavenworth, Kansas, which was the federal military prison for deserters and soldiers who had committed various felony crimes. Our sentence was to be 20 years. At the time, the military had a policy saying blacks were not allowed to fight. The reasoning was that blacks could not be trained and disciplined to become good soldiers or airmen. The military hired a Harvard psychology professor to support this reasoning and further state that blacks were intellectually inferior to whites.

The NAACP heard about our situation and appealed to President Truman. President Truman and Thurgood Marshall, who was the first black Supreme Court justice, reversed the decision, and we were granted honorable discharges. However, we were told our military records would include a written reprimand for refusing to follow orders of a commanding officer. It would say that we were not capable of being good soldiers. The 101 Tuskegee officers who refused to sign the paper were discharged and sent home. The other 445 airmen were returned to their assignments. I never got my chance to become a combat bomber pilot. I went back home and returned to teaching high school Latin.

It is a little-known fact that over 600,000 black men served in various capacities during World War II; however, most of them were assigned to minor tasks in all branches of the military. Many of them wanted to fight for their country but were denied the opportunity. The majority of black soldiers, airmen, and sailors were forced to live in segregated units and were not permitted to associate with white soldiers.

It was not until 1948, over two years after World War II had ended, that President Truman signed a law desegregating the military. I would like to think that the "101" of us black officers who refused to sign the order at Freeman Field helped bring attention to the racial discrimination that was taking place in our military.

18

THE BOMB

"Sixteen hours ago an American airplane dropped one bomb on Hiroshima. It is an atomic bomb."

—Harry S. Truman

The Buck Stops Here

"We turned back to look at Hiroshima. The city was hidden by that awful cloud, mushrooming, terrible and incredibly tall."
—Colonel Paul Tibbets

On August 14, 1945, Japanese citizens, stunned by the devastation that had befallen their country, tuned in to their radios to hear, for the first time, the voice of their leader, Emperor Hirohito. As they listened in, they learned of his decision to surrender. The war was over!

What helped bring Hirohito to this decision was the development of the most destructive weapon in the world—the atomic bomb. In 1939, Albert Einstein, the famous German physicist and scientist, informed President Roosevelt that German scientists were working on developing atomic power. To counter Hitler's initiative, Roosevelt ordered the implementation of a program that would put this powerful weapon in the hands of the United States first.

This top-secret mission became known as the Manhattan Project. A massive research laboratory was developed in Oak Ridge, Tennessee, with the purpose of developing an atomic bomb. From 1939 to 1945, some of the world's greatest scientific minds of the time worked to develop the bomb. Chief scientist of the project was Robert Oppenheimer, who was responsible for developing the bomb.

On April 12, 1945, Vice President Harry S. Truman was sworn in as president of the United States. The new president, along with millions of Americans, was still in shock over the death of Franklin D. Roosevelt. The voice that had delivered "Fireside Chats" during the Great Depression, the voice that told of a day of "infamy," the voice that had led the country in prayer on June 6, 1944, was now silent. When Truman became president, he learned for the first time of a new and powerful weapon that had been under development per the direction of President Roosevelt.

High-ranking military officers and top scientists gathered in the New Mexico desert at Alamogordo in July 1945 to witness the testing of an atomic device. They watched in amazement as a bright flash filled the sky along with a mushroom cloud that rose to 10,000 feet. Scientists had given President Truman the most destructive weapon in the world. As commander in chief, it was his decision alone on whether it should be utilized.

In isolated and top-secret conditions, Colonel Paul Tibbets oversaw the training of a selected few who would lead the bombing missions over Hiroshima and Nagasaki, Japan. While Tibbets's personnel trained for their mission on the island of Tinian, another secret mission was also under way in the Pacific. A large wooden crate, with its contents unknown to its crew members, was sitting on the deck of the USS *Indianapolis*, guarded by U.S. Marines.

The *Indianapolis* made it safely to Tinian, where it delivered key components of the weapon that would soon end the war. As the *Indianapolis* sailed away, with its mission complete, a Japanese submarine lay in wait. Just minutes after midnight on July 30, torpedoes sped through the quiet waters toward the *Indianapolis*. At 12:05 a.m., the tragic ordeal at sea for the sailors of the *Indianapolis* began.

On August 6, 1945, the *Enola Gay*, piloted by Colonel Tibbets, flew over Hiroshima and dropped the first atomic bomb. Three days later, with no Japanese surrender, the United States dropped the second bomb on Nagasaki. For the soldiers, sailors, airmen, and Marines, there was no invasion of Japan. Harry S. Truman had ended the war.

The crew of the *Enola Gay* one day before their historic flight over Hiroshima.
The bomb dropped by the *Enola Gay* was called "Little Boy." Pilot Paul Tibbets is in the center.

Carl Arnold

Army: Corporal, 41st Infantry Division
Hometown: Zanesville, Ohio
Career: Small-business owner

I tried to enlist in the Marines at sixteen but was turned down due to my eyes. I was drafted into the army at eighteen and sent to basic training at Camp Robinson in Little Rock, Arkansas. I was assigned to the 41st Infantry Division, and headed to the Pacific in May 1945. When we stopped in New Guinea for water, supplies and to pick up mail, I saw a coffin being loaded into a truck. I thought this was strange, since the war had moved north. I learned the GI was killed when he flipped his Jeep hitting a large snake. It made me think that there were other ways you could die besides combat.

I will never forget the terrible food we ate. Our food was dehydrated, and water needed to be added. The water we used was swamp water. Much of it was polluted, and many guys would eat the food and then become sick and vomit.

After about five weeks we moved to Zamboanga, a city in the southwest corner of Mindanao, an island in the Philippine Islands chain. Our battalion commander wanted to make a name for himself, so he volunteered to take our unit and spearhead a drive against the Japs in Devour. He lost seventy-five percent of the men, either dead or wounded. After returning to our base, some of the guys said, "Next time in battle, he won't survive." This meant one of our own soldiers would shoot him.

On the way to Japan, we stopped at Okinawa, but we were unable to land due to a large typhoon. It lasted for three days, and our ship was constantly rolling from side to side. Our troopship had about 3,500 troops with only four life rafts. I guess they didn't count on too many of us surviving, if our ship went down.

We finally made it to Japan and docked at Kure in mid-September 1945. The city had been leveled by our incendiary bombs. Only a few concrete structures protruded from the rubble. I saw the rugged mountains rising from the sea where the Japs had built their heavy military fortifications. The Japanese were prepared to fight to their death. I think President Truman made the right decision to drop the bomb. If the bombs had not been dropped, there probably would have been millions of casualties on both sides. It was about ten days before the Japanese civilians came out of their homes and villages. They had been told we would massacre them.

Stationed at a former Japanese naval base, our job was to be a part of the American Occupation Force setting up camps and providing security. Many of our guys were sick with malaria when we arrived and some contracted jaundice. We built a cemetery for the 30 to 35 who died due to illness. For three weeks, I pulled guard duty of the cemetery to protect it from any possible desecration.

I asked for a transfer and was assigned to an amphibious engineer unit close to Tokyo. I saw a job posting seeking a chaplain's assistant, so I applied for the job and got it. After about three weeks, the chaplain asked me to drive him to Hiroshima to see a group of priests. This was in September 1945, only a month after the bombs had been dropped. We had no protective gear of any kind and gave no thought to radiation exposure, and no one informed us about it. My first impression upon arriving in the city was the sight of massive destruction. Huge piles of rubble were everywhere, and the shells of some buildings were all that remained. It was not much different than what I saw in Kure.

We drove up a mountain road to meet with a priest. He told us the American air force had dropped thousands of leaflets the day before the bombing encouraging the Japanese to leave the city. The leaflets explained the Americans would be dropping a bomb on the city the next day. Some residents left, but most stayed. When the *Enola Gay* flew over Hiroshima on August 6, 1945, people heard the noise and looked up to see the plane. They thought more leaflets were being dropped.

I later learned there were three categories of those killed on that day. One was those killed by the bomb blast. The second was people who were burned by the atomic firestorm and died from their burns, including those who jumped into canals and drowned. The third way people died was drowning, due to a large tsunami that happened on that day. Many people never heard this tsunami.

In January 1946, I joined a survey outfit in Tokyo. A few weeks later, I was sent to Seoul, Korea, where my job was to do survey work at the 38th Parallel. This became the dividing line between North and South Korea. The army ordered this work done because the American government and military anticipated our next military conflict would be with the Communists in Korea. They were right. The Korean War began in 1950.

In August 1946, we headed home on one of the older troop ships which had transported troops to and from the Pacific. One day a chaplain said to me, "If you haven't yet prayed during the war, you had better pray this ship gets us home." He was referring to the age and condition of the ship. On our return, we hit another bad storm in the Aleutian Islands. It was so bad the bow of the ship would rise several feet out of the water and slap back down. The noise was so loud we thought we had hit mines, which were still floating in the Pacific. I did pray that I would get home safely, because I knew my mother was expecting me.

In the military, we were trained to kill, before we got killed. Not everyone was willing to kill someone else, even the enemy. War affects your personality, and you need time to adjust to civilian life and learn to love one another.

James E. O'Donnell

Navy: Machinist Mate Third Class, USS *Indianapolis*
Hometown: Indianapolis, Indiana
Career: Firefighter

USS *Indianapolis*

I served on the USS *Indianapolis*, a heavy cruiser that was the pride of the United States Navy. She was the flagship of the Fifth Fleet. Our ship had earned ten battle stars for combat in Saipan, Tinian, Guam, and Iwo Jima, and had participated in the key battles of Midway and the Philippine Sea. Of her ten battle stars, I served in five of those combat missions.

On March 31, 1945, while engaged in the battle of Okinawa, the USS *Indianapolis* was hit by a kamikaze pilot. I remember the whole ship being rocked by the explosion; nine crew members were killed. We had to return to the States for repairs.

On July 16, 1945, little did we know that the USS *Indianapolis* would become involved in the navy's worst tragedy at sea, and the 1,190 men and the ship would become part of history. We were assigned a top-secret mission. We were dispatched to San Francisco, California, where two large crates were loaded onto the ship and locked in the hanger deck. None of us knew what was in the crates. The atomic bomb was one of the war's best-kept secrets.

Our orders were to deliver these crates to the Tinian Airfield on the island of Tinian in Japan. We later learned that we had delivered the components of the atomic bomb, which launched an event that not only brought an end to the war but also changed history. After we unloaded our payload, we were sent to Guam and then to Leyte to be a part of the invasion of mainland Japan.

On our way to Guam, a Japanese submarine hit us with two torpedoes. They hit us at low and midship, and the explosion and fire were horrendous. The torpedoes caused complete electrical damage. Almost immediately, the ship rolled over on its side. I walked along the side of the ship, grabbed a life jacket and jumped into the oil-filled water. It's estimated that the ship sank in about twelve minutes. We believe that some 800 men made it into the water before it sank. Those of us who survived the sinking floated in the oil in the pitch black Pacific Ocean.

I remember men screaming and praying. Many of us linked together to help keep each other afloat. The one comfort we had was thinking help would arrive soon. It did not come for nearly five days. During this time, many men gave up and drowned. Others were killed by sharks. Over the course of five days, many of the groups floated miles apart.

After 72 hours, nearly half of the 800 plus survivors were dead. Removing life vests from the dead and passing them on to the living was common. One sailor found his best buddy floating dead in his life vest. He refused to take it and clung to his friend's lifeless body. I don't know if he was rescued or not.

As time went on we began praying louder for survival and that rescue ships would come. Finally, on August 2, an American bomber was in the area and spotted the oil slick. The pilot radioed for help. The first to arrive was a PBY seaplane, and as the first rescue craft, it was able to pick up 56 men. Later in the night the USS *Cecil Doyle* arrived and started rescuing more survivors. The USS *Bassett* also arrived that night, and one of its rescue boats found my group. We were in the water together for 108 hours.

I was one of the 317 fortunate ones to survive. Over 800 sailors lost their lives. It was a terrible experience that I will never forget.

On August 2, 1995, 50 years to the day after the ship was sunk, the monument to the USS *Indianapolis* was unveiled in Indianapolis, Indiana. One of my lasting memories as a survivor is that freedom does not come cheap. Have faith and never give up! That is why I am still alive.

President Harry S. Truman

"America was not built on fear. America was built on courage and an unbeatable determination to do the job at hand."

The vice president of the United States, Harry S. Truman, and the entire nation were stunned with the death of President Roosevelt. Truman told reporters, "I feel like the moon, the stars, and all of the planets have fallen on me." During the war, Truman made some crucial decisions, with the most notable being the decision to drop the atomic bomb on Hiroshima and Nagasaki, Japan, in August 1945. This decision led to the Japanese surrender and the end of World War II.

Wally Yakey

Marine Corps: Second Lieutenant, 3rd Division
Hometown: Indianapolis, Indiana
Career: Owner commercial painting company

Marine Corp Boot Camp at Parris Island, 1944

After my freshman year at Indiana University, I left school to enlist in the Marine Corps. My boot camp was on Parris Island, South Carolina. We were very well trained and had to endure hard drills, marches with full gear, physical training, and harassment. All of this was done to prepare us for combat.

In the Marine Corps, you learn to work as a unit and not as individuals. After completing my boot camp, I attended Officer Training School in Quantico, Virginia. Our daily schedule started at 5:00 a.m., and we finished around 7:30 p.m. Everything we did in training was on the run. All of us wanted to be good officers, and we were prepared to lead our men to fight the Japanese.
After graduating from Officer Training School, I was commissioned a 2nd lieutenant and was assigned as platoon leader with the 3rd Division.

While the war was still going on and our soldiers were fighting the Japanese, our troop carrier departed for the Pacific. Our ship traveled in blackout mode for fear of Japanese submariners. Although we did not know where we were going, we were ready for combat. On our way, the atomic bombs were dropped on Hiroshima and Nagasaki, so we never got to experience combat. We continued on and landed at Guam Island.

I feel I was very fortunate and was proud to be a U.S. Marine. The Marines taught us, no matter what your job is, forward or rear, you are all the same, a "Marine." During my service, I met some great fellow Marines and friends that I will never forget. I would later serve in the Korean War with the Marine Corps and fought in the battle of the Chosin Reservoir.

I believe in our form of government and was proud to serve my country. I believe immensely in patriotism! I was never a hero. I just tried to be a good Marine.

Leslie Zoss

Army: Tech Sergeant, Military Police
Hometown: Lockport, New York
Career: Engineering professor and consultant for Eli Lilly

The Hiroshim Exhibition Hall after the atomic bomb was dropped. The Hall is about 350 meters from the center of the blast.

During my basic training, some of us were pulled out of basic training at Fort Benning, Georgia, and sent to the University of Pennsylvania for nine months to learn the Japanese language, history, and geography.

After the atomic bombs were dropped on Hiroshima and Nagasaki, Japan, I was sent to Nagasaki as part of a special unit of the military police called the Criminal Investigation Division (CID). Our job was to expose and arrest members of the U.S. military and the Japanese who were selling food, supplies, and equipment on the black market to the Chinese. We also investigated murders. This was very dangerous work, and I was afraid of being killed.

I will never forget the mass destruction of Nagasaki. Dead, decomposing bodies were still in the streets, and the buildings were in piles of rubble. The worst part was seeing the burned and crippled children walking through the streets looking for food. We gave them any food we had. Many of their parents and family members had been killed in the blast. At the time, we did not know that we had been exposed to the radiation from the bomb. Many of our soldiers who were in Nagasaki after the war suffered from radiation poisoning. Later, many of them developed various cancers and died. I have had several skin cancers.

19

THE LIBERATORS

V for Victory

"Today the guns are silent. A great tragedy has ended. A great victory has been won. The skies no longer rain death—the seas bear only commerce—men everywhere walk upright in the sunlight. The entire world is quietly at peace."
—General Douglas MacArthur

On an overcast and gray day, American and British ships filled Tokyo Bay for the long awaited end to World War II. Throughout the morning, Allied delegations had been boarding the floating piece of American soil known as the USS *Missouri*. While the deck was crowded with sailors and high-ranking officials, crowds of ordinary people, men and women, young and old, were gathered around radios throughout the world to hear the historic proceedings.

On September 2, 1945, with microphones and surrender documents ready, the solemn delegation of Japan boarded the *Missouri*. General Douglas MacArthur oversaw the surrender proceedings, and it was his words that ushered in peace to a war-torn world.

Before America entered the war, millions of people worldwide watched as the armies of Japan and Germany invaded their lands, killed their people, destroyed their military, and took over their government. In brutal fashion, these countries had been conquered!

When the boys of America went on the march, they followed the war torn paths to countries and islands around the world. American boys sailed into enemy-controlled waters of the Atlantic and Pacific. American boys flew into the skies ruled by the Empire of Japan and Nazi Germany. American boys saw combat in Burma, North Africa, Italy, Guadalcanal, the Philippines, Saipan, Iwo Jima, Okinawa, France, Holland, and Belgium. The "torch of liberty" was taken by American boys to the homelands of Germany and Japan.

Our American boys fought and died, so we could live in freedom.

When American boys went on the march, they went not as conquerors, but as liberators!

Bless Them All

Their Legacy Will Live Forever ...

Earl Anderson

"I was not far from the front gate, and I saw the German swastika flag being taken down by our troops, and the American flag was raised. I still become emotional thinking about this experience."

Jim Baize

"I saw this kid who had taken on some lead ... he had about half of his side hanging out and was holding his side. He still had his rifle pointing out, and he kept on going."

Dr. Raymond Beights, Sr.

"If there had been any doubt as to the seriousness of what we were doing, the tragedies we witnessed made us realize the dangers involved."

Arthur Carter, Sr.

"I am a patriot and proud that I served my country and am proud to be an American."

Les Cheesman

"You don't fight for medals; you fight to save your buddies. A lot of guys died trying to save someone."

Gene Cogan

"In combat, every day is a lifetime."

Averitte Corley

"Once you are trained as a Marine,
you feel you can do anything."

Phyllis Funk

"As I look back, I think my nurse friends and I were young and dumb, but we were also brave."

Mark Griffin

"In WW II, we had a common cause and a defined purpose. We were in it to win, and we did!"

Irving Heath

"If Germany had discovered how to make the atomic bomb before the United States, it would be a different world today."

Bernard Heeke

"A German plane dropped bombs on one of our platoons, killing most of the men. I was so close, the blast bounced me off the ground."

Everett Hodgin

"A buddy asked me to go with him to headquarters. I told him no because I had too much work to do. A few hours later, he was brought back in an ambulance dead. He had been shot by a Japanese sniper."

(Author Duane Hodgin with his father on his ninety-fifth birthday)

Kathryn "Katy" Huehl

"I never worked harder in my life, but it was the most worthwhile service I have ever done."

William Jefferies

"Combat was about instinct and survival.
As Marines, we were trained to hit hard and hit fast."

Eva Mozes Kor

"We must never forget, and we must never let it happen again."

Dr. Gadi Lawton

"I wasn't a hero. I did what I had to do as did my men."

Harry Leavell

"With B. O. Davis, it was all about *duty*, *honor*, and *country*, and he made sure we all understood that."

Gene Liston

"I gazed over the beaches and the thousands of white Allied Crosses at Normandy. I cried, as I thought, 'There, but for the grace of God, go I.'"

Harry Macy

"The Japanese abandoned their dead, and we never did."

Joe McAndrews

"When I returned home and knocked on my front door, my mother opened it, and we hugged each other and cried."

Eddie Mode

"When we landed on Okinawa, I was a seventeen-year old kid. It scared the shit out of me."

Ed Moss

"I served my country for a purpose greater than myself."

Harry and Florence Phariss

"What impressed me were the spirit, perseverance, and integrity of the American soldiers and people."

Florence Phariss

Ken Rash

"My submarine service ranged from boredom to stark terror."

Carl Scott

"I heard someone say, 'Don't step there.' I looked down and saw an enemy mine exposed in the sand. I turned around to see who had warned me, and no one was around. Some guys called these incidents, 'Angels looking over us.'"

William Swift

"We have to know what's going on in the world and pay attention because at that time we weren't."

Walter Umbarger

"There was never any doubt in my mind that we would win the war."

In memory of those buried on foreign
soil who never returned home ...

Corporal Robert V. Reno,
father of Brigitt Caito

"Our debt to the heroic men and valiant women in the service of our country can never be repaid.

They have earned our undying gratitude. America will never forget their sacrifices."

—Harry S. Truman
April 16, 1945

Acknowledgments

This is a project of love for the men and women of World War II. We wish to thank them for the hours they spent interviewing and answering questions, and we appreciate their wives, daughters, and sons who helped arrange interviews and sat with us as their fathers and mothers recounted their experiences.

We extend a special thank you to Sara Heiny, who designed the book cover and the introductory photos at the beginning of the book. Sara is a senior at Lawrence Central High School in Indianapolis, Indiana. She is working toward an international baccalaureate (IB) diploma and is a member of the National Honor Society. She plays varsity soccer, the cello, and is a staff member for the *Cub Reporter*, her school's student-run newspaper. Her plans are to attend Columbia or Stanford University.

We want to express appreciation to our wives, Cathy Hardwick and Sandi Hodgin, for their advice, assistance, and patience during the course of this project. The hours are too numerous to count for the time away from home interviewing, typing, and editing the manuscript.

Many individuals along this journey have provided advice, support, and their own expertise in helping us write this book, including: Gina Apple, our friend and colleague, Tom Applegate, Jack Eder, Chuck Heintzelman, Kathryn Lerch, and Dr. John Shively. We especially wish to acknowledge Allen Andrews, who helped with the historical review of the manuscript.

From Duane:
This book is a tribute to my father Everett Hodgin who, at 94 years old, was the first veteran I interviewed in January 2010. Due to his death, I regret that he is unable to see the finished book.

From Steve:
I would like to thank my wonderful children Grace and Grant. As you have grown up, I have spent many hours preparing the World War II Tributes, visiting veterans, and writing this book to preserve their memoirs. Through these projects, you have met many veterans, and you

have always treated them with respect and kindness. I am proud of you. Thank you for sharing your Dad with the men and women of the Greatest Generation.

Steve would like to thank two of his close World War II friends who are no longer with us. Sergeant Garry Quackenbush served with the 291st Combat Engineers during the Battle of the Bulge and was one of the men who cleared and carried away the frozen dead GIs from the Malmedy Massacre. Garry and Steve spent many hours together, and Garry's advice will always be valued.

Corporal Gerald Stoner was with the 80th Infantry Division during the Battle of the Bulge. "Stoner" was one of a kind. His war stories and sense of humor kept Steve laughing for many hours. When the stories subsided, "Stoner" would reach out and grab Steve's elbow, lean in and say with a chuckle, "Now remember, 80 percent of what I told you is true."

Bibliography

Ambrose, Stephen E. *Band of Brothers: E Company, 50th Regiment*. New York: Touchstone, 2001.

———. *Citizen Soldiers: The U.S. Army from the Normandy Beaches to the Bulge to the Surrender of Germany June 7, 1944 to May 7, 1945*. New York: Simon & Schuster, 1997.

———. *D-Day June 6, 1944: The Climactic Battle of World War II*. New York: Simon & Schuster, 1994.

———. *The Good Fight: How World War II Was Won*. New York: Byron Preiss Visual Publications, 2001.

———. *The Victors—Eisenhower and His Boys: The Men of World War II*. New York: Simon and Schuster, 1998.

Bard, Mitchell G., PhD. *The Complete Idiot's Guide to World War II*. 3rd Ed. New York: Penguin Books, 2010.

Bernstein, Mark, and Alex Lubertozzi. *World War II on the Air: Edward R. Murrow and the Broadcasts that Riveted a Nation*. Naperville, IL: Sourceboks, 2003.

Bowman, Martin. *Great American Air Battles of World War II*. Shrewsbury: Airlife Publishing, 1994.

Brinkley, Douglas, and Michael Haskew. *The World War II Desk Reference*. New York: Harper Collins, 2004.

Brinkley, Douglas. *The World War II Memorial: A Grateful Nation Remembers*. Washington: Smithsonian Books, 2004.

Brokaw, Tom. *The Greatest Generation*. New York: Random House, 1998.

Churchill, Winston S. *Memoirs of the Second World War: An Abridgment of the Six Volumes of The Second World War*. Boston: Houghton Mifflin, 1987.

Eisenhower, John S. D. *The Bitter Woods: The Battle of the Bulge.* New York: Da Capo, 1995.

Hechler, Ken. *The Bridge at Remagen.* Missoula, MT: Pictorial Histories, 2001.

Hildebrandt, Laura. *Unbroken: A World War II Story of Survival, Resilience and Redemption.* New York: Random House, 2010.

Keegan, John. *Who was Who in World War II.* New York: Crescent, 1984.

Life Magazine Editors. *Our Finest Hour: Voices of the World War II Generation.* Des Moines, IA: Time, 2000.

MacDonald, Charles. *A Time for Trumpets: The Untold Story of the Battle of the Bulge.* New York: HarperCollins, 1985.

Moser, Don. *China-Burma-India.* Alexandria, VA: Time-Life Books, 1978.

Moskin, J. Robert. *The U.S. Marine Corps Story.* 3rd ed. New York: Little, Brown, 1992.

Mozes Kor, Eva. *Echoes from Auschwitz: Dr. Mengele's Twins, The Story of Eva and Miriam Mozes.* Terre Haute, IN: CANDLES, 2002.

Province, Charles M. *The Unknown Patton.* New York: Bonanza Books, 1983.

Pyle, Ernie. *Brave Men.* New York: Henry Holt, 1944.

Richardson, Robert C., Jr., Lieutenant General. *Your Victory: History of Battles in the Pacific Theater.* No publisher listed.

Rozett, Robert, and Shmuel Spector. *Encyclopedia of the Holocaust.* New York: Facts On File, 2000.

Stewart, Graham. *His Finest Hours: The War Speeches of Winston Churchill.* London: Quercus, 2007.

Toland, John. *Adolf Hitler.* New York: Doubleday, 1976.

———. *Battle: The Story of the Bulge.* Lincoln: University of Nebraska Press, 1999.

Truman, Harry S. *Memoirs by Harry S. Truman: 1945: Year of Decisions.* Garden City, NY: Doubleday, 1955.

About the Authors

DUANE HODGIN was an educator for forty-three years, serving as an elementary, middle, and high school teacher and administrator. He authored two books and coauthored another one on character education for teachers. His experiences include presenting at numerous state and national conventions and speaking with students in schools, colleges and universities. He has received numerous awards and recognition including Indiana's highest civilian award, The Sagamore of the Wabash, presented by the governor of Indiana. His Ph.D. was earned from Miami University in Oxford, Ohio. Special interests include books on World War II, Abraham Lincoln and collecting and writing inspirational quotes on life, character, and education.

STEVE HARDWICK has been a 5th grade teacher for seventeen years in Lawrence Township in Indianapolis, Indiana. Prior to becoming a teacher, he served in the U.S. Army and Indiana National Guard. For twelve years, he and his students have hosted a World War II USO show to honor the men and women of World War II. He is the recipient of the Preserve America Teacher of the Year award for Indiana, the Indiana Daughters of the American Revolution Outstanding Teacher of American History award, and, in 2011, he was awarded the Indiana Distinguished Service Medal by the governor of Indiana.